MW00893899

CROCHET

Edgings & More
from Turn-of-the-Century Sources

edited by Jules & Kaethe Kliot

The latter half or the nineteenth century reflected great achievements in lace making, with the true hand made laces of bobbin lace and needle lace giving way to the much easier-to-execute techniques of crochet, and tape lace. These "simpler" laces which initially tried to mimic the true laces, eventually came into their own, developing designs unique to the technique. The success of this development is evidenced by the many crochet pattern books printed for the mass market from the 1880's to 1918 recording the rich designs inspired by a previous era, most manuals displaying the talents of the popular contemporary artists. These works essentially disappeared by the mid teens, not to resurface till the mid 30's and then with the much simpler anonymous designs of a new era.

The work of this book is taken from several manuals of crochet designs from the early years and should serve as a valuable resource for the crocheter as well as historian and collector.

CONTENTS

Note: Numbers in [ ] refer to page numbers of this book. Other page references are from original publications.

SUPPLIES: Fine crochet hooks, to size 16, Novelty Braid and fine crochet threads available from:
LACIS, 2982 Adeline Street, Berkeley, CA 94703

LACIS
PUBLICATIONS
3163 Adeline Street, Berkeley, CA 94703

© 1996, LACIS
ISBN 0-916896-81-1

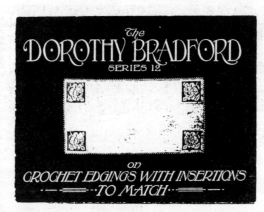

The DOROTHY BRADFORD
SERIES 12

on
CROCHET EDGINGS WITH INSERTIONS
TO MATCH

BOOK NUMBER ONE

1. CROCHETED EDGINGS AND INSERTIONS
With Instructions
BY
Augusta Pfeuffer
PRICE TEN CENTS

BOOK NUMBER TWO

2. CROCHETED EDGINGS AND INSERTIONS
With Instructions
BY
Augusta Pfeuffer
PRICE TEN CENTS

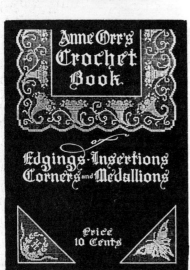

Anne Orr's Crochet Book.
Edgings · Insertions
Corners and Medallions
Price
10 Cents

The SELF INSTRUCTOR
IN
SILK KNITTING
CROCHETING
& EMBROIDERY
published by
BELDING BROS. & Co.
Revised Edition
1891
New York.
Cincinnati.
Boston.
St Paul
Montreal
Chicago.
Philadelphia.
St Louis.
San Francisco.
New Orleans.

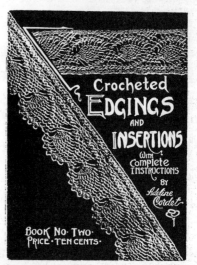

Crocheted EDGINGS AND INSERTIONS
With Complete INSTRUCTIONS
BY
Adeline Cordet
BOOK NO. TWO
PRICE · TEN CENTS

CROCHET & TATTING CRAFT
Book No. 1 By ANNA VALEIRE
EDGINGS MEDALLIONS & INSERTIONS
WITH FULL INSTRUCTIONS ON OVER SIXTY PIECES
FOR USE IN LINGERIE & THE HOME

T. B. C. Designs for Crocheting
Edges   Yokes
Insertions   Medallions
Published by T. BUETTNER & CO., Incorporated
Art Needlework Specialists :: Importers and Manufacturers
CHICAGO, ILLINOIS   HAMBURG, GERMANY
PRICE 25 CENTS

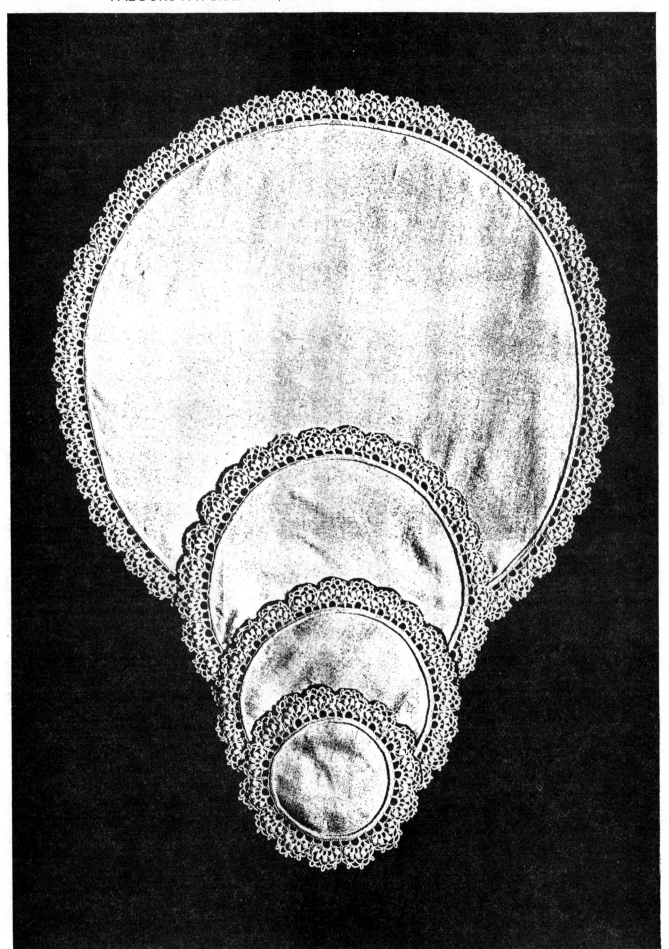

Fig. 1. Edging used on this Luncheon Set is described in Fig. 28.

ABBREVIATION OF TERMS.

ch. = Chain Stitch.
sl. st. = Slip Stitch.
s. c. = Single Crochet.
d. c. = Double Crochet.
t. c. = Treble Crochet.
l. t. c. = Long Treble Crochet.

c. t. c. = Crossed Treble Crochet.
ppc. st. = Popcorn Stitch.
p. = Picot.
p. l. = Picot Loop.
st. = Stitch.
C. B. = Coronation Braid.

Repetition Mark means:

To repeat directions printed between these two stars as many times as stated in each case.

Fig. 2, Chain Stitch (ch. st.). To start, tie a slip knot over hook — *thread over hook — and draw through a loop* — continue this until the required length is reached.

Fig. 2.

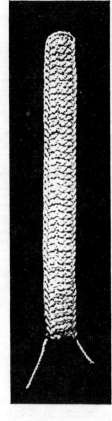

Fig. 3, Slip Stitch (sl. st.). On a chain — put hook through both, stitch and loop on hook at the same time.

Fig. 3.

Fig. 4, Single Crochet (s. c.). On a chain — put hook through the work — thread over hook — draw through work — thread over hook — and draw through both loops.

Fig. 4.

Fig. 5, Double Crochet (d. c.). On a chain — thread over hook — put hook through the work — **thread over hook — draw through the work — thread over hook —** put hook through the next stitch — **thread over hook**

showing 3 stitches on hook — thread over hook — draw through 2 loops — thread over hook — draw through 2 loops.

Fig. 5.

Fig. 6, Treble Crochet (t. c.). On a chain — thread over hook twice — put hook through the work — thread over hook — draw through work, showing 4 stitches on hook — thread over hook — draw through 2 loops — thread over hook — draw through 2 loops — thread over hook — draw through 2 loops.

Fig. 6.

Fig. 7, Long Treble Crochet (l. t. c.). On a chain — thread over hook 3 times — put hook through the work — thread over hook — draw through work, showing 5 stitches on hook — *thread over hook — draw through 2 loops* — 4 times in all.

Fig. 8, Crossed Treble Crochet (c. t. c.). On a chain — thread over hook twice — put hook through the 11th st., counting back from last ch. st. — *thread over hook — draw through work, showing 4 stitches on hook — thread over hook — draw through 2 loops* — thread over hook — draw through 2 loops — thread over hook — **skip 1 stitch — put hook through the next stitch — thread over hook**

Fig. 7.

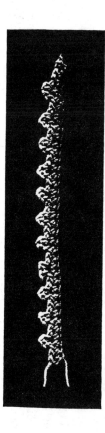

Fig. 8.

— draw through work — thread over hook — draw through 2 loops — thread over hook — draw through 2 loops — thread over hook — draw through 2 loops — thread over hook — draw through the last 2 loops — ch. 2 — thread over hook — put hook through the middle stitch of the t. c. — thread over hook — draw through work — thread over hook — draw through 2 loops — thread over hook — draw through the last 2 loops — ch. 2 — thread over hook twice — skip 2 stitches — put hook through the 3rd stitch — repeat from*.

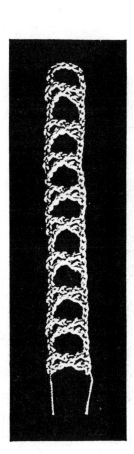

Fig. 11.

Fig. 11, Picot Loop (p. l.). On a chain — 3 s. c. — *ch. 4 — 3 s. c. in the next 3 st. of the chain — repeat from*. The loop thus formed by the ch. of 4 is the Picot Loop.

Fig. 12, Edging, matching Fig. 13, Insertion.
FIRST ROW: Chain 14 — and join by 1 s. c.
SECOND ROW: 9 s. c. over ch. — turn.
THIRD ROW: *Ch. 11 — fasten with 1 s. c. in the 5th s. c. — turn.
FOURTH ROW: 9 s. c. over ch. of 11 — turn — repeat from*.

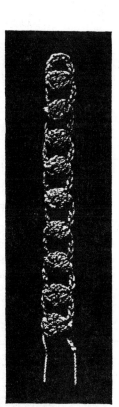

Fig. 12.

Fig. 13, Insertion, matching Fig. 12, Edging.
FIRST ROW: Chain 18.
SECOND ROW: 1 s. c. in the 14th st. of ch., counting back from the last st. — ch. 6 — 1 d. c. in the first st. of ch. — turn.

Fig. 13.

Fig. 9.

Fig. 9, Popcorn Stitch (ppc. st.). On a chain — 6 d. c. in the 8th stitch, counting back from last ch. st., all in the same stitch — *take out hook — put hook through the top stitch of the first d. c. — draw last lo p through, to form a pocket — ch. 5 — skip 4 st. — 6 d. c., all in the 5th stitch — repeat from*.

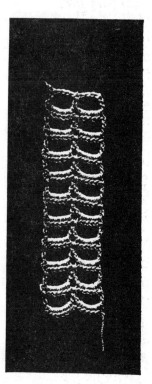

Fig. 10.

Fig. 10, Picot (p.). On a chain — join the last 4 ch. sts., by putting hook through the 4th stitch, counting back from hook, with 1 s. c. — then continue work.

[5]

5

THIRD ROW: Ch. 8 — 1 c. t. c. in the 3rd and 4th d. c. of preceding row —*ch. 4—1 c. t. c. in the 2nd and 3rd d. c.—repeat from* until the end of the row—turn.
FOURTH ROW: Ch. 4 — skip 1 st.—*1 d. c. in the 2nd st. of preceding row—ch. 1—skip 1 st.—repeat from*.

Fig. 16.

Fig. 16, Edging, matching Fig. 17, Insertion.
FIRST ROW: Make a ch. of the desired length.
SECOND ROW: 1 d. c. in the 6th st., counting back from last ch. st. —3 d. c. in the next 3 st. —*ch. 3 — skip 3 ch. st. — 5 d. c. in the next 5 ch. st. —repeat from*—break off thread at the end of the row.
THIRD ROW: 1 s. c. in the 3rd d. c. of preceding row — ch. 6 — *2 d. c. over ch. of 3 — 3 p. — 2 d. c. over same ch. of 3 — ch. 2 — 1 s. c. in the 3rd d. c. — ch. 2 — repeat from*.

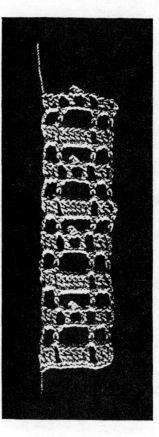

Fig. 17.

Fig. 17, Insertion, matching Fig. 16, Edging.
FIRST ROW: Chain 19.
SECOND ROW: 1 d. c. in the 6th ch. st., counting back from the last ch. st. — 1 d. c. in the next st. — ch. 2 — skip 2 ch. — 5 d. c. in the next 5 ch. st. — ch. 2 — skip 2 ch. — 3 d. c. — turn.

THIRD ROW: *Ch. 2 — 6 s. c. over ch. of 6 — ch. 1 — 6 s. c. over next ch. — turn.
FOURTH ROW: Ch. 9 — 1 s. c. over ch. of 1 of preceding row — ch. 6 — 1 d. c. over ch. of 2 — turn — repeat from*.

Fig. 14.

Fig. 14, Edging, matching Fig. 15, Insertion.
FIRST ROW: Make a ch. of the desired length.
SECOND ROW: 1 d. c. in the 8th st., counting back from the last ch. st. —*ch. 1 — skip 1 ch. — 1 d. c. in the second ch. — repeat from* to the end of the row — turn.
THIRD ROW: Ch. 8 — 1 d. c. in the third d. c. of preceding row — 1 d. c. in the next d. c. —*ch. 7 — 1 d. c. in the 2nd and d. c. of preceding row — 1 d. c. in the next d. c. — repeat from* until the end of the row — turn.
FOURTH ROW: 10 s. c. over ch. of 7 — *9 s. c. over next ch. of 7 — repeat from*.

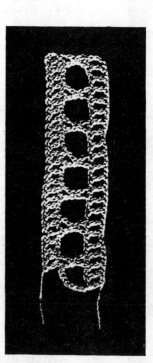

Fig. 15.

Fig. 15, Insertion, matching Fig. 14, Edging.
FIRST ROW: Make a ch. of the desired length.
SECOND ROW: 1 d. c. in the 8th st., counting back from the last ch. st. — *ch. 1 — skip 1 ch. — 1 d. c. in the next ch. — repeat from* until the end of the row — turn.

[6]

THIRD ROW: Ch. 6 — 1 d. c. over ch. of 2 of preceding row — ch. 6 — 1 d. c. over next ch. of 2 of preceding row — ch. 2 — skip 2 st. — 1 d. c. in the 3rd st. — turn.

FOURTH ROW: Ch. 4 — 2 d. c. over ch. of 2 — ch. 2 — 1 d. c. in the 2nd st. of ch. of 6 of preceding row — 1 p. — skip 2 st. — 1 d. c. in the 3rd st. — ch. 2 — 3 d. c. over ch. of 6 — turn.

FIFTH ROW: Ch. 6 — 1 d. c. over ch. of 2 of preceding row — ch. 6 — 1 d. c. over next ch. of 2 — ch. 2 — skip 2 st. — 1 d. c. in the 3rd st. — turn.

SIXTH ROW: Ch. 4 — 2 d. c. over ch. of 2 — ch. 2 — 6 d. c. over ch. of 6 — ch. 2 — 3 d. c. over ch. of 6 — turn — repeat from*.

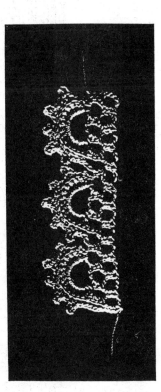

Fig. 18. Edging used on the Scarf of the Cover page.

Fig. 18, Edging, matching Fig. 19, Insertion.
FIRST ROW: Make a ch. of the desired length.
SECOND ROW: 1 s. c. in the 5th st., counting back from last ch. st. — 1 s. c. in the next st. — 1 p. 1. — *6 s. c. in the next 6 st. of ch. — turn — ch. 9 — skip 3 s. c. — 1 s. c. in the 4th s. c. — turn — 6 s. c. over ch. of 9 — 1 p. 1. — 6 s. c. over same ch. of 9 — 2 s. c. in the next 2 st. of foundation ch. — 1 p. 1. — repeat from*.

Fig. 19, Insertion, matching Fig. 18, Edging.
FIRST ROW: Make a ch. of the desired length.

Fig. 19.

SECOND ROW: 1 s. c. in the 5th st., counting back from last ch. st. — pick up each following ch. st. with a s. c. — break off thread at the end of each row.

THIRD ROW: 1 s. c. in the 1st s. c. of preceding row — *ch. 6 — skip 2 s. c. — 1 s. c. in the 3rd st. — repeat from* until the end of the row.

FOURTH ROW: 1 s. c. over the center of ch. of 6 — *ch. 6 — 1 s. c. over the center of next ch. of 6 — repeat from* until the end of the row.

FIFTH ROW: 1 s. c. over the center of ch. of 6 — *ch. 4 — 1 s. c. over the center of next ch. of 6 — repeat from* until the end of the row.

SIXTH ROW: 3 s. c. over ch. of 4 — *3 s. c. over next ch. of 4 — repeat from* until the end of the row.

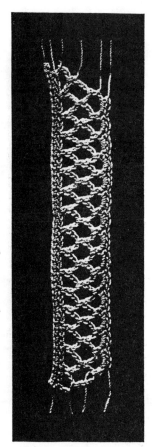

Fig. 20.

Fig. 20, Edging, matching Fig. 21, Insertion.
FIRST ROW: Chain 10.
SECOND ROW: 1 s. c. in the 8th st., counting back from hook — 1 s. c. in the next 2 st. — turn.
THIRD ROW: Ch. 6 — 3 s. c. over ch. of 7 — turn.
FOURTH ROW: Ch. 6 — 3 s. c. over ch. of 6 — turn.
FIFTH ROW: Ch. 6 — 3 s. c. over ch. of 6 — turn.
SIXTH ROW: Ch. 6 — 3 s. c. over ch. of 6 — ch. 10 — fasten with 1 s. c. in the 4th last row over ch. of 6 on side of border — turn.
SEVENTH ROW: 14 s. c. over ch. of 10 — 4 — 3 s. c. over ch. of 6 of preceding row — turn.
EIGHTH ROW: Ch. 6 — 3 s. c. over ch. of 4 of preceding row — fasten with 1 s. c. over ch. of 6 — 14 s. c. in the 14 s. c. of preceding row — turn.
NINTH ROW: Skip 1 s. c. — 3 s. c. in the next 3 s. c. — 1 p. — *1 s. c. in the last st. of the 3 s. c. — 2 s. c. in the next 2 st. — 1 p. — repeat from* until there are 5 p. — 1 s. c. in the last st. of the 3 s. c. — 2 s. c. in next 2 st. — ch. 4 — 3 s. c. over ch. of 6 — turn.

TENTH ROW: Ch. 6 — 3 s. c. over ch. of 4 of preceding row — turn.

ELEVENTH ROW: Ch. 6 — 3 s. c. over ch. of 6 — turn — repeat from Fourth Row.

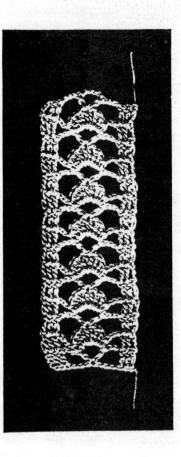

Fig. 21.

Fig. 21, Insertion, matching Fig. 20, Edging.
FIRST ROW: Chain 16.
SECOND ROW: 1 s. c. in the 8th st., counting back from hook — 2 s. c. in the next 2 st. — ch. 4 — skip 3 st. — 3 s. c. in the last 3 st. of first row — turn.
THIRD ROW: Ch. 6 — 3 s. c. over ch. of 4 — ch. 4 — 3 s. c. over next ch. — turn.
FOURTH ROW: *Ch. 6 — 3 s. c. over ch. of 4 — ch. 4 — 3 s. c. over ch. of 6 — turn — repeat from*.

Fig. 22.

Fig. 22, Edging, matching Fig. 23, Insertion.
FIRST ROW: Ch. 12 and join with 1 s. c. — turn.
SECOND ROW: *1 s. c. over ch. of 12 — 8 d. c. over same ch. — turn — ch. 12 — fasten with 1 s. c. in the last d. c. — turn — repeat from* until the desired length is reached — break off thread.
THIRD ROW: Start with 4 s. c. over ch. of 12 of preceding row — *ch. 4 — 4 s. c. over next ch. of 12 — repeat from* until the end of the row.

Fig. 23, Insertion, matching Fig. 22, Edging.
FIRST ROW: Chain 17.
SECOND ROW: 1 d. c. in the 6th st., counting back from hook — 1 d. c. in the next st. — ch. 3 — skip 3 st. — 1 d. c. in the 4th st. — ch. 5 — 1 d. c. in same place as last d. c. — ch. 3 — skip 3 st. — 3 d. c. in the next 3 st. — turn.

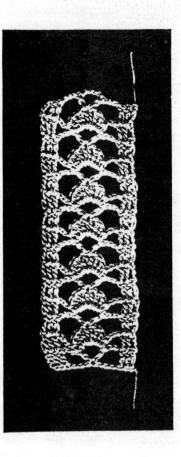

Fig. 23.

THIRD ROW: *Ch. 4 — skip 1 st. — 2 d. c. in the next 2 st. — ch. 3 — 1 s. c. over ch. of 5 — 7 d. c. — 1 s. c. over same ch. of 5 — ch. 4 — 3 d. c. over the 3 d. c. of preceding row — turn.
FOURTH ROW: Ch. 4 — skip 1 st. — 2 d. c. — ch. 3 — 1 d. c. in the 4th d. c. — ch. 5 — 1 d. c. in same place as last d. c. — ch. 3 — 3 d. c. over the 3 d. c. — turn — repeat from*.

Fig. 24.

Fig. 24, Edging, matching Fig. 25, Insertion.
FIRST ROW: Ch. 3 — 1 p. — ch. 16 — join with 1 s. c. in the 1st st. — have p. in center of the half circle — turn.
SECOND ROW: *3 s. c. over ch. of 16 — 1 p. — 4 s. c. — 1 p. — 4 s. c. — 1 p. — 3 s. c. — turn. — ch. 5 — 1 p. — ch. 16 — 1 s. c. in center of ch. of 5 — turn — repeat from*.
Fig. 25, Insertion, matching Fig. 24, Edging.
FIRST ROW: Chain 23.

SECOND ROW: 1 p. — ch. 2 — skip 7 st. on ch. — 1 s. c. in next st. — *ch. 2 — 1 p. — ch. 2 — 1 p. — ch. 2 — skip 4 st. on ch. — 1 s. c. in the 5th stitch — repeat from*, until there are 4 p. — turn.

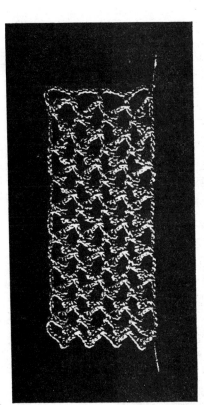

Fig. 25.

THIRD ROW: Ch. 5 — 1 p. l. — ch. 2 — 1 s. c. over ch. of 2, after the last p. — *ch. 2 — 1 p. l. — ch. 2 — 1 s. c. over ch. of 2, after the next p. — repeat 2 more times from* — turn — and repeat from Third Row until the required length is reached.

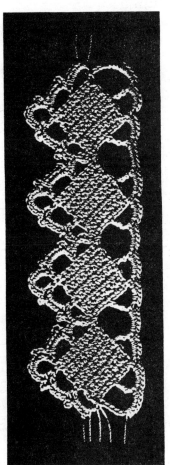

Fig. 26.

Fig. 26, Edging, matching Fig. 27, Insertion.
Make the squares first.
FIRST ROW: Chain 11.
SECOND ROW: 1 s. c. in the 4th st., counting back from hook —

7 s. c., picking up the next 7 ch. st. — turn.

THIRD ROW: *Ch. 2 — skip 1 st. — 8 s. c. — turn — repeat from*, until there are 8 rows of s. c., which completes one square — then start again from First Row, until the desired number of squares is made — then break off thread.

For Inside Edge, start
FIRST ROW: With 1 s. c. in the center point of the square (the very first chain made) — ch. 10 — 1 t. c. in the center of the side of same square — ch. 4 — 1 t. c. in the center of next side of the next square — *ch. 4 — 1 s. c. in the next point of same square — ch. 4 — 1 s. c. in the center of the side of the next square — ch. 4 — 1 t. c. in the center of next side of same square — repeat from* — break off thread at end of each row.

SECOND ROW: 5 s. c. over ch. of 10 of preceding row — *ch. 1 — 5 s. c. over ch. of 4 — repeat from*, until the end of the row.

For Outside Edge, start
FIRST ROW: With 1 s. c. in the center point of the square (the very first chain made) — *ch. 7 — 1 s. c. in the center of the side of same square — ch. 7 — 1 s. c. in the next point of same square — ch. 8 — 1 s. c. in the same place as last s. c. — ch. 7 — 1 s. c. in the center of next side of same square — ch. 7 — 1 s. c. between the two squares — repeat from*.

SECOND ROW: 5 s. c. over ch. of 7 of preceding row — 1 p. l. — *5 s. c. over next ch. of 7 — 1 p. l. — 7 s. c. over ch. of 8 — 1 p. l. — 5 s. c. over next ch. of 7 — 1 p. l. — 2 s. c. over next ch. — 2 s. c. over next ch. — 1 p. l. — repeat from*.

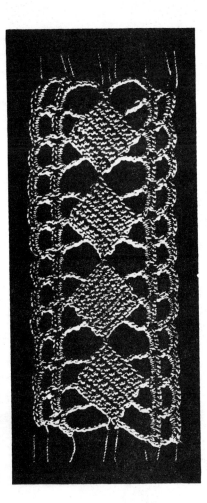

Fig. 27.

Fig. 27, Insertion, matching Fig. 26, Edging.
For the Edge, start
FIRST ROW: With 1 s. c. in the center point of the square (the very first chain made) — ch. 10 — 1 t. c. in center of the side of same square — ch. 4 — 1 t. c. in the next point of same square — ch. 4 — 1 t. c. in the center of next side of same square — *ch. 4 — 1 t. c. in the center

of the side of the next square — ch. 4 — 1 s. c. in the next point of same square — ch. 4 — 1 t. c. in the center of next side of same square — repeat from*.

SECOND ROW: On opposite side — same as First Row.

THIRD ROW: 1 s. c. over ch. of 10 of preceding row — 1 p. l. — 5 s. c. over same ch. of 10 — 1 p. l. —*5 s. c. over next ch. of 4 — 1 p. l. — repeat from*.

FOURTH ROW: On opposite side — same as Third Row.

FIFTH ROW: 1 s. c. over p. l. of preceding row — ch. 7 — 1 s. c. over next p. l. —*ch. 5 — 1 s. c. over next p. l. — repeat from*.

SIXTH ROW: On opposite side — same as Fifth Row.

SEVENTH ROW: 5 s. c. over ch. of 7 — *ch. 1 — 5 s. c. over next ch. of 5 — repeat from*.

EIGHTH ROW: On opposite side — same as Seventh Row.

1 ppc. st. over ch. of 7 of preceding row — *ch. 7 — 1 ppc. st. over next ch. of 7 — ch. 7 — 1 ppc. st. over next ch. of 7 — ch. 7 — 1 ppc. st. over next ch. of 7, until there are 5 ppc. st. — ch. 5 — 1 s. c. over ch. of 7 of preceding row — 1 s. c. over next ch. of 7 — repeat from*.

FIFTH ROW: 1 s. c. over ch. of 7 of preceding row — ch. 5 — 1 s. c. over next ch. of 7 — *ch. 7 — 1 s. c. over next ch. of 7 — repeat from*, until there are 3 loops of the ch. of 7 in all — ch. 5 — 1 s. c. over next ch. of 5 — ch. 5 — 1 s. c. over ch. of 5 of preceding row — 1 s. c. over next ch. of 5 — ch. 5 — 1 s. c. over ch. of 7 — continue as before.

SIXTH ROW: 1 s. c. over ch. of 5 of preceding row — ch. 7 — *1 s. c. over ch. of 7 — ch. 7 — 1 s. c. over same ch. of 7 — ch. 7 — 1 s. c. over next ch. of 7 — ch. 7 — 1 s. c. over same ch. — ch. 7 — 1 s. c. over the 3rd ch. of 7 — ch. 7 — 1 s. c. over same ch. — ch. 5 — 1 s. c. over next ch. of 5 — ch. 5 — repeat from*.

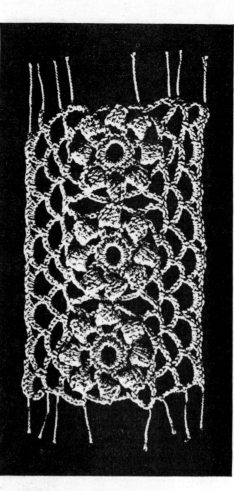

Fig. 29.

Fig. 29, Insertion, matching Fig. 28, Edging.

Make each medallion with popcorn stitch separately — and join to the previous one.

FIRST ROW: Ch. 10 — and join with 1 s. c.

SECOND ROW: 16 s. c. over ch. of 10 — join with a sl. st.

THIRD ROW: *Ch. 7 — skip 1 s. c. — 1 s. c. in the 2nd st. — repeat from*, until there are 8 loops of the ch. of 7.

FOURTH ROW: Ch. 10 — 1 ppc. st. over ch. of 7 — *ch. 7 — 1 ppc. st. over next ch. of 7 — repeat from*, until there are 8 ppc. st.

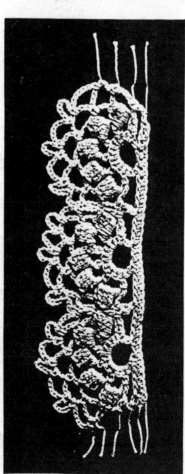

Fig. 28. Edging used on Luncheon Set, Fig. 1.

Fig. 28, Edging, matching Fig. 29, Insertion.

FIRST ROW: Make a chain of the desired length.

SECOND ROW: 1 s. c. in each ch. st. — break off thread after each row.

THIRD ROW: 1 s. c. in 1st s. c. of preceding row — ch. 9 — skip 3 st. — 1 s. c. in the 4th st. — turn — 11 s. c. over ch. of 9 — 1 s. c. over next ch. of 9 — turn — ch. 7 — skip 1 s. c. — 1 s. c. in the 2nd s. c. — ch. 7 — skip 1 s. c. — 1 s. c. in the 2nd s. c. — ch. 7 — skip 1 s. c. — 1 s. c. in the 2nd s. c. — ch. 7 — skip 1 s. c. — 1 s. c. in the 2nd s. c., making 5 loops of the ch. of 7 in all — ch. 7 — skip 4 s. c. of second row — 1 s. c. in the 5th s. c. — ch. 7 — skip 4 s. c. of second row — 1 s. c. in the 5th s. c. — repeat from*, until the end of the row.

FOURTH ROW: 1 s. c. over ch. of 9 of preceding row — 7

For making Borders:

FIRST ROW: On side of medallion — 1 s. c. over ch. of 7 — ch. 9 — 2 s. c. over next ch. of 7 — 2 s. c. over next ch. of 7 — *ch. 4 — 1 t. c. over next ch. of 7 — 1 t. c. over ch. of 7 of the 2nd medallion — ch. 4 — 2 s. c. over next ch. of 7 — ch. 7 — 2 s. c. over next ch. of 7 — repeat from*, until the end of the row.

SECOND ROW: On opposite side of medallion — same as First Row.

THIRD ROW: 1 s. c. over ch. of 9 — *ch. 7 — 1 s. c. over ch. of 7 — ch. 7 — 1 s. c. over ch. of 4 — ch. 7 — 1 s. c. over next ch. of 4 — repeat from*, until the end of the row.

FOURTH ROW: On opposite side of medallion — same as Third Row.

FIFTH ROW: 1 s. c. over ch. of 7 — ch. 7 — *1 s. c. over next ch. of 7 — ch. 7 — repeat from* until the end of the row.

SIXTH ROW: On opposite side — same as Fifth Row.

SEVENTH ROW: 4 s. c. over ch. of 7 — ch. 2 — continue same, until the end of the row.

EIGHTH ROW: On opposite side — same as Seventh Row.

Fig. 30, Edging, matching Fig. 31, Insertion.

Make each medallion separately — and then join to the previous one.

FIRST ROW: Ch. 10 — and join by 1 s. c.

SECOND ROW: Ch. 2 — 24 d. c. over ch. of 10 — join with a **sl. st.**

THIRD ROW: *Ch. 8 — skip 2 st. of preceding row — 1 s. c. in the 3rd st. — repeat from*, until there are 8 loops.

FOURTH ROW: 4 s. c. over ch. of 8 — *1 p. l. — 4 s. c. over same ch. of 8 — 4 s. c. over next ch. of 8 — repeat from* around.

FIFTH ROW: Ch. 13 — *1 s. c. in the center of the 8 s. c. (after the 1st loop of preceding row) — ch. 13 — repeat from*.

SIXTH ROW: 4 s. c. over ch. of 13 — *1 p. l. — 4 s. c. — 1 p. l. — 4 s. c. — 1 p. l. — 4 s. c. over same ch. — 4 s. c. over next ch. of 13 — repeat from*.

For the **Border,** begin

FIRST ROW: On the side with 1 s. c. over center p. l. — ch. 6 — 1 s. c. over next p. l. — ch. 5 — 1 s. c. over next p. l. — ch. 5 — 1 s. c. over next p. l. — ch. 5 — 1 s. c. over next p. l. — *ch. 13 — skip 2 p. l. — 1 s. c. over next p. l. — ch. 5 — 1 s. c. over next p. l. — ch. 5 — 1 s. c. in the 1st st. of ch. of 13 — 7 d. c. in ch. of 13, picking up each ch. st. — turn — ch. 10 — skip 1 p. l. of this medallion — skip 1 p. l. of next medallion — 1 s. c. over next p. l. — turn — 1 s. c. in the 1st st. of ch. of 10 — 7 d. c. in ch. of 10, picking up each ch. st. — ch. 5 — skip 2 p. l. — 1 s. c. over next p. l. — ch. 5 — 1 s. c. over next p. l. — ch. 5 — 1 s. c. over next p. l. — repeat from*.

SECOND ROW: 1 s. c. over ch. of 6 of preceding row — ch. 6 — 1 s. c. over ch. of 5 — ch. 6 — 1 s. c. over next ch. of 5 — continue same.

THIRD ROW: 1 s. c. over ch. of 6 of preceding row — ch. 3 — 2 d. c. over same ch. — *ch. 3 — 3 d. c. over next ch. of 6 — repeat from*.

FOURTH ROW: 1 s. c. in the 3rd ch. st. of preceding row — ch. 3 — 2 d. c. in the 2 d. c. — *2 d. c. over ch. of 3 — 3 d. c. in the 3 d. c. — repeat from*.

Fig. 30.

Fig. 31, Insertion, matching Fig. 30, Edging.

Same as Edging in Fig. 30, the border on both sides of the medallions to be made alike, namely:

Finish First Row on the one side — then First Row on opposite side.

Finish Second Row on the one side — then Second Row on opposite side, and so on.

Fig. 31.

solid mesh; to 2 solid meshes there are 7 d. c.; to 3 solid meshes there are 10 d. c., and so on.

Attention is drawn to Figs. 34 to 39, inclusive, which have been designed especially for bedspreads; handsome effects can be obtained by using these edgings and insertions in connection with some good Russian linen in a narrow width in either white, cream or ecru.

Fig. 32, Edging, matching Fig. 33, Insertion.

For the 7 meshes, make ch. of 25.

FIRST ROW: Skip 4 st. — 1 d. c. in the 5th st., counting back from hook — 2 d. c. in the next 2 st. — 6 open meshes — turn — ch. 5.

For the balance of this design, follow the illustration and the general directions given above for Filet Crochet — and bear in mind to always make a ch. of 5 for turning at the end of each row.

For the scallop on its increase, make ch. of 6 — skip 4 st. — 1 d. c. in the 5th st., counting back from hook — 1 d. c. in the next st. — 1 d. c. in the 1st d. c. of preceding row — then continue from illustration.

For the scallop on its decrease, complete the solid mesh — then turn — ch. 2 — skip 1 d. c. — 3 s. c. in the 3 d. c. of preceding row — ch. 3 — 2 d. c. over ch. of 2 — 1 d. c. over 1 d. c. — then continue from illustration.

GENERAL DIRECTIONS FOR FILET CROCHET.

Figs. 32 to 39, inclusive, represent the style of crochet which is commonly known as Filet Crochet. A few explanatory remarks about the principal features of this style may seem appropriate, as they will facilitate the understanding of the directions.

Two kinds of square meshes are used, namely: the **open** and the **solid mesh.**

In order to make a number of **open** meshes, say 10 open meshes, make a ch. of 3 times the number of meshes, namely, a ch. of 30 — add 1 ch. — then 5 more ch. — and turn — skip 8 ch. st. — 1 d. c. in the 9th st., counting back from hook (thus completing the first open mesh) — *ch. 2 — skip 2 ch. st. — 1 d. c. in the 3rd ch. st. (thus completing the next open mesh) — repeat from*, until there are 10 open meshes. For second row of open meshes, if you wish, turn the work — make a ch. of 5 — 1 d. c. in the 2nd d. c. of preceding row — *ch. 2 — skip 2 st. — 1 d. c. in the next d. c. — repeat from*.

For a solid mesh, you would continue after 1 d. c. with — 2 d. c. over ch. of 2 — 1 d. c. over next d. c., thus showing 4 d. c. for one separate

Fig. 33.

Fig. 33, Insertion, matching Fig. 32, Edging.

For the 13 meshes, make ch. of 45.

FIRST ROW: Skip 8 ch. st. — 1 d. c. in the 9th st., counting back from hook — make 12 more open meshes.

For the balance of this design, follow the illustration and general directions given above for Filet Crochet — and bear in mind to always make a ch. of 5 for turning at the end of each row.

Fig. 34, Edging, matching Fig. 35, Insertion.

For the 18 meshes, make ch. of 58.

FIRST ROW: Skip 4 st. — 1 d. c. in the 5th st., counting back from hook — 2 d. c. in the next 2 st. — 9 open meshes — 1 solid mesh — 7 open meshes — turn — ch. 5.

For the balance of this design, follow the illustration and general directions given above for Filet Crochet — and bear in mind to always make a ch. of 5 for turning at the end of each row.

For the scallop on its increase, make ch. 6 — skip 4 st. — 1 d. c. in the 5th st., counting back from hook — 1 d. c. in the next st. — 1 d. c. in the first d. c. of preceding row — then continue from illustration.

For the scallop on its decrease, complete the solid mesh — then turn — ch. 2 — skip 1 d. c. — 3 s. c. in the next 3 d. c. of preceding row — ch. 3 — 2 d. c. over ch. of 2 — 1 d. c. over d. c. — then continue from illustration.

Fig. 35, Insertion, matching Fig. 34, Edging.

For the 20 meshes, make ch. of 66.

FIRST ROW: Skip 8 ch. st. — 1 d. c. in the 9th st., counting back from hook — make 6 more open meshes.

For the balance of this design, follow the illustration and general directions given above for Filet Crochet — and bear in mind to always make a ch. of 5 for turning at the end of each row.

Fig. 36, Edging, matching Fig. 37, Insertion.

For the 26 solid meshes, make ch. of 82.

FIRST ROW: Skip 4 ch. st. — 1 d. c. in the 5th st., counting back from hook — 1 d. c. in each of the 77 ch. st. — turn.

SECOND ROW: Ch. 3 — skip 1 d. c. — 1 d. c. in the 2nd d. c. of preceding row — 2 d. c. in the next 2 d. c. — 1 d. c. in each d. c. of preceding row.

For the scallop on its increase, make ch. 6 — skip 4 st. — 1 d. c. in the 5th st., counting back from hook — 1 d. c. in the next st. — 1 d. c. in the 1st d. c. of preceding row — then continue from illustration.

For the balance of this design, follow the illustration and general directions given above for Filet Crochet. For turning, follow directions of Second Row.

Fig. 32.

Fig. 34 above.   Fig. 35 below.

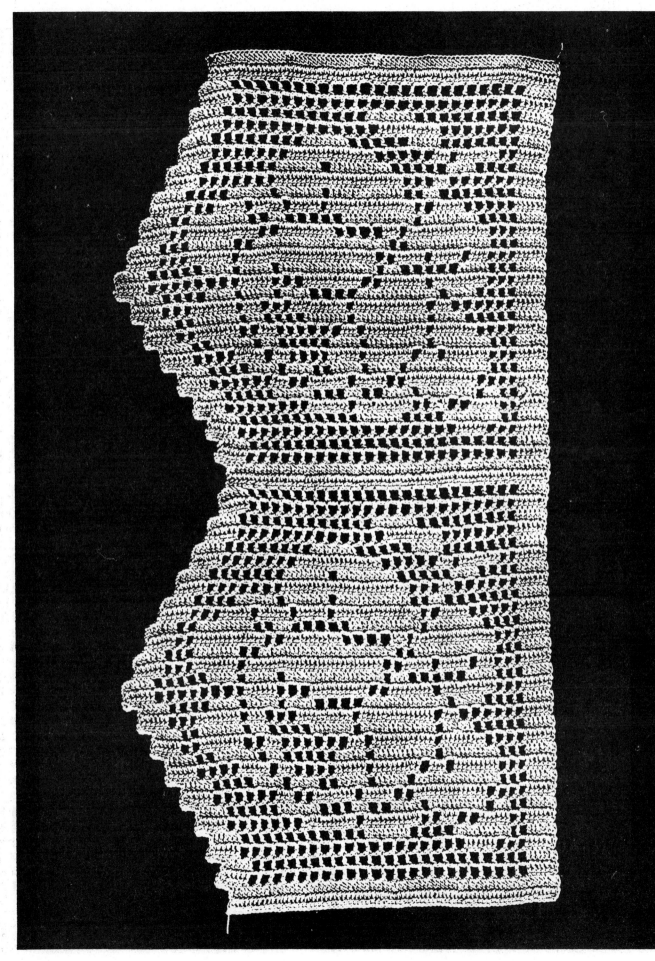

Fig. 36.

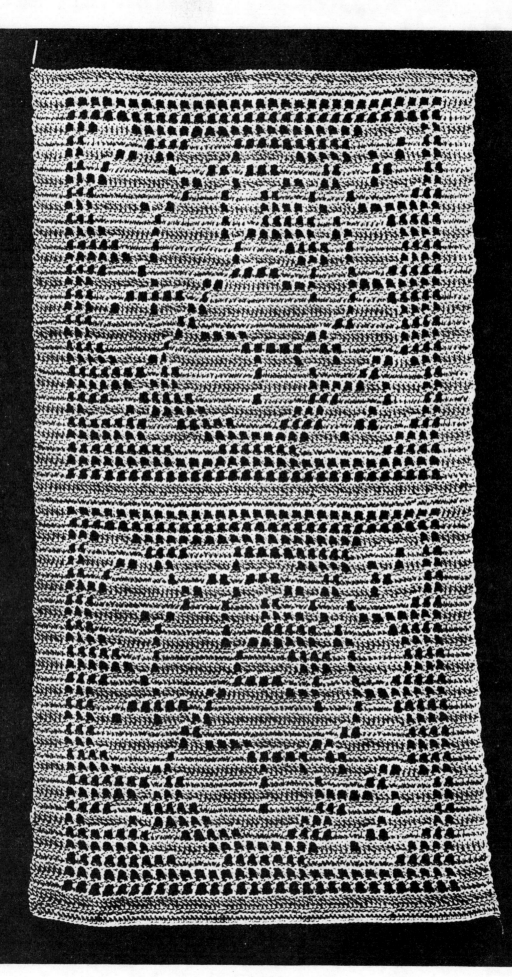

Fig. 37. Design used for the corners of the Scarf on the Cover page.

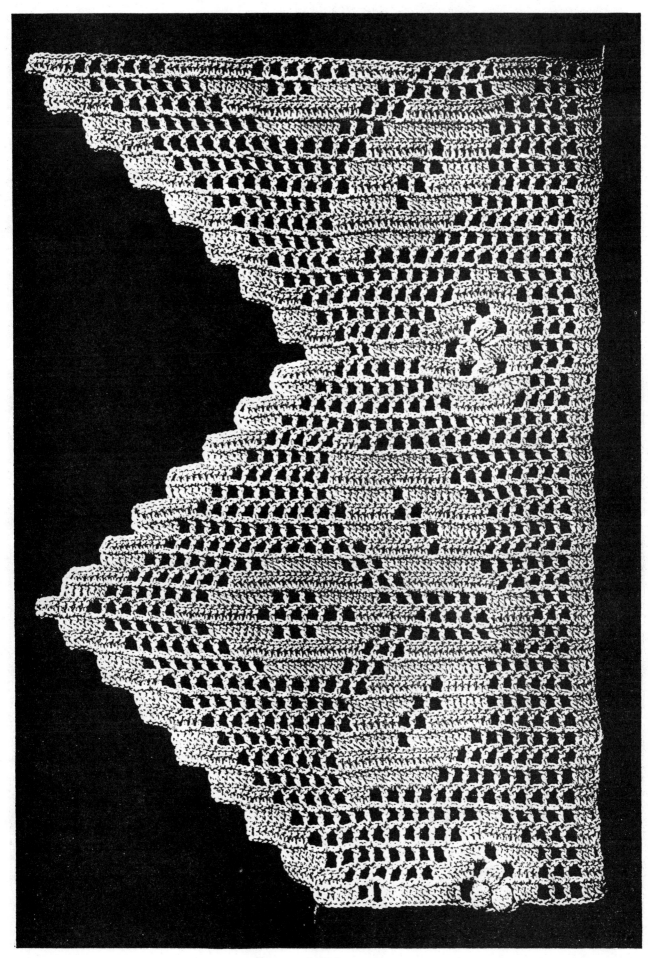

Fig. 38.

Fig. 39.

For the scallop on its decrease, complete the solid mesh — then turn — ch. 2 — skip 1 d. c. — 3 s. c. in the next 3 d. c. of preceding row — ch. 3 — 3 d. c. over 3 d. c. of preceding row — 2 d. c. over ch. of 2 — 1 d. c. over 1 d. c. — then continue from illustration.

Fig. 37, Insertion, matching Fig. 36, Edging.

For the 34 solid meshes, make ch. of 106.

FIRST ROW: Skip 4 ch. st. — 1 d. c. in the 5th st., counting back from hook — 1 d. c. in each of the 101 ch. st. — turn.

SECOND ROW: Ch. 3 — skip 1 d. c. — 1 d. c. in the 2nd d. c. of preceding row — 2 d. c. in the next 2 d. c. — 1 d. c. in each d. c. of preceding row.

For the balance of this design, follow the illustration and general directions given above for Filet Crochet. For turning, follow directions of Second Row.

Fig. 38, Edging, matching Fig. 39, Insertion.

Make a ch. of 52.

FIRST ROW: Skip 4 ch. st. — 1 d. c. in the 5th st., counting back from hook — 2 d. c. in the next 2 st. — 3 open meshes — 1 solid mesh — ch. 5 — skip 2 st. — 1 ppc. st. in the 3rd st. — ch. 5 — skip 2 st. — 1 ppc. st. in the 3rd st. — ch. 5 — skip 2 st. — 1 d. c. in the 3rd st. — 12 d. c. in the next 12 st. — 2 open meshes — 2 solid meshes — turn.

For the balance of this design, follow the illustration and general directions given above for Filet Crochet.

For the scallop on its increase, make ch. of 9 — skip 4 st. — 1 d. c. in the 5th st., counting back from hook — 4 d. c. in the next 4 st. — 4 d. c. in the 1st 4 d. c. of preceding row — ch. 2 — skip 2 st. — 1 d. c. in the 3rd st. — then continue from illustration.

For turning, make ch. of 3 — 1 d. c. in the 2nd d. c. of preceding row — 2 d. c. in the next 2 d. c. — then continue from illustration.

Before and after each ppc. st., make ch. of 5.

Fig. 39, Insertion, matching Fig. 38, Edging.

Make ch. of 79.

FIRST ROW: Skip 4 ch. st. — 1 d. c. in the 5th st., counting back from hook — 2 d. c. in the next 2 st. — 3 open meshes — 18 d. c. in the next 18 st., making 19 d. c. in all — *ch. 5 — skip 2 st. — 1 ppc. st. in the 3rd st. — repeat from*, until there are 4 ppc. st. — ch. 5 — skip 2 st. — 19 d. c. in the next 19 st. — 3 open meshes — 1 solid mesh — turn.

For the balance of this design, follow the illustrations and general directions given above for Filet Crochet.

For turning, make ch. of 3 — 1 d. c. in the 2nd d. c. of preceding row — 2 d. c. in the next 2 d. c. — then continue from illustration.

Before and after each ppc. st., make a ch. of 5.

NOTE: Anyone who is particularly interested in the application of Coronation Braid for crocheting will find a complete book on this subject in the "DOROTHY BRADFORD" Series 7. This splendid little book shows a large number of articles for wearing apparel and decorative house linens, with full instructions for working them.

Fig. 40, Edging, matching Fig. 41, Insertion.

C. B. used is Size 1.

FIRST ROW: 2 s. c. over fine part of braid — *form a loop of 3 knots of braid — 2 s. c., leaving these 3 knots of braid between — ch. 4 — 2 s. c., leaving 1 knot of braid between — repeat from*.

SECOND ROW: On opposite side of braid — same as First Row.

THIRD ROW: 1 s. c. over ch. of 4 of preceding row — *ch. 3 — 3 d. c. over same ch. — ch. 3 — 4 d. c. over next ch. of 4 — repeat from*.

FOURTH ROW: On opposite side of braid — 3 s. c. over ch. of 4 — *1 p. l. — 3 s. c. over same ch. of 4 — ch. 1 — 3 s. c. over next ch. of 4 — repeat from*.

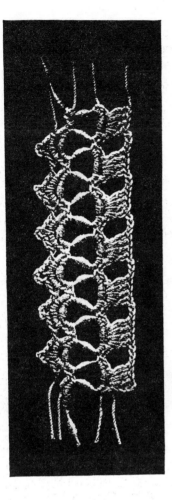

Fig. 40.

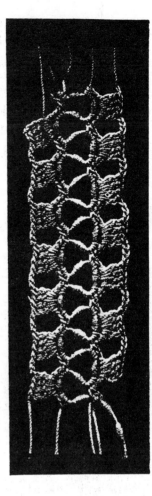

Fig. 41.

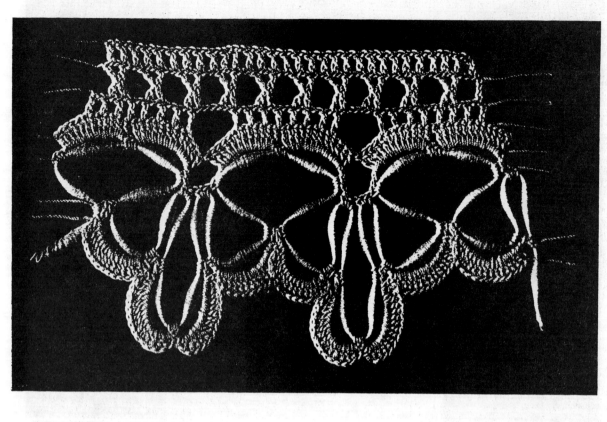

Fig. 43, Edging, matching Fig. 44, Insertion.
C. B. used is Size 5.

FIRST ROW: 2 s. c. over fine part of braid — form a loop of 3 knots of braid — 2 s. c., leaving these 3 knots of braid between — *ch. 10 — 2 s. c., leaving 1 knot of braid between — ch. 10 — 2 s. c., leaving 1 knot of braid between — form a loop of 3 knots of braid — 2 s. c., leaving these 3 knots between — form a loop of 4 knots of braid — 2 s. c., leaving these 4 knots of braid between — form a loop of 3 knots of braid — 2 s. c., leaving these 3 knots of braid between — repeat from*.

SECOND ROW: On opposite side of braid — 2 s. c. over fine part of braid — *2 s. c., leaving 4 knots of braid between — ch. 10 — 2 s. c., leaving 1 knot of braid between — 2 s. c., leaving 2 knots of braid between — ch. 10 — 2 s. c., leaving 1 knot of braid between — ch. 10 — 2 s. c., leaving 2 knots of braid between — ch. 10 — 2 s. c., leaving 1 knot of braid between — repeat from*.

THIRD ROW: 1 s. c. over ch. of 10 of preceding row — 14 d. c. over same ch. of 10 — 1 s. c. over same ch. of 10 — *1 s. c. over next ch. of 10 — 14 d. c. — 1 s. c. — repeat from*.

FOURTH ROW: On opposite side of braid — 1 s. c. over ch. of 10 — ch. 3 — 11 d. c. over same ch. of 10 — *12 d. c. over next ch. of 10 — repeat from*.

FIFTH ROW: 1 s. c. in the 5th d. c. of preceding row — ch. 4 — *skip 1 st. — 1 d. c. in the 2nd st. — ch. 1 — repeat from*, until there are 7 d. c. — ch. 5 — 1 d. c. in the 5th d. c. of next 12 d. c. of preceding row — *ch. 1 — skip 1 st. — 1 d. c. in the 2nd st. — repeat from*, until there are 8 d. c.

SIXTH ROW: 1 s. c. in the 3rd ch. st. of preceding row — ch. 7 — *skip 2 st. — 1 c. t. c. — ch. 2 — repeat from*.

SEVENTH ROW: 1 s. c. in the 6th ch. st. of preceding row — ch. 4 — skip 1 st. — 1 d.c. in the 2nd st. — *ch. 1 — skip 1 st. — 1 d. c. in the 2nd st. — repeat from*.

Fig. 44, Insertion, matching Fig. 43, Edging.
C. B. used is Size 5.

FIRST ROW: 2 s. c. over fine part of braid — *form a loop of 3 knots of braid — 2 s. c., leaving these 3 knots of braid between — 2 s. c., leaving a loop of 4 knots of braid between — 2 s. c., leaving a loop of 3 knots of braid between — ch. 9 — 2 s. c., leaving 1 knot of braid between — repeat from*.

SECOND ROW: 2 s. c. over fine part of braid, in the 1st loop of braid — *ch. 10 — 2 s. c., leaving 1 knot between — 2 s. c., leaving 2 knots

Fig. 43.

21

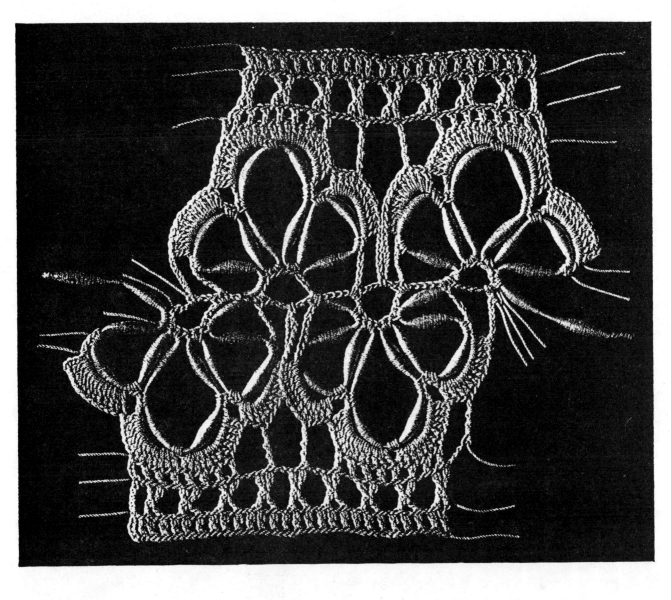

Fig. 44.

of braid between — ch. 10 — 2 s. c., leaving 1 knot of braid between — ch. 10 — 2 s. c., leaving 1 knot of braid between — 2 s. c., leaving 2 knots of braid between — ch. 10 — 2 s. c., leaving 1 knot of braid between — ch. 5 — turn the next 3 loops of braid on the opposite side — make 2 s. c. over ch. of 9 — ch. 5 — 2 s. c. over next ch. of 9 — turn the next 3 loops of braid on the opposite side — ch. 5 — 2 s. c. over fine part of braid in the 1st loop of braid — repeat from*.

THIRD ROW: On opposite side of braid — same as Second Row, but without turning the loops of braid, which are now in their proper position.

FOURTH ROW: 1 s. c. over ch. of 10 of preceding row — ch. 3 — 11 d. c. over same ch. of 10 — *12 d. c. over next ch. of 10 — repeat the same twice from* — ch. 8 — 1 s. c. over ch. of 5 of preceding row — ch. 8 — 12 d. c. over ch. of 10 of preceding row — *12 d. c. over next ch. of 10 — repeat the same twice from* — and continue with ch. of 8 — and so on, same as before.

FIFTH ROW: On opposite side of braid — same as Fourth Row.

SIXTH ROW: Skip first 12 d. c. of preceding row — 1 s. c. in the 6th d. c. of next 12 d. c. of preceding row — ch. 5 — *skip 1 st. — 1 d. c. in the 2nd st. — ch. 1 — repeat from*, until there are 7 d. c. — ch. 4 — 1 l. t. c. in the 4th d. c. of next 12 d. c. — ch. 4 — 1 l. t. c. in the 9th d. c. of next 12 d. c. — ch. 4 — 1 d. c. in the 5th d. c. of next 12 d. c. — *ch. 1 — skip 1 st. — 1 d. c. in the 2nd st. — repeat from*, until there are 8 d. c. — ch. 4 — 1 l. t. c. — and so on — same as before.

SEVENTH ROW: On opposite side of braid — same as Sixth Row.

EIGHTH ROW: 1 s. c. in the 4th ch. st. of preceding row — ch. 7 — *skip 2 st. — 1 c. t. c. — ch. 2 — repeat from*.

NINTH ROW: On opposite side of braid — same as Eighth Row.

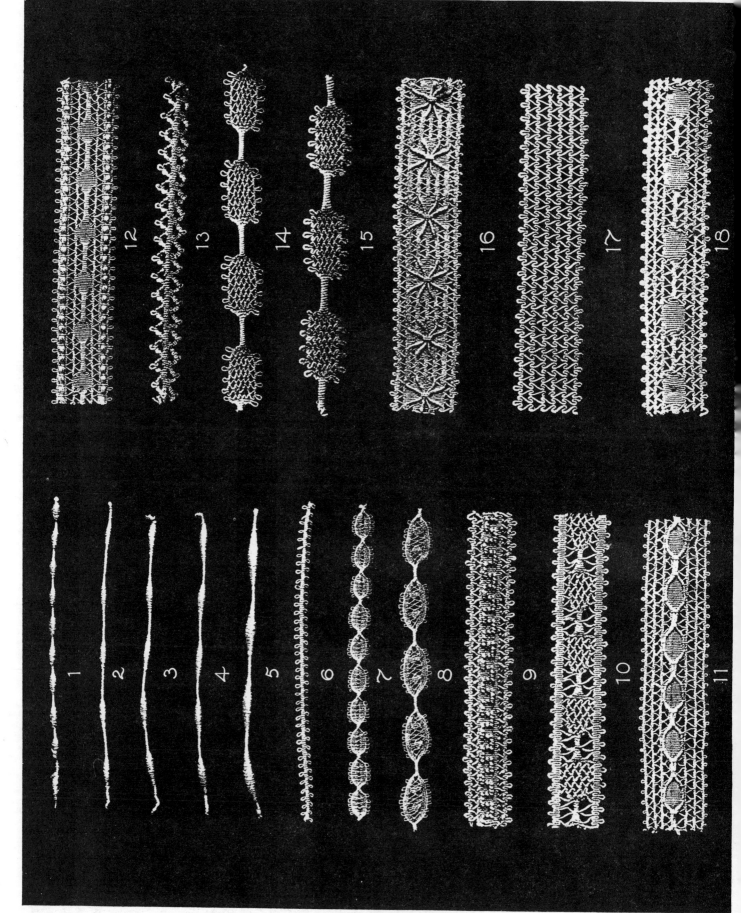

TENTH ROW: 1 s. c. in the 5th st. of preceding row — ch. 4 — *skip 1 st. — 1 d. c. in the 2nd st. — ch. 1 — repeat from*.

ELEVENTH ROW: On opposite side of braid — same as Tenth Row.

AN ITEM OF INTEREST TO EVERY NEEDLEWORKER.

There is a style of needlework, which has been known to a great many generations, which has fascinated every woman who ever attempted it and which is deserving of the widest possible use by everybody interested in decorating her home or beautifying her wearing apparel or her children's and infants' clothes by a dainty touch of needlework. The work is known under a number of names and is illustrated and explained in series 5 and 6 of the "DOROTHY BRADFORD" publications, which are obtainable at every art needlework department and art specialty shop.

Each series shows 12 colored patterns on one sheet (from simple conventionals to fancy florals) with directions for working. In these publications the work is called

HAND WEAVING

with the intention of indicating by its name the nature of the work; it consists of drawn work and weaving in over the remaining threads any of the illustrated designs.

The work is simple, very simple; the counting of threads is required only at the starting of the group or stem as the weaving is put in; it requires less counting than knitting or crocheting and will positively outlast any other kind of embroidery because it renders the material worked on very firm.

And what wealth of suggestions is now offered to the needleworker! The wonderful achievement of producing fast colors in the leading brands of embroidery threads has opened up fields of unlimited opportunities. Let your fancy have free sway now, arrange the colors suggested by series 5 and 6 of "DOROTHY BRADFORD" publications to suit your own tastes, to match your dresses, your furniture, your wall papers. These HAND WEAVING sheets (series 5 and 6), showing 12 patterns each, can be arranged by the tasteful and thinking needleworker for uncounted color schemes. Let us as an example take Fig. X (Series 6) which is shown in two lavenders, one yellow and one green; can you imagine the daintiness of this design on a hemstitched scarf in three blues and white or in three greens and white shading from the deep into the delicate hues?

Can you imagine Fig. H (Series 5) in a light yellow and white or in a baby blue and white on a baby pillow slip with the baby's initials embroidered above it?

Can you imagine Fig. Q (Series 6) in two pinks and white or in two lavenders and white on a guest towel with a pretty basket above it embroidered in cross stitch, or Fig. B (Series 5) in some delicate shade with white to offset it, for a band on your new shirtwaist?

It is a safe prediction to make that any one once attempting this work and recognizing its simplicity will do it again and again. Its daintiness makes it fascinating, its durability makes it practical, its simplicity has made it popular.

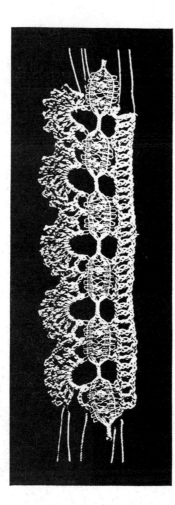

Fig. 46.

Fig. 46, Edging, matching Fig. 47, Insertion.

FIRST ROW: 1 s. c. in the last loop of first petal of braid — *ch. 8 — 1 s. c. in the 1st loop of next petal — ch. 5 — skip 2 loops — 1 s. c. in the 3rd loop — ch. 5 — skip 2 loops — 1 s. c. in the last loop — repeat from* — break off thread at end of each row.

SECOND ROW: On opposite side of braid — 1 s. c. in the 1st loop of first petal — *1 s. c. in the next loop — ch. 5 — skip 3 loops — 2 s. c. in the last 2 loops — ch. 5 — 1 s. c. in the 1st loop of next petal — repeat from*.

THIRD ROW: 1 s. c. in the 1st st. of preceding row — ch. 5 — *skip 1 st. — 1 d. c. in the 2nd st. — ch. 1 — repeat from*.

FOURTH ROW: On opposite side of braid — 1 s. c. over ch. 7 — ch. 6 — 1 d. c. — *ch. 1 — 1 d. c. — repeat from*, until there are 6 d. c. over ch. of 7 — ch. 2 — 2 s. c. over ch. of 5 — ch. 5 — 2 s. c. over next ch. of 5 — ch. 2 — 1 d. c. over next ch. of 7 — *ch. 1 — 1 d. c. — repeat from*, until there are 7 d. c. over same ch. — and so on.

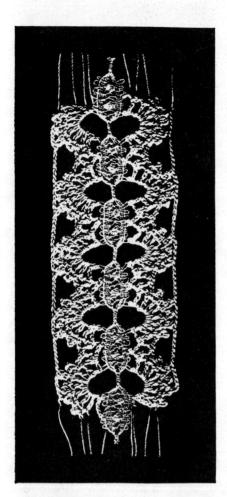

Fig. 47.

SECOND ROW: On opposite side of braid — same as First Row.

THIRD ROW: 1 s. c. over ch. of 5 of preceding row — ch. 3 — 1 ppc. st. over same ch. — *ch. 5 — 1 ppc. st. over next ch. of 5 — repeat from*.

FOURTH ROW: 1 s. c. in the 1st st. of preceding row — ch. 5 — *skip 2 st. — 2 d. c. in the next 2 st. — ch. 3 — repeat from*.

FIFTH ROW: On opposite side of braid — 1 s. c. over ch. of 5 — ch. 3 — 1 ppc. st. over same ch. — *2 p. — 1 ppc. st. over next ch. of 5 — repeat from*.

Fig. 50, Edging, matching Fig. 51, Insertion.

FIRST ROW: 1 s. c. in the 2nd loop of braid — *ch. 6 — skip 1 loop — 1 s. c. in the 2nd loop — repeat from* — break off thread at the end of each row.

SECOND ROW: On opposite side of braid — same as First Row.

THIRD ROW: *2 s. c. over ch. of 6 of preceding row — 1 p. l. — 1 s. c. — 1 p. l. — 1 s. c. — 1 p. l. — 2 s. c. over same ch. — 4 s. c. over next ch. of 6 — repeat from*.

FOURTH ROW: On opposite side of braid — 1 s. c. over ch. of 6 — *ch. 5 — 1 s. c. over same ch. — ch. 4 — 1 s. c. over next ch. of 6 — repeat from*.

FIFTH ROW: 2 s. c. over ch. of 5 of preceding row — *ch. 4 — 2 s. c. over next ch. of 5 — repeat from*.

SIXTH ROW: 2 s. c. over the 2 s. c. of preceding row — *3 s. c. over ch. of 4 — 2 s. c. over the next 2 s. c. — repeat from*.

Fig. 49.

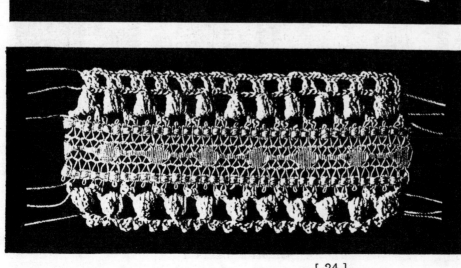

Fig. 48.

FIFTH ROW: 1 s. c. over ch. of 6 of preceding row — 1 p. — 1 s. c. over ch. of 1 — *1 p. — 1 s. c. over next ch. of 1 — repeat from*, until there are 5 p. in all — ch. 2 — 2 s. c. over ch. of 5 — ch. 2 — 1 s. c. over 1st ch. of 2nd scallop — 1 p. — 1 s. c. over next ch. of 1 — and so on.

Fig. 48, Edging, matching Fig. 49, Insertion.

FIRST ROW: 1 s. c. in the next 2 loops — ch. 5 — *skip 1 loop — 2 s. c. in the next 2 loops — ch. 5 — repeat from* — break off thread at the end of each row.

Fig. 52, Edging, matching Fig. 53, Insertion.

FIRST ROW: 1 s. c. in the 1st loop of first petal of braid — *ch. 7 — 1 s. c. in the 5th loop of next petal — ch. 5 — skip 3 loops — 1 s. c. in the last loop of same petal — repeat from* — break off thread at end of each row.

SECOND ROW: *3 s. c. over ch. of 7 of preceding row — 1 p. l. — 3 s. c. — 1 p. l. — 3 s. c. over same ch. — 2 s. c. over ch. of 5 — repeat from*.

THIRD ROW: On opposite side of braid — 1 s. c. in the 1st loop of petal — ch. 5 — *skip 3 loops — 1 s. c. in the last loop of same petal — ch. 3 — 1 s. c. in the 1st loop of next petal — ch. 4 — repeat from*.

Fig. 53, Insertion, matching Fig. 52, Edging.

FIRST and SECOND ROWS: Same as in Fig. 52, Edging.

THIRD and FOURTH ROWS: On opposite side of braid — same as First and Second Rows.

FIFTH ROW: 1 s. c. in the center of the 1st p. l. — ch. 5 — 1 s. c. in the next p. l. — *ch. 5 — 1 s. c. in the next p. l. — ch. 3 — 1 s. c. in the next p. l. — repeat from*.

SIXTH ROW: On opposite side of braid — same as Fifth Row.

Fig. 54, Edging, matching Fig. 55, Insertion.

FIRST ROW: 1 s. c. in the 1st loop of braid — 4 s. c. in the next 4 loops — ch. 5 — *1 s. c. in the next loop — ch. 5 — repeat from*, until there are 5 loops of ch. of 5 in all — 4 s. c. in the next 4 loops, giving 5 s. c. in all — ch. 5 — 1 s. c. in the next loop — and so on — break off thread at end of each row.

SECOND ROW: On opposite side of braid — same as First Row. Arrange to have the center loops of ch. of 5 of this row directly opposite the 5 s. c. of First Row.

THIRD ROW: 1 s. c. over ch. of 5 of preceding row — ch. 5 — 1 d. c. over next ch. of 5 — *ch. 3 — 1 d. c. over same ch. — ch. 3 — 1 d. c. over next ch. of 5 — ch. 3 — 1 d. c. over same ch. — ch. 3 — 1 d. c. over the 4th ch. of 5 — ch. 3 — 1 d. c. over same ch. — ch. 3 — 1 d. c. over next ch. of 5 — ch. 3 — 1 d. c. over next ch. of 5, leaving the 5 s. c. between — ch. 3 — 1 d. c. over next ch. of 5 — repeat from*.

FOURTH ROW: On opposite side of braid — same as Third Row.

FIFTH ROW: 1 s. c. over ch. of 5 of preceding row — ch. 5 — 4 d. c. over 1st ch. of 3 — ch. 2 — skip next ch. of 3 — 4 d. c. over next ch. of 3 — ch. 2 — skip ch. of 3 — 4 d. c. over next ch. of 3 — ch. 7 — skip 3 ch. of 3 — 4 d. c. over ch. of 3, between the 2 d. c. of next scallop — and so on.

SIXTH ROW: 1 s. c. in the 4th ch. st. of preceding row — ch. 3 —

63

Fig. 50.

Fig. 51.

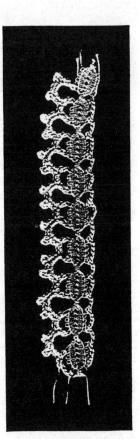

Fig. 52.

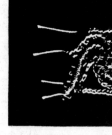

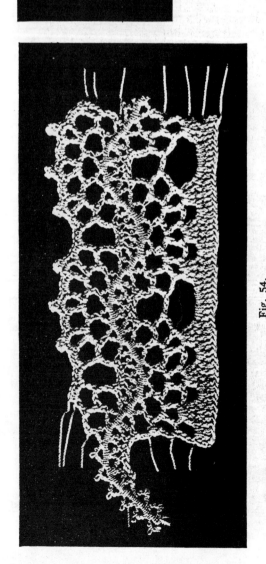

Fig. 53.

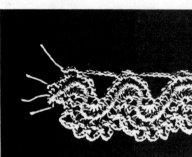

Fig. 57.

Fig. 56.

Fig. 54.

2 d. c. over same ch. — 4 d. c. in the 4 d. c. — 3 d. c. over ch. of 2 — 4 d. c. — continue same; over ch. of 7, make 7 d. c.

SEVENTH ROW: On opposite side of braid — 3 s. c. over 1st ch. of 5 — 2 s. c. over ch. of 3 — 1 p. — 2 s. c. over same ch. — *3 s. c. over next ch. of 3 — 2 s. c. over ch. of 3 — 1 p. — 2 s. c. over same ch. — repeat from* — 2 s. c. over next ch. of 3 — 3 s. c. over next ch. of 3, between the scallops — 2 s. c. over next ch. of 3 — 2 s. c. over next ch. of 3 — 1 p. — and so on.

Fig. 55.

Fig. 56, Edging, matching Fig. 57, Insertion.

FIRST ROW: 1 s. c. in the 1st loop of braid — ch. 1 — *put hook through the next loop of braid — thread over hook — draw through the loop — repeat from*, until there are 8 loops on hook — thread over hook — and draw through the 8 loops — ch. 1 — *1 s. c. in the next loop — ch. 1 — repeat from*, until there are 7 s. c. in all — ch. 1 — draw thread through 7 loops — and so on — break off thread at end of each row.

SECOND ROW: On opposite side of braid — same as First Row.

THIRD ROW: 1 s. c. over ch. of 1, after the first 3 s. c. of preceding row — ch. 3 — *1 s. c. over next ch. of 1 — ch. 6 — 1 s. c. over ch. of 1, after the 3 s. c. of 2nd scallop — ch. 3 — repeat from*.

FOURTH ROW: On opposite side of braid — 1 s. c. over ch. of 1 — ch. 2 — 1 s. c. over ch. of 1, leaving 1 s. c. between — *ch. 5 — 1 s. c. over next ch. of 1, leaving 1 s. c. between — repeat from*, until there are 5 loops of the ch. of 5 — 1 s. c. over ch. of 1 of the 2nd scallop, between the 1st and 2nd s. c. of the 7 s. c. — ch. 5 — 1 s. c. over next ch. of 1 — and so on.

Fig. 58, Edging, matching Fig. 59, Insertion.

FIRST ROW: 1 s. c. in the 2nd loop of braid — ch. 3 — 1 d. c. in the same loop — *ch. 2 — skip 1 loop — 2 d. c. in the next loop — repeat from* — break off thread at the end of each row.

SECOND ROW: On opposite side of braid — same as First Row.

THIRD ROW: 1 s. c. over ch. of 2 of preceding row — *4 d. c. — 1 s. c. over same ch. — 1 s. c. over next ch. of 2 — repeat from*.

Fig. 60, Edging, matching Fig. 61, Insertion.

FIRST ROW: 1 s. c. in the 1st loop of petal — ch. 5 — *1 d. c. in the next loop — ch. 2 — repeat from*, until there is 1 d. c. in each loop — ch. 4 — 1 s. c. over stem, between petals — ch. 4 — 1 d. c. in the 1st loop of next petal — ch. 2 — 1 d. c. in the next loop — repeat same until there are 6 d. c. — and so on — break off thread at the end of each row.

SECOND ROW: On opposite side — same as First Row.

THIRD ROW: 1 s. c. over ch. of 5 of preceding row — ch. 4 — 1 d. c. over same ch. — *ch. 4 — 2 d. c. over next ch. of 2 — repeat from*, until there are 5 times 2 d. c. — then ch. 3 — 2 d. c. over 1st ch. of 2 of the 2nd scallop — and so on.

FOURTH ROW: On opposite side of braid — same as Third Row.

FIFTH ROW: 2 s. c. over ch. of 4 of preceding row — *1 p. l. — 2 s. c. over same ch. — 2 s. c. over next ch. of 4 — repeat from*, until there are 4 p. l. — 3 s. c. over ch. of 3, between scallops — continue same.

SIXTH ROW: On opposite side of braid — same as Fifth Row.

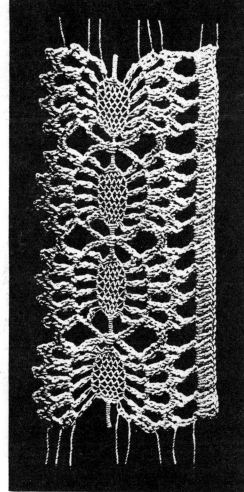

Fig. 60.

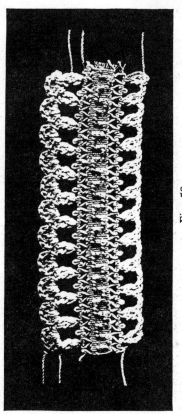

Fig. 58.

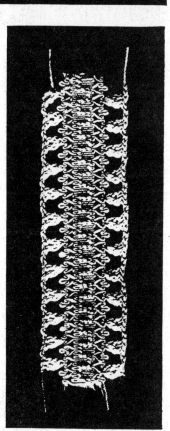

Fig. 59.

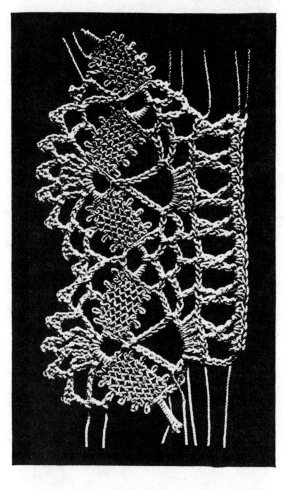

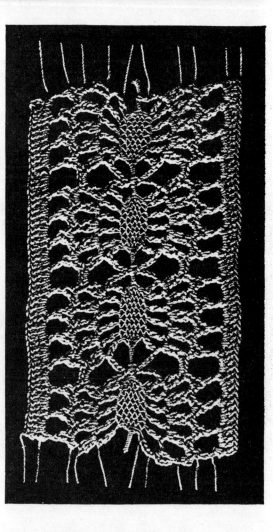

Fig. 62. Edging used on Luncheon Set, Fig. 42.

Fig. 63.

Fig. 61.

SEVENTH ROW: 1 s. c. in the 1st p. l. of preceding row — ch. 6 — 1 d. c. in the 2nd p. l. — *ch. 4 — 1 d. c. in the next p. l. — repeat from*.

EIGHTH ROW: 1 s. c. over ch. of 6 of preceding row — ch. 3 — 3 d. c. over same ch. — *1 d. c. over the 1 d. c. — 3 d. c. over ch. of 4 — repeat from*.

Fig. 62, Edging, matching Fig. 63, Insertion.

FIRST ROW: 1 s. c. in the 1st loop of petal — *ch. 10 — skip 4 loops — put hook through the last loop — then through the first loop of 2nd petal — thread over hook — draw thread through both loops — thread over hook — draw through the 2 loops on hook — ch. 10 — skip 4 loops — 1 s. c. in the last loop — ch. 4 — 1 s. c. over stem, between petals — ch. 4 — 1 s. c. in the 1st loop of next petal — repeat from* — break off thread at end of each row.

SECOND ROW: 1 s. c. over ch. of 10 of preceding row — ch. 6 — 1 s. c. over next ch. of 10 — *ch. 6 — 1 s. c. over ch. of 4 — repeat from*.

THIRD ROW: 1 s. c. over ch. of 6 of preceding row — ch. 3 — 6 d. c. over same ch. — ch. 3 — 1 d. c. over next ch. of 6 — *ch. 3 — 1 d. c. over next ch. of 6 — repeat from*, until there are 4 ch. of 3 — then 7 d. c. — and so on.

FOURTH ROW: 1 s. c. in the 2nd ch. st. of preceding row — ch. 7 — skip 2 st. — *1 c. t. c. — ch. 2 — skip 2 st. — repeat from*.

FIFTH ROW: 2 s. c. over ch. 7 of preceding row — *2 s. c. in ch. between c. t. c. — 2 s. c. over ch. of 2 — repeat from*.

[28]

Fig. 64.

Fig. 66.

SEVENTH ROW: 1 s. c. over ch. of 7 of preceding row — 1 p. — *1 s. c. over next ch. of 7 — ch. 2 — 1 p. — ch. 2 — 1 s. c. over next ch. of 7 — repeat ch. 2 — 1 p. — ch. 2 — 1 s. c. over ch. — 6 times in all — 1 p. — repeat from*.

Fig. 67.

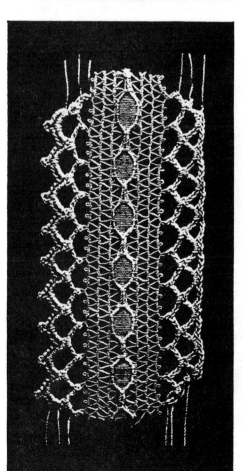

Fig. 65.

SIXTH ROW: On opposite side of braid — 1 s. c. in the 3rd loop of first petal — *ch. 7 — skip 2 loops — put hook through the last loop — then through the 1st loop of 2nd petal — thread over hook — draw thread through both loops — thread over hook — draw through 2 loops on hook — ch. 7 — skip 2 loops — 1 s. c. in the next loop — ch. 7 — 1 s. c. over stem, between petals — ch. 6 — 1 s. c. over same place — ch. 6 — 1 s. c. over same place — ch. 6 — 1 s. c. over same place — ch. 7 — skip 2 loops — 1 s. c. in the 3rd loop — repeat from*.

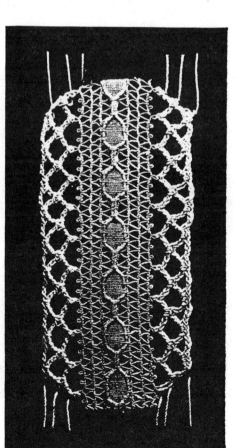

FOURTH ROW: On opposite side of braid — same as Third Row.

FIFTH ROW: 3 s. c. over ch. of 6 of preceding row — *ch. 3 — 3 s. c. over next ch. of 6 — repeat from*.

SIXTH ROW: On opposite side of braid — 4 s. c. over ch. of 6 — *1 p. l. — 4 s. c. over same ch. — 4 s. c. over next ch. of 6 — repeat from*.

Fig. 66, Edging, matching Fig. 67, Insertion.

FIRST ROW: 1 s. c. in the 2nd loop of braid — ch. 3 — *1 d. c. in the next loop — ch. 1 — repeat from* — break off thread at the end of each row.

SECOND ROW: On opposite side of braid — same as First Row.

THIRD ROW: 1 s. c. over ch. of 3 of preceding row — ch. 6 — *skip 2 st. — 3 d. c. in the next 3 st. — ch. 3 — repeat from*.

FOURTH ROW: On opposite side of braid — same as Third Row.

FIFTH ROW: 2 s. c. over ch. of 6 of preceding row — *ch. 5 — 2 s. c. over ch. of 3 — repeat from*.

SIXTH ROW: On opposite side of braid — same as Fifth Row.

SEVENTH ROW: 1 s. c. over ch. of 5 of preceding row — ch. 3 — 2 d. c. over same ch. — *ch. 3 — 3 d. c. over next ch. of 3 — repeat from*.

EIGHTH ROW: On opposite side of braid — 6 s. c. over ch. of 5 — 6 s. c. over next ch. of 5 — repeat same.

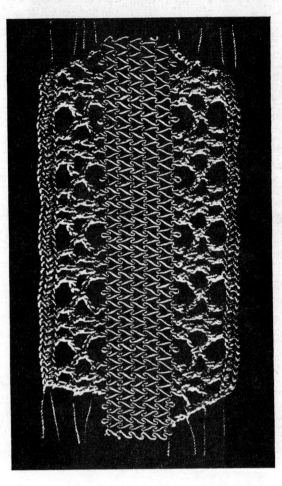

Fig. 69.

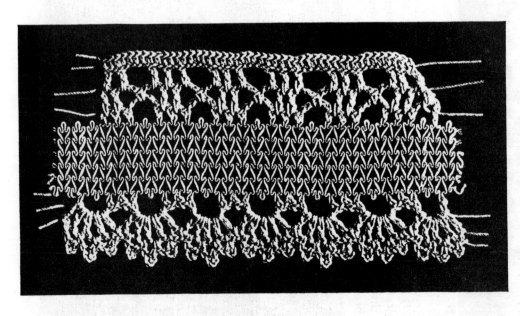

Fig. 68.

Fig. 64, Edging, matching Fig. 65, Insertion.

FIRST ROW: 1 s. c. in the 3rd loop of braid — ch. 6 — *skip 2 loops — 1 s. c. in the 3rd loop — ch. 6 — repeat from* — break off thread at end of each row.

SECOND ROW: On opposite side of braid — same as First Row.

THIRD ROW: 2 s. c. over ch. of 6 of preceding row — *ch. 6 — 2 s. c. over next ch. of 6 — repeat from*.

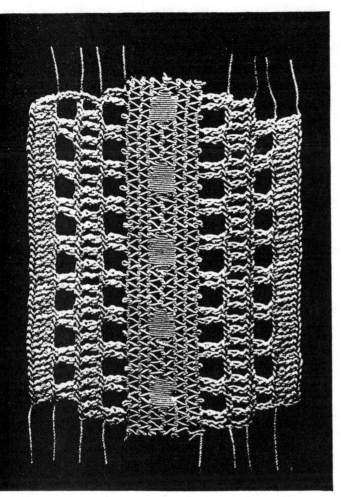

Fig. 68, Edging, matching Fig. 69, Insertion.

FIRST ROW: 1 s. c. in the 2nd loop of braid — *ch. 6 — skip 1 loop — 1 s. c. in the next loop — ch. 1 — 1 s. c. in the next loop — ch. 1 — 1 s. c. in the next loop — repeat from* — break off thread at end of each row.

SECOND ROW: On opposite side of braid — same as First Row.

THIRD ROW: 1 s. c. over ch. of 6 of preceding row — ch. 3 — *1 d. c. over same ch. — ch. 1 — repeat from*, until there are 4 d. c. — 1 d. c. over next ch. of 6 — ch. 1 — 1 d. c. — repeat ch. 1 — 1 d. c. until there are 5 d. c. in all.

FOURTH ROW: 1 s. c. over ch. of 3 of preceding row — ch. 2 — *1 p. — 1 s. c. over ch. of 1 — 1 p. — 1 s. c. over next ch. of 1 — 1 p. — 1 s. c. over next ch. of 1 — 1 s. c. between scallops — 1 s. c. over ch. of 1 of next scallop — repeat from*.

FIFTH ROW: On opposite side of braid — 1 s. c. over ch. of 6 — ch. 3 — *1 d. c. over ch. of 1 — ch. 1 — 1 d. c. over next ch. of 1 — ch. 3 — 1 s. c. over ch. of 6 — ch. 3 — repeat from*.

SIXTH ROW: 1 s. c. over ch. of 3 of preceding row — ch. 3 — *1 d. c. over ch. of 1 — ch. 1 — 1 d. c. over ch. of 3 — ch. 4 — 1 d. c. over next ch. of 3 — ch. 1 — repeat from*.

Fig. 71.

SEVENTH ROW: 1 s. c. in the 2nd ch. st. of preceding row — 1 s. c. in each stitch until the end of the row.

Fig. 70, Edging, matching Fig. 71, Insertion.

FIRST ROW: 1 s. c. in the 2nd loop of braid — ch. 4 — 1 d. c. in the next loop — *ch. 4 — skip 1 loop — 2 d. c. in the next 2 loops — repeat from* — break off thread at the end of each row.

SECOND ROW: On opposite side of braid — same as First Row.

THIRD ROW: 1 s. c. in the 3rd ch. st. of preceding row — ch. 4 — *skip 1 st. — 1 d. c. in the next st. — ch. 1 — repeat from*.

FOURTH ROW: 1 s. c. over 1st ch. of 1 of preceding row — ch. 5 — *skip 3 st. — 1 d. c. in the 4th st. — skip 1 st. — 1 d. c. in the 2nd st. — ch. 4 — repeat from*.

FIFTH ROW: 1 s. c. in the 3rd ch. st. of preceding row — ch. 2 — 1 d. c. in each st. until the end of the row.

SIXTH ROW: On opposite side of braid — 3 s. c. over loop of ch. of 4 — *3 p. — 3 s. c. over next ch. of 4 — 1 p. — 3 s. c. over next ch. of 4 — repeat from*.

Fig. 70.

No. 100.

1ST. ROW—1 s in br, ch 1, 1 s in br.
2ND ROW—1 d in br, * ch 4, 1 d in same l of br, 1 d in next 3rd l of br; repeat from *.

No. 101.

CHAIN 11—1ST ROW—1 t in 6th ch, 3 t in next 3 ch, ch 7, sl st to begining of 11 ch.
2ND ROW—11 s in 7 ch, 1 s in each of t.

No. 102.

CHAIN 12, JOIN—ch 3, 6 d, 1 p, 6 d, ch 3, sl st in ring of 12 ch.
TOP ROW—2 t, ch 3, 1 t.

No. 103.

UPPER EDGE—1 d in br, ch 2, 1 d in br.
1ST LOWER EDGE—4 t in br, ch 1, 4 t in 4th l of br.
2ND ROW—1 s in 1 ch, ch 2, 3 p, ch 2, 1 s in next 1 ch.

No. 104.

UPPER EDGE—1 s in br, ch 2, 1 s in br.
1ST LOWER EDGE—sl st to br, ch 6, sl st to 2nd l of br, ch 8, sk 1 l of br, sl st to br, ch 8.
2ND ROW—1 s in 6 ch., 7 d, ch 2, 7 d in 8 ch., 1 s in 6 ch.
3RD ROW—1 d in d, * ch 1, sk 1 d, 1 d in d; repeat from * 9 times.
4TH ROW—1 s in 1 ch, ch 4, 1 s in next 1 ch.

No. 105.

UPPER EDGE—1 s in br, ch 4, 1 s in br.
1ST LOWER EDGE—1 s in point of br., 1 t, * ch 1, 1 t; repeat from * once in point of br, ch 3, 1t, * ch 1, 1 t; repeat from * once in same point of br., 1 s in next point of br.
2ND ROW—1 d in s., ch 4, 2 d, ch 1, 1 p, ch 1, 2 d in 3 ch., ch 4, 1 d in s.

No. 106.

LOWER EDGE—1 s in br., 3 d, 1 p, 3 d in next 1 of br.
1ST UPPER EDGE—3 d in br, 3 d in next l of br.
2ND ROW—1 d in 2nd of 3 d, ch 2, sk 2 d, 1 d in next d.

No. 107

CHAIN 21—1ST ROW—5 d in 4th ch, 6 d in next 6 ch., ch 2, sk 2 ch, 3 d in 3 ch., * ch 2, sk 2 ch, 1 d in ch; repeat from * once.
2ND ROW—ch 5, 1 d in d, ch 2, 3 d in 3 d., * ch 2, 1 d; repeat from * twice.
3RD ROW—ch 3, 5 d in d, 2 d in 2 ch, 1 d in d, 2 d in 2 ch, 1 d in d., ch 2, 3 d in 3 d., * ch 2, sk 2 ch, 1 d in d; repeat from * once.

No. 108.

WORK DESIRED LENGTH IN SPACES.
1ST ROW—3 s in each of 5 sp, ch 7, turn, sl st to 6th s., 2 s, 1 p, 7 s, 1 p, 2 s in 7 ch., 3 s in next sp, ch 7, turn, sk 1 p, 1 s., 5 d in 5 s., ch 7, sk 1 s, 1 p, sl st to 4th s., 2 s, 1 p, * 4 s, 1 p; repeat from * once, 4 s in 7 ch., 1 s over each of 5 d, ch 5, turn, 1 t over 3rd s, ch 5, sl st to 1 st s., 4 s, 1 p, 4 s in 5 ch, 3 p, 4 s, 1 p, 4 s in next 5 ch., 2 s, 1 p, * 4 s, 1 p; repeat from * once, 2 s in 7 ch., 3 s in each of 5 sp before starting next scl.

No. 109.

CHAIN 18—1ST ROW—1 d in 8th ch, 2 d in next 2 ch., ch 2, sk 2 ch., 2 d in ch, ch 2, 2 d in next ch., ch 2, 1 d in last ch.
2ND ROW—ch 3, 5 d in d., ch 2, 2 d, ch 2, 2 d in 2 ch., ch 2, 3 d in 3 d., ch 2, 1 d in d.

No. 110.

CHAIN 29—1ST ROW—1 d in 4th ch, 11 d in next 11 ch., ch 5, sk 3 ch, 12 d in 12 ch.
2ND ROW—ch 3, 9 d in 9 d., ch 5, 1 s in 5 ch, ch 5, sk 2 d, 10 d in 10 d.
3RD ROW—ch 3, 7 d in 7 d., ch 5, 1 s in 5 ch, ch 5, 1 s in next 5 ch, ch 5, sk 2 d, 8 d in 8 d.
4TH ROW—ch 3, 5 d in 5 d., * ch 5, 1 s in 5 ch; repeat from * twice, ch 5, sk 2 d, 6 d in 6 d.
5TH ROW—ch 3, 3 d in 3 d., * ch 5, 1 s in 5 ch; repeat from * 3 times, ch 5, sk 2 d, 4 d in 4 d.
6TH ROW—Like 4th.
7TH ROW—Like 3rd.
8TH ROW—Like 2nd.
9TH ROW—Like 1st.

No. 111.

CHAIN DESIRED LENGTH—1ST ROW—1 d in each ch.
2ND ROW—1 d in d, ch 1, sk 1 d, 1 d in next d.
3RD ROW—1 d in d, 1 d in 1 ch, 1 d in d.
4TH ROW—sl st in d, ch 8, * 2 ds in 3rd ch catching 1 thread only, ch 2 sl st in same 3rd ch., ch 2; repeat from * twice, ch 5, sl st in 6th d., ch 8, 1 d in 3rd ch, catching only 1 thread, sl st to petal, 1 d in same 3rd ch, ch 2, sl st to same 3rd ch, finish flower like before.
5TH ROW—sl st to lower petal, ch 7, sl st to next lower petal.
6TH ROW—12 s in each of 7 ch.

No. 112.

UPPER EDGE—1 d in br, ch 2, 1 d in next 1 of br.
1ST LOWER ROW—1 s in br, ch 2, 1 s in next 1 of br.
2ND ROW—3 d in 2 ch, 3 d in next 2 ch., ch 5, sk 1 s, 2 ch, 1 s., 3 d in next 2 ch.
3RD ROW—4 d, ch 3, 4 d in 5 ch., sk 6 d, 4 d, ch 3, 4 d in next 5 ch.
4TH ROW—6 d in 3 ch, ch 5.
5TH ROW—4 d, ch 2, 4 d in 5 ch., ch 1, sk 6 d.
6TH ROW—1 s in 1 ch, ch 1, * 2 d, 1 p; repeat from * twice, 2 d in 2 ch, ch 1, 1 s in 1 ch.

No. 113.

CHAIN 17—1ST ROW—1 d in 4th ch, 2 d in next 2 ch, ch 3, sk 3 ch, 1 d in next ch., 3 d, ch 2, 3 d in next 3rd ch, ch 2, 1 d at end of ch.
2ND ROW—ch 3, 2 d in 2 ch., ch 2, 3 d, ch 2, 3 d in 2 ch., 1 d in d, ch 3, 4 d in 4 d.
3RD ROW—ch 3, 3 d in 3 d, ch 3, 1 d in d., 3 d, ch 2, 3 d in 2 ch., ch 2, 3 d in 2 ch, ch 2, 1 d in 3rd d. Each succeeding row is made like explained before, adding only an extra ch of 2 and 3 ds in each row.
1ST LOWER EDGE—1 s in o m, ch 5, 1 s in next o m, ch 5, 1 s in point, ch 5, 1 s in next o m; repeat.
2ND ROW—8 s in each 5 ch.

No. 114.

CHAIN 18—1ST ROW—1 d in 4th ch, 14 d in next 14 ch.
2ND ROW—ch 3, 3 d in 3 d., * ch 2, sk 2 d ,1 d in d; repeat from * twice, 3 d in 3 d.
3RD ROW—ch 3, 3 d in 3 d, ch 2, sk 2 ch, 1 d in d, 2 d in 2 ch, 1 d in d, ch 2, 4 d in 4 d.
4TH ROW—Like 2nd.
5TH ROW—Like 1st.
1ST LOWER EDGE—3 s in each sp.
2ND LOWER EDGE—2 t in 2 s, sk 4 s, 2 t in next 2 s, ch 5, 2 t in next 2 s, sk 4 s.
3RD ROW—3 d, 3 p, 3 d in 5 ch.

6

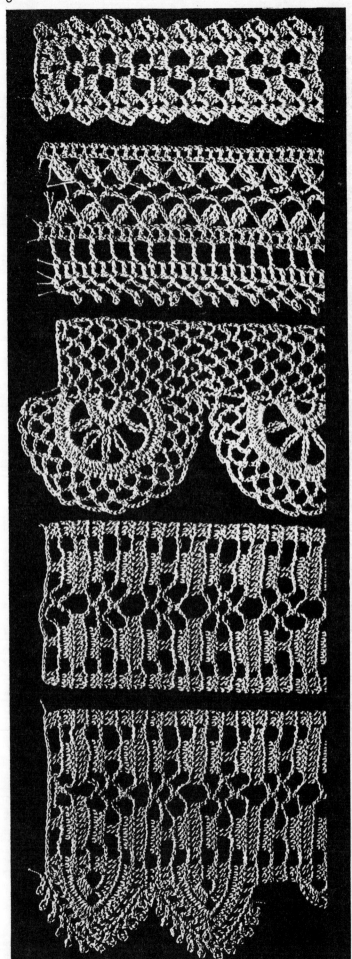

No. 115.

CHAIN 14—1ST ROW—2 d in 4th ch, ch 2, 3 d in next ch., ch 2, sk 2 ch, 3 d in next 3 ch, ch 2, sk 2 ch, 3 d in next ch, ch 2, 3 d in next ch.
2ND ROW—ch 3, 3 d, ch 2, 3 d in 2 ch., 3 d in next 2 ch, ch 2, 3 d in next 2 ch., 3 d, ch 2, 3 d in next 2 ch.
3RD ROW—ch 3, 3 d, 2 ch, 3 d in 2 ch., ch 2, 3 d in next 2 ch, ch 2, 3 d, ch 2, 3 d in 2 ch.

No. 116.

CHAIN DESIRED LENGTH—1ST ROW—1 d in ch, ch 1, sk 1 ch, 1 d in ch.
2ND ROW—1 cl of 2 t, ch 4, sl st in d., ch 4, sk 2 d, 1 cl of 2 t, ch 4, sl st in 3rd d.
3RD ROW—sl st to cl, ch 7, sl st to cl.
5TH AND 6TH ROWS—Worked like 1st and 2nd.
4TH ROW—sl st to cl, ch 3, 1 s over 7 ch, ch 3, sl st to next cl.
7TH ROW—1 t in d, ch 3, sk 1 d, 1 t in d.
8TH ROW—1 d in t, ch 1, 1 d in 2nd ch, ch 1, 1 d in t.
9TH ROW—sl st to d, ch 5, sk 1 d, sl st to next d.
10TH ROW—1 s in 5 ch., ch 2, 1 p, ch 2, 1 s in next 5 ch.

No. 117.

CHAIN 18.—1ST ROW—1 s in 8th ch, * ch 5, 1 s in next 3rd ch; repeat from * twice.
2ND ROW—* ch 5, 1 s in 5 ch; repeat from * twice, ch 5, 1 s in 8 ch.
3RD, 4TH AND 5TH ROWS—Like 1st and 2nd.
5TH ROW, CONTINUE—ch 5, 1 d in s, ch 3, 1 s in 5 ch, * ch 5, 1 s; repeat from * 3 times
6TH ROW—* ch 5, 1 s; repeat from * 3 times, ch 3, 6 d, ch 2, 6 d in 5 ch., sl st to s.
7TH ROW—ch 10, sl st to 4th d, ch 5, sl st to 5th ch., * ch 10, sl st to 2 ch between 6 ds., ch 5, sl st to 5th ch; repeat from * twice, ch 10, sl st to 3rd d, ch 5, sl st to 5th ch, ch 5, 1 s in 3 ch., * ch 5, 1 s in 5 ch; repeat from * 3 times.
8TH ROW—* ch 5, 1 s in 5 ch; repeat from * 3 times, * 7 d in 5 ch; repeat from * 5 times, sl st to 5 ch.
9TH ROW—* ch 5, 1 s in 3rd d; repeat from * 13 times, * ch 5, 1 s in 5 ch; repeat from * 3 times.
10TH ROW—* ch 5, 1 s in 5 ch; repeat from * 17 times.
11TH ROW—Like 10th.

No. 118.

CHAIN 33—1ST ROW—1 d in 4th ch, 1 d in next ch, ch 5, sk 4 ch, 2 d in 2 ch, ch 5, sk 3 ch, 1 s in ch, ch 5, sk 4 ch , 1 s in ch, ch 5, sk 4 ch, 2 d in 2 ch, ch 5, sk 4 ch, 3 d in 3 ch.
2ND ROW—ch 3, 2 d in 2 d., ch 3, 2 d in 2 ch, 2 d in 2 d, 2 d in 2 ch., ch 5, 1 s in 5 ch., ch 5, 2 d in 2 ch, 2 d in 2 d, 2 d in 2 ch., ch 3, 3 d in 3 d.
3RD ROW—ch 3, 2 d in 2 d, ch 1, 1 d in each of 2 ch, 6 d and 2 ch., ch 5, 1 d in each of 2 ch, 6 d and 2 ch., ch 1, 3 d in 3 d.
4TH ROW—ch 3, 2 d in 2 d, ch 3, sk 2 d, 6 d in 6 d, ch 5, 1 s in 5 ch, ch 5, sk 2 d, 6 d in 6 d, ch 3, 3 d in 3 d.
5TH ROW—ch 3, 2 d in 2 d, ch 5, sk 2 d, 2 d in 2 d, ch 5, 1 s in 5 ch, ch 5, 1 s in next 5 ch, ch 5, sk 2 d, 2 d in 2 d, ch 5, 3 d in 3 d.
6TH ROW—Like 2nd.

No. 119.

WORK 4 ROWS LIKE NO. 118, CONTINUE ON 4TH ROW—ch 5, sl st to 3rd row, now sl st to 2nd row.
5TH ROW—5 d, ch 3, 5 d in 5 ch., 3 d in 3 d, ch 5, sk 2 d, 2 d in 2 d, * ch 5, 1 s in 5 ch; repeat from * once, ch 5, sk 2 d, 2 d in 2 d, ch 5, 3 d in 3 d.
6TH ROW—Like 2nd row down to 3 d in 3 d., 1 d in each of 5 d, 5 d in 3 ch, ch 1, 5 d in same 3 ch, 5 d in 5 d, sl st to next row.
7TH ROW—* ch 1, sk 1 d, 1 d in 1 d; repeat from * 4 times, * ch 1, 1 d in 1 ch; repeat from * 2 times, ch 1, 1 d in 1 d, * ch 1, sk 1 d, 1 d in 1 d; repeat from * 3 times, ch 1, 3 d in 3 d, finish row like 3rd row.
LOWER EDGE—1 s in 1 ch, ch 1, 1 p, ch 1, 1 s in next 1 ch.

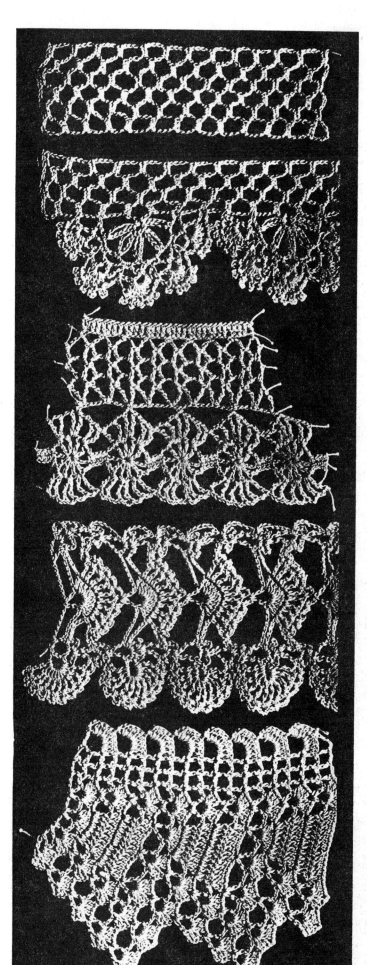

No. 120.

CHAIN 26.—1ST ROW—1 s in 12th ch, 2 s in next 2 ch, * ch 5, sk 3 ch, 3 s; repeat from * once.
2ND ROW—ch 8, sk 3 s, 3 s in 5 ch, * ch 5, sk 3 s, 3 s in 5 ch; repeat from * once.

No. 121.

WORK 8 ROWS like 1st and 2nd of No. 120, now ch 12, sl st in 10th ch, * ch 10, sl st in 10th ch; repeat from * 3 times, sl st together, * ch 5, sk 3 s, 3 s in 5 ch; repeat from * once.
9TH ROW—ch 8, sk 3 s, 3 s in 5 ch., ch 5, sk 3 s, 3 s in 5 ch.
10TH ROW—Like 9th.
11TH ROW—ch 8, sk 3 s, 3 s in 5 ch., ch 5, sk 3 s, 3 s in 8 ch., ch 2, 1 s in loop of 10 ch, * ch 4, 1 s in next loop of 10 ch; repeat from * 3 times, ch 2, 1 s in 1 s.
12TH ROW—* ch 5, sk 1 loop, 3 s in 4 ch; repeat from * 3 times, ch 5, sl st in 1st s, ch 8, 3 s in 5 ch, ch 5, sk 3 s, 3 s in 5 ch.
13TH ROW—ch 8, sk 3 s, 3 s in 5 ch., ch 5, sk 3 s, 3 s in 8 ch., * ch 2, 1 d, ch 3, 1 d in 3rd of 5 ch, ch 2, 1 s in 3 s; repeat from * 4 times, sl st to s.
14TH ROW—ch 2, * 1 d, 1 p; repeat from * 4 times in 3 ch., ch 2, 1 s in s; repeat from 1st * 4 times, ch 8, 3 s in 5 ch, ch 5, 3 s in 5 ch.

No. 122.

CHAIN DESIRED LENGTH. LOWER EDGE IS WORKED FIRST—1ST ROW—4 s in 4 ch, * ch 2, 1 d in 4th ch; repeat from * 3 times, ch 2, sk 3 ch, 4 s in 4 ch.
2ND ROW—1 t in 2 ch, ch 2, 1 t in same ch., * ch 2, sk 3 s, 1 t, ch 2, 1 t in next 2 ch; repeat from * once, sk 4 s.
Opposite side worked like rows 1 and 2.
UPPER EDGE—1ST ROW—1 s in 2 ch, ch 9, sk 6 t, 1 s in next 2 ch.
2ND ROW—1 t in ch, sk 3 ch, 1 t in ch., ch 5, 1 t in same ch, sk 3 ch, 1 t.
3RD ROW—1 d in 5 ch, * 1 d in next 5 ch, ch 5, 1 d in same 5 ch; repeat from *.
4TH ROW—Same like 3rd.
5TH ROW—1 s in 5 ch, ch 3, 1 s in next 5 ch.
6TH ROW—1 d in each ch.

No. 123.

CHAIN 23—1ST ROW—1 d in 8th ch, ch 7, sk 7 ch, 1 d in ch, ch 3, 1 d in same ch., ch 7, 1 d in last ch, ch 6, sl st in last ch.
2ND ROW—ch 7, 1 s in 3rd ch, ch 3, 1 s in 3 ch, ch 5, 1 s in 3 ch., ch 5, sk 7 ch, 10 d in 3 ch., ch 5, 1 s in 3 ch, ch 5, 1 s in same 3 ch, ch 5, 1 s in same 3 ch, ch 8.
3RD ROW—1 t in 2nd s, ch 3, 1 t in same 2nd s., ch 4, sk 5 ch, 1 d in d, * ch 1, 1 d in 1 d; repeat from * 8 times, ch 4, 1 t in 2nd s, ch 3, 1 t in 2nd s, * ch 1, 1 t in 7 ch; repeat from * 9 times.
4TH ROW—* ch 3, 1 s in 1 ch; repeat from * 9 times, ch 5, 1 s in 3 ch, ch 5, 1 s in same 3 ch, ch 2, sk 2 ch, 1 s in 1 ch, * ch 3, 1 s in 1 ch; repeat from * 9 times, ch 2, 1 s in 3 ch, ch 5, 1 s in same 3 ch, ch 5, 1 s in same 3 ch.

No. 124.

CHAIN 23—1ST ROW—1 d in 8th ch, ch 2, sk 2 ch, 1 d in ch, * ch 2, sk 2 ch, 1 d in ch, ch 2, 1 d in same ch; repeat from * 3 times.
2N DROW—ch 3, 2 d, ch 2, 3 d in 2 ch., 3 d, ch 2, 3 d in next 2 ch., 6 d in next 2 ch., 3 d, ch 2, 3 d in next 2 ch., 1 d in d, * ch 2, 1 d in d; repeat from * once, ch 5, 1 d in d.
3RD ROW—ch 3, 7 d in 5 ch, 1 d in d, * ch 2, 1 d; repeat from * once, ch 2, 1 d, ch 2, 1 d in 2 ch, ch 2, 2 d in next d, * 1 d in d; repeat from * 3 times, 2 d in d, * ch 2, 1 d, ch 2, 1 d in 2 ch; repeat from * once.
4TH ROW—ch 3, 2 d, ch 2, 3 d in 2 ch., 3 d, ch 2, 3 d in next 2 ch., 2 d in d, * 1 d in d; repeat from * 5 times, 2 d in d., 3 d, ch 2, 3 d in 2 ch, 1 d in d, * ch 2, 1 d; repeat from * once, ch 5, sl st to 4th d.
5TH ROW—ch 3, 7 d in 5 ch, 1 d in d, * ch 2, 1 d; repeat from * once, ch 2., 1 d, ch 2, 1 d in 2 ch, ch 2, 2 d in d, * 1 d in d; repeat from * 7 times, 2 d in d., * ch 2, 1 d, ch 2, 1 d in 2 ch; repeat from * once.
6TH ROW—ch 3, 2 d, ch 2, 3 d in 2 ch., 3 d, ch 2, 3 d in next 2 ch., 2 d in d, * 1 d in d; repeat from * 9 times, 2 d in d., 3 d, ch 2, 3 d in 2 ch., 1 d in d, * ch 2, 1 d in d; repeat from * once, ch 5, sl st to 4th d.
7TH ROW—ch 3, 7 d in 5 ch, 1 d in d, * ch 2, 1 d in d; repeat from * once, ch 2, 1 d, ch 2, 1 d in 2 ch., ch 2, 1 d, ch 2, 1 d in d, * ch 2, 1 d, ch 2, 1 d in 7th d; repeat from * once, * ch 2, 1 d, ch 2, 1 d in 2 ch; repeat from * once.
8TH ROW—ch 3, 2 d, ch 2, 3 d in 2 ch., * 3 d, ch 2, 3 d in next 2 ch; repeat from * 2 times, 6 d in next 2 ch., 3 d, ch 2, 3 d in next 2 ch., 1 d in d, * ch 2, 1 d in d; repeat from * once, ch 5, sl st to 4th d.
9TH ROW—Like 7th row, only work 8 d in 6 d.
10TH ROW—Like 8th row, only work 10 d in 8 d.

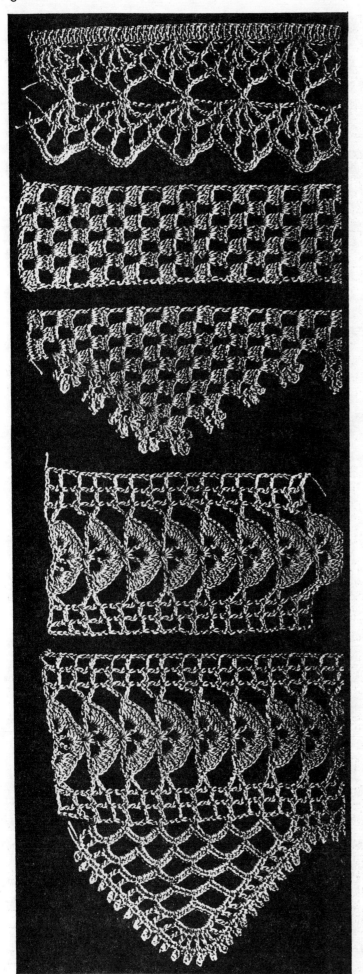

No. 125.

CHAIN DESIRED LENGTH—1ST ROW—1 d in each ch.
2ND ROW—1 s in d., * ch 2, 1 t in 5th d; repeat from * 3 times, ch 2, 1 s in 5th d.
3RD ROW—1 d in t, ch 3, 1 d in next t, ch 5, 1 d in next t, ch 3, 1 d in next t.
4TH ROW—1 s in 5 ch, ch 8, 1 s in next 5 ch.
5TH ROW—Like 2nd.
6TH ROW—Like 3rd.
7TH ROW—5 s in 3 ch, 9 s in 5 ch, 5 s in 3 ch.

No. 126.

CHAIN 16.—1ST ROW—1 d in 4th ch, 2 d in 2 ch., * ch 2, sk 2 ch, 3 d in 3 ch; repeat from * once., ch 2, 4 d in 4 ch.
2ND ROW—ch 5, sk 4 d, 3 d in 2 ch., * ch 2, sk 3 d, 3 d in 2 ch; repeat from * once., ch 2, 1 d in 4th d.
3RD ROW—ch 3, 3 d in 2 ch., * ch 2, sk 3 d, 3 d in 2 ch; repeat from * once, ch 2, 4 d in 5 ch.

No. 127.

CHAIN 12—1ST ROW—1 d in 4th ch, 2 d in 2 ch, ch 2, sk 2 ch, 4 d in 4 ch.
2ND ROW—ch 5, sk 4 d, 3 d in 2 ch, ch 2, sk 3 d, 1 d in d.
3RD ROW—ch 3, 3 d in 2 ch., ch 2, sk 3 d, 3 d, ch 2, 3 d in 5 ch.
4TH ROW—3 p, 3 d, ch 2, 3 d in 2 ch., ch 2, sk 3 d, 3 d in 2 ch., ch 2, 1 d in d.
5TH ROW—ch 3, 3 d in 2 ch, ch 2, sk 3 d, 3 d, ch 2, sk 3 d, 3 d, ch 2, 3 d in 2 ch.
6TH ROW—Like 4th, only ch 2 and 3 d extra.
7TH ROW—Like 5th, only add ch 2 and 3 d extra.
8TH ROW—Like 4th, only add necessary ch 2 and 3 d.
9TH ROW—Like 5th, only add necessary ch 2 and 3 d.
10TH ROW—3 p, 3 d, 3 p, 3 d in 2 ch., * ch 2, sk 3 d, 3 d in 2 ch; repeat from * 3 times, ch 2, 1 d in d.
11TH ROW—ch 3, 3 d in 2 ch., * ch 2, sk 3 d, 3 d in 2 ch; repeat from * 3 times.
12TH ROW—3 p, sk 3 d, 3 d in 2 ch., * ch 2, sk 3 d, 3 d in 2 ch; repeat from * 2 times, ch 2, 1 d in d.
Other rows are worked accordingly only leaving the 1 ch of 2 and ds off.

No. 128.

CHAIN 19—sl st in 13th ch., * ch 6, sl st in 1st of 6 ch; repeat from * once, ch 18.
1ST ROW—1 d in 8th ch, ch 2, sk 2 ch, 1 d in d, ch 2, 1 s over 10 ch, 6 d in loop of 6 ch., 3 d, ch 2, 3 d in next l of 6 ch., 6 d in next l, 1 s over ch, * ch 2, sk 2 ch, 1 d in ch; repeat from * once.
2ND ROW—ch 5, 1 d in d, ch 2, sk 2 ch, 1 d in d, ch 6., * 1 d, ch 3; repeat from * 2 times, 1 d in 2 ch., ch 6, 1 d in d, * ch 2, sk 2 ch, 1 d; repeat from * once.
3RD ROW—Like 1st.

No. 129.

Work 14 rows like 1st and 2nd of No. 128, now continue.—14TH ROW—* ch 7, sk 2 sp, sl st to d; repeat from * 5 times, turn, and in next 5 scallops crochet 12 s in each, 6 s in next scl, turn, * ch 7, sl st to next scl; repeat from * 4 times, turn, work like before, always decreasing the scallop till you have only one, now crochet the whole scallop up, filling in with singles.
1ST LOWER EDGE—1 d, ch 1, all around scallop.
2ND ROW—2 s in 1 ch, 1 p, sk 1 d., 2 s in 1 ch; repeat.

No. 130.

CHAIN DESIRED LENGTH—1ST ROW—1 d in ch, ch 2, sk 2 ch, 1 d in ch.
2ND ROW—1 s in d, ch 9, sk 2½ m, 1 s.
3RD ROW—4 s, 1 p, 4 s, 1 p, 4 s in 9 ch.
4TH ROW—sl st to scl, ch 9, sl st to next scl.
5TH ROW—Like 3rd.
6TH ROW—Like 4th.
7TH ROW—* 4 s, 1 p, 4 s, 1 p, 4 s in 9 ch; repeat from * once, 4 s, 1 p, 2 s in next 9 ch, turn, * ch 9, sl st to next scl; repeat from * once, 4 s, 1 p, 4 s, 1 p, 4 s in 9 ch, 4 s, 1 p, 2 s in next 9 ch, ch 9, turn, sl st to next scl, 4 s, 1 p, 2 s, 1 p, 2 s, 1 p, 4 s in 9 ch., * 2 s, 1 p, 4 s in next scl; repeat from * once.

No. 131.

UPPER EDGE—1 s in br, ch 4, 1 s in br, ch 4, 1 d between 2 med of br, ch 4.
LOWER EDGE—Same.
MIDDLE ROW—3 t in br, 3 t in br, ch 5, sl st to br, ch 9, sl st to br, ch 5, 3 t in br, 3 t in br.
Other row the same, only sl st to 9 ch, and after crocheting ts, sl st together.

No. 132.

CHAIN 33.—1ST ROW—1 d in 8th ch., * ch 2, sk 2 ch, 1 d; repeat from * 7 times.
2ND ROW—ch 3, * 2 d in 2 ch, 1 d in d; repeat from 8 times.
3RD ROW—ch 5, 1 d in 4th d, * ch 2, 1 d in 3rd d; repeat from * 7 times.
4TH ROW—Meshes.
5T HROW—Same.
6TH ROW—Like 2nd.

No. 133.

CHAIN 36—Works 1st 3 rows like No. 132, only making an extra mesh in width, now continue on 3rd row—ch 7, 1 d in d, * ch 2, 1 d in d; repeat from * 9 times.
4TH ROW—ch 5, 1 d in d, * ch 2, sk 2 ch, 1 d in d; repeat from * 8 times, * ch 1, 1 d; repeat from * 9 times in 7 ch., sl st to d.
5TH ROW—* 1 s, 1 p, 1 s in 1 ch; repeat from * 10 times, sl st to d, ch 3, * 2 d in 2 ch, 1 d in d, repeat from * 9 times.

No. 134.

CHAIN 31—1ST ROW—1 d in 4th ch, 26 d in 26 ch.
2ND ROW—ch 3, 2 d in 2 d., * ch 2, sk 2 ch, 3 d in 3 d; repeat from * 4 times.
3RD ROW—Like 1st.
4TH ROW—Like 2nd.
5TH ROW—Like 1st.
6TH ROW—Like 2nd.
7TH ROW—Like 1st.
8TH ROW—Like 2nd.
9TH ROW—Like 1st, continue—ch 10, sl st to 7th row.
10TH ROW—ch 3, 19 d in 10 ch., 3 d in 3 d, * ch 2, sk 2 d, 3 d in 3 d; repeat from * 4 times.
11TH ROW—ch 3 and work ds down to scl., * ch 1, sk 1 d, 1 d in d; repeat from * 9 times, sl st to 4th row.
12TH ROW—ch 5, * sk 1 d, 1 d, ch 1, 1 d in 1 ch, ch 1; repeat from * 9 times, 3 d in 3 d., * ch 2, sk 2 d, 3 d in 3 d; repeat from * 4 times.
13TH ROW—ch 3 and work ds down to scl., * ch 1, sk 1 d, 1 d in 1 ch; repeat from * 19 times, sl st to 2nd row.
14TH ROW—ch 3, 2 d in 1 ch, * sk 1 d, 3 d in 1 ch; repeat from * 19 times, 3 d in 3 d., * ch 2, sk 2 d, 3 d in 3 d; repeat from * 4 times.
15TH ROW—ch 3 and work down ds to scl., * ch 2, sk 2 d, 1 d in d; repeat from * 20 times., sl st to 1st row.
16TH ROW—* ch 1, 1 p, ch 1, 1 s in d; repeat from * 20 times., ch 3, 3 d in 3 d., * ch 2, sk 2 d, 3 d in 3 d; repeat from 4 times.

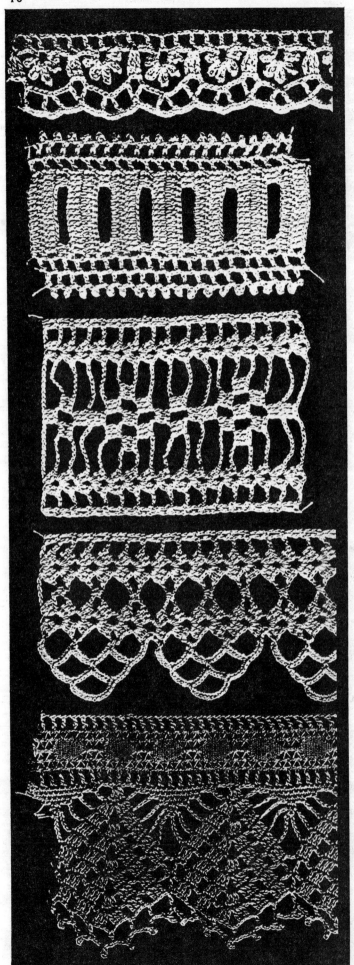

No. 135.

CHAIN DESIRED LENGTH—1ST ROW—1 d in ch, ch 2, sk 2 ch, 1 d in ch.

2ND ROW—3 s in sp, 1 p of 6 ch, 1 p of 7 ch, 1 p of 8 ch, 1 p of 7 ch, 1 p of 6 ch, sk 1 d, 3 s in next sp, 3 s in each of next 2 sp.

3RD ROW—3 t in 1 s, ch 12, sk flower, 3 t in 7th s.

4TH ROW—1 d in 2nd of 12 ch, ch 3, sk 3 ch, 1 d, ch 3, 1 d in middle of ch, ch 3, 1 d in 2nd last of 12 ch, 1 d in 2nd ch of next 12 ch.

5TH ROW—5 s in each 3 ch.

No. 136.

CHAIN 18—1ST ROW—1 d in 4th ch, 14 d in 14 ch.

2ND ROW—ch 3, 15 d in 15 d.

3RD ROW—ch 3, 2 d in 2 d., ch 10, sk 10 d, 3 d in 3 d.

4TH ROW—ch 3, 2 d in 2 d, 10 d in 10 ch, 3 d in 3 d.

5TH ROW—ch 3, 15 d in 15 d.

1ST LOWER EDGE—1 d in d, ch 2, 1 d in next d.

2ND ROW—1 d in 2 ch, ch 1, 1 p, ch 1, sk 1 d, 1 d in next 2 ch.

No. 137.

CHAIN 40—1ST ROW—1 d in 4th ch, ch 3, sk 3 ch, 2 d, ch 2, 2 d in 2 ch, ch 10, sk 10 ch, 3 d in 1 ch, ch 10, sk 10 ch, 2 d, ch 2, 2 d in 1 ch, ch 3, sk 3 ch, 2 d in ch.

2ND ROW—ch 3, 1 d in d, ch 3, sk 3 ch., 2 d, ch 2, 2 d in 2 ch., ch 7, sk 7 ch, 3 d in 3 ch, ch 3, sk 3 d, 3 d in 3 ch, ch 7, sk 7 ch, 2 d, ch 2, 2 d in 2 ch, ch 3, sk 3 ch, 2 d in 2 d.

3RD ROW—Like 1st.

4TH ROW—Same.

5TH ROW—Like 2nd.

6TH ROW—ch 3, 1 d in d, ch 3, sk 3 ch, 2 d, ch 2, 2 d in 2 ch., ch 4, sk 4 ch, 3 d in 3 ch, * ch 3, sk 3 d, 3 d in 3 ch; repeat from * once, ch 4., 2 d, ch 2, 2 d in 2 ch., ch 3, sk 3 ch, 2 d in 2 d.

7TH ROW—Like 5th.

No. 138.

CHAIN 18—1ST ROW—2 d in 4th ch, ch 3, 3 d in next ch., ch 5, 3 d in 6th ch, ch 3, 3 d in next ch, ch 2, sk 2 ch, 2 d in next 2 ch.

2ND ROW—ch 3, 1 d in d, ch 2., 3 d, ch 3, 3 d in 3 ch., ch 2, 1 s over 5 ch, ch 2., 3 d, ch 3, 3 d in 3 ch.

3RD ROW—ch 3, 3 d, ch 3, 3 d in 3 ch, ch 5., 3 d, ch 3, 3 d in 3 ch., ch 2, sk 2 ch, 2 d.

4TH ROW—Like 2nd.

5TH ROW—Like 3rd.

6TH ROW—Like 2nd, continue on 6th row—* ch 7, sl st to 3 ch; repeat from * twice, * 12 s in scl; repeat from * once, 6 s in next scl, * ch 7, turn, sl st to 2nd scl; repeat from * once, 12 s in 1st scl., repeat from * in 2nd, ch 7, turn, sl st to scl., turn, 12 s in scl, * 6 s in next scl; repeat from * once, sl st up to 2 ch., ch 3, 2 d, ch 3, 3 d in 3 ch, ch 5., 3 d, ch 3, 3 d in 3 ch, ch 2, sk 2 ch, 2 d.

No. 139.

UPPER EDGE.—1 d in br, ch 1, 1 d in br.

1ST LOWER EDGE—Same.

2ND ROW—3 d in 1 ch., ch 3, sk 2 d, * 1 s in d, 1 s in ch; repeat from * 13 times, ch 3, sk 2 d, 3 d in 1 ch.

3RD ROW—1 d in d, 2 d in d, * ch 4, sk 3 s, 10 s in 10 s, ch 4., 2 d in d, 1 d in d, ch 3, 1 d in d, ch 3., 1 d in d, 2 d in d; repeat from *.

4TH ROW—3 d in 3 d, * ch 5, sk 2 s, 6 s in 6 s, ch 5, 3 d in 3 d, ch 2, 3 d in 3 ch, ch 2, 3 d in 3 d; repeat from *

5TH ROW—3 d in 3 d, ch 6, sk 2 s, 2 s in 2 s, ch 6, 3 d in 3 d, ch 2, 2 d in 1 d, 1 d in d, ch 3, 1 d in d, 2 d in d, ch 2, 3 d in d.

6TH ROW—3 d in 3 d, ch 6, 2 s in 2 s, ch 6, 3 d in 3 d, ch 2, 3 d in 3 ch, * ch 2, 3 d in 3 d; repeat from * once.

7TH ROW—3 d in 3 d, * ch 2, 3 d in 3 d; repeat from * once, ch 2, 2 d in d, 1 d in d, ch 3, 1 d in d, 2 d in 2 d, * ch 2, 3 d in d; repeat from *.

8TH ROW—1 d in 2nd d, 1 d in 2nd d of next 3 d., * ch 2, 3 d in 3 d; repeat from * once, ch 2, 3 d in 3 ch., * ch 2, 3 d in 3 d; repeat from * once. ch 2, 1 d in d.

9TH ROW—1 d in 2 d., 3 d in 3 d, ch 2, 3 d in 3 d, ch 2, 2 d in d, 1 d in d, ch 3, 1 d in d, 2 d in d. * ch 2, 3 d in 3 d; repeat from * once, 1 d in d.

10TH ROW—1 d in d, * ch 2, 1 p, ch 2, 1 d in sp; repeat from *

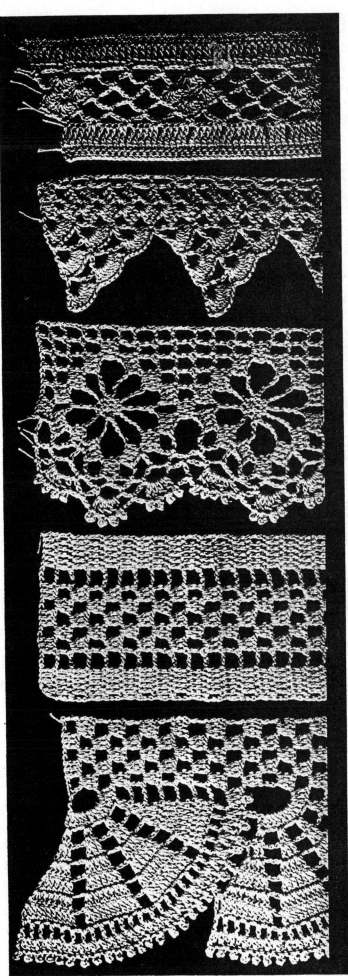

No. 140.

CHAIN DESIRED LENGTH—1ST ROW—1 s in each ch.

2ND ROW—1 s in each s.

3RD ROW—1 t in each s.

4TH ROW—1 s in t, ch 7, sk 4 t, 1 s in t.

5TH ROW—1 s in 7 ch, * ch 7, 1 s in next 7 ch; repeat from * twice, 5 d in s, 1 s in 7 ch, ch 7, 1 s in next 7 ch.

6TH ROW—1 s in 7 ch, * ch 7, 1 s in next 7 ch; repeat from * once, 5 d in s, 1 s in 3rd d, 5 d in next s, ch 7, 1 s in 7 ch.

7TH ROW—1 s in 7 ch, ch 7, 1 s in 3rd d, 5 d in s, 1 s in 3rd d, ch 7, 1 s in 7 ch.

8TH ROW—1 s in 7 ch, ch 4, 1 s in 3rd d, ch 4, 1 s in 7 ch.

9TH ROW—1 t in each ch.

10TH ROW—1 s in each t.

11TH ROW—1 s in each s.

No. 141.

CHAIN 9—1ST ROW—1 d in 4th ch, sk 1 ch, 3 d in next ch, ch 2, 3 d in next ch., ch 3, 1 d in last ch.

2ND ROW—ch 3, 7 d in 3 ch, 3 d, ch 2, 3 d in 2 ch, 1 d in d, ch 1, sk 1 ch, 1 d.

3RD ROW—ch 4, 1 d in d., 3 d, ch 2, 3 d in 2 ch., 1 d, ch 3, 1 d in d., ch 2, sk 6 d., 1 d, ch 3, 1 d in last d.

4TH ROW—Like 2nd, making one extra shell.

5TH ROW—Like 3rd, making one extra of 1 d, ch 3, 1 d in d.

6TH ROW—same like 4th, making one extra shell.

No. 142.

CHAIN 23—1ST ROW—1 d in 8th ch, * ch 2, sk 2 ch, 1 d in ch; repeat from * 3 times, 3 d in 3 ch.

2ND ROW—ch 11, sk 8 ch, 3 d in 3 ch, 1 d in d, ch 2, sk 2 d, 1 d in d, 2 d in 2 ch, 1 d in d., * ch 2, sk 2 ch, 1 d in d; repeat from * 3 times.

3RD ROW—ch 5, 1 d in d, * ch 2, sk 2 ch, 1 d in d; repeat from * once, 2 d in 2 ch, 1 d in 1 d, ch 4, 1t in 2 ch, ch 4, 1 d in d, 3 d in 3 ch.

4TH ROW—ch 11, sk 8 ch., 3 d in 3 ch, 1 d in 1 d., ch 4, sk 3 ch., 1 s in t, 1 s in ch., ch 4, sk 3 d, 1 d in d, 2 d in 2 ch, 1 d in d., * ch 2, sk 2 ch, 1 d in d; repeat from * once.

5TH ROW—ch 5, 1 d in d, 2 d in 2 ch, 1 d in d., ch 7, 5 s, ch 7., 1 d in d, 3 d in 3 ch.

6TH ROW—ch 5., 1 d in d, 2 d in 2 ch, 1 d in d., ch 7, sk 1 s, 3 s in 3 ch, ch 7, sk 4 d, 3 d in 3 ch, 1 d in d., ch 2, sk 2 d, 1 d in d, ch 2, sk 2 ch, 1 d in d.

7TH ROW—ch 5, 1 d in d, ch 2, sk 2 ch, 1 d in d., ch 2, sk 2 d, 1 d in d, 3 d in 3 ch., ch 4, 1 t in 2nd s., ch 4, sk 4 ch, 3 d in 3 ch, 1 d in d.

8TH ROW—ch 5, sk 3 d, 1 d in d, 3 d in 3 ch., ch 2, sk 1 ch, 1 t, 1 ch, 3 d in 3 ch, 1 d in d., ch 2, sk 2 d, 1 d in d, * ch 2, sk 2 ch, 1 d in d; repeat from * twice.

1ST LOWER EDGE—1 d in s m, ch 5, 1 s in o m., ch 5, 1 d in next s m.

2ND ROW—1 s in 5 ch, ch 5, 1 s in next 5 ch.

3RD ROW—1 s in 5 ch, ch 2, 1 d, * 1 p, 1 d; repeat from * 3 times in next 5 ch, ch 2, 1 s in next 5 ch.

No. 143.

CHAIN 33—1ST ROW—1 d in 4th ch, 4 d in 4 ch., ch 3, sk 3 ch, 3 d in 3 ch., * ch 2, sk 2 ch, 3 d in 3 ch; repeat from * once, ch 3, sk 3 ch, 6 d in 6 ch.

2ND ROW—ch 3, 5 d in 5 d, ch 3, sk 3 ch, 1 d in d, ch 2, sk 2 d, 3 d in 2 ch, ch 2, sk 3 d, 3 d in 2 ch, ch 2, sk 3 d, 1 d in 3rd d., ch 3, sk 3 ch, 6 d in 6 d.

No. 144.

CHAIN 18—1ST ROW—1 d in 8th ch, 2 d in next 2 ch., ch 2, sk 2 ch, 3 d in 3 ch, ch 2, sk 2 ch, 1 d in ch.

2ND ROW—ch 3, 3 d in 2 ch, * ch 2, sk 3 d, 3 d in 2 ch; repeat from * once, ch 7, 1 d in o m.

3RD ROW—ch 3, 12 d in 7 ch., * ch 2, sk 3 d, 3 d in 2 ch; repeat from * once, ch 2, 1 d in last d.

4TH ROW—ch 3, 3 d in 2 ch, * ch 2, sk 3 d, 3 d in 2 ch; repeat from * once., * ch 3, sk 2 d, 2 d in 1 d; repeat from * 7 times.

5TH ROW—ch 3, 2 d in 2 d., * ch 3, 3 d in 2 d; repeat from * twice, ch 3, 1 d in 1st d, * ch 2, sk 3 d, 3 d in 2 ch; repeat from * once, ch 2, 1 d in last d.

6TH ROW—ch 3, 3 d in 2 ch, * ch 2, sk 3 d, 3 d in 2 ch; repeat from * once, * ch 3, 2 d in d, 1 d in d, 2 d in d; repeat from * 3 times.

7TH ROW—ch 3, 6 d in 5 d, * ch 3, 7 d in 5 d; repeat from * twice, ch 3, 1 d in d, * ch 2, sk 3 d, 3 d in 2 ch; repeat from * once., ch 2, sk 3 d, 1 d in d.

8TH ROW—ch 3, 3 d in 2 ch., * ch 2, sk 3 d, 3 d in 2 ch; repeat from * once, * ch 3, 9 d in 7 d; repeat from * 3 times.

9TH ROW—ch 3, 10 d in 9 d, * ch 3, 11 d in 9 d; repeat from * twice, ch 3, 1 d in d, * ch 2, sk 3 d, 3 d in 2 ch; repeat from * once, ch 2, 1 d in last d

10TH ROW—ch 3, 3 d in 2 ch., * ch 2, sk 3 d, 3 d in 2 ch; repeat from * once, ch 3, * 1 d in d, ch 1, sk 1 d, 1 d in d and also 1 d, ch 1 in 3 ch. Repeat along * the whole scl along.

11TH ROW—ch 3, * 1 p, 2 d in 1 ch; repeat from * up to 3d., * ch 2, sk 3 d, 3 d in 2 ch; repeat from * once; ch 2, 1 d in last d. Next scl is caught with sl st to every other p.

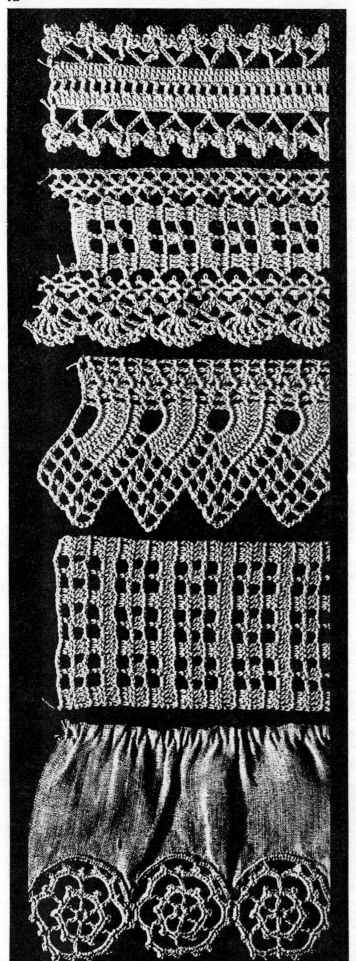

No. 145.

Work like No. 111, leaving 5th and 6th rows off and crocheting 4th row to other side of ds.

No. 146.

UPPER EDGE—1 s in br, ch 2, 1 s in br.
MIDDLE PART—1ST ROW—sl st to br, ch 16, sl st to 2nd piece of br, ch 2, sk 2 ch, 13 d in 13 ch.
2ND ROW—ch 3, 2 d in 2 d., ch 3, sk 3 d, 1 d in d., ch 3, sk 3 d., 3 d in 3 d.
3RD ROW—ch 2, sl st to br., ch 2, 3 d in 3 d., ch 2, 3 d in 1 d., ch 2, 3 d in 3 d.
4TH ROW—ch 2, sl st to 2nd piece of br, ch 2, 3 d in 3 d., ch 3, 1 d in 2nd d., ch 3, 3 d in 3 d.
5TH ROW—ch 2, sl st to br, ch 2., 3 d in 3 d, 3 d in 3 ch, 1 d in d, 3 d in 3 ch, 3 d in 3 d.
1ST LOWER EDGE—2 d, ch 3, 2 d in 1 of br, sk 1 l, 2 d, ch 3, 2 d in next l of br.
2ND LOWER EDGE—* 1 t, 1 ch; repeat from * 5 times in 3 ch, sl st to next 3 ch.
3RD ROW—1 s in 1 ch, ch 3, sk 1 t, 1 s in next 1 ch.

No. 147.

CHAIN 30—1ST ROW—1 d in 8th ch., * ch 2, sk 2 ch, 1 d in ch; repeat from * twice., ch 7, sk 5 ch, 1 d in ch., ch 1, sk 1 ch, 2 d, ch 2, 2 d in ch., ch 1, 1 d in ch.
2ND ROW—ch 4, 1 d in d., 2 d, ch 2, 2 d in 2 ch., 1 d in d, ch 1, 1 d in next d, 12 d in 7 ch, * ch 2, sk 2 ch, 1 d in d; repeat from * 3 times.
3RD ROW—ch 5, 1 d in d, * ch 2, sk 2 ch, 1 d in next d; repeat from * twice, 12 d in 12 d, ch 1, 1 d in d., 2 d, ch 2, 2 d in 2 ch., 1 d in d, ch 1, sk 1 ch, 1 d in d.
4TH ROW—ch 4, 1 d in d., 2 d, ch 2, 2 d in 2 ch., 1 d in d, ch 1, 1 d in next d, 12 d in 12 d, * ch 2, sk 2 ch, 1 d in d; repeat from * 3 times.
5TH ROW—ch 5, 1 d in d., * ch 2, sk 2 ch, 1 d in d; repeat from * twice, * ch 2, sk 1 d, 1 d in d; repeat from * 3 times., ch 7, sk 3 d, 1 d in d., ch 1, 1 d in d., 2 d, ch 2, 2 d in 2 ch., 1 d in d, ch 1, 1 d in d.

No. 148.

CHAIN 37—1ST ROW—1 d in 4th ch, 2 d in next 2 ch., * ch 3, sk 3 ch, 1 d in ch, ch 3, sk 3 ch, 3 d in 3 ch; repeat from * once, ch 3, sk 3 ch, 1 d in ch, ch 3, sk 3 ch, 4 d in 4 ch.
2ND ROW—ch 3, 3 d in 3 d., * ch 2, 3 d in next 1 d, ch 2, 3 d in next 3 d; repeat from * once, ch 2, 3 d in next 1 d, ch 2, 4 d in 4 d.
3RD ROW—ch 3, 3 d in 3 d., * ch 3, 1 d in 2nd d, ch 3, 3 d in 3 d; repeat from * once, ch 3, 1 d in 2nd d., ch 3, 4 d in 4 d.
4TH ROW—ch 3, 3 d in 3 d, 3 d in 3 ch, 1 d in d; repeat all the way up.

No. 149.

CHAIN 6. JOIN—1ST ROUND—ch 6, 1 d in ring, * ch 3, 1 d in ring; repeat from * 3 times, ch 3, sl st to 3rd ch.
2ND ROUND—* 3 s, 1 p, 3 s in 3 ch; repeat from * 5 times, sl st to 1st s.
3RD ROUND—ch 10, 1 d over d., * ch 7, 1 d over d; repeat from * 3 times, ch 7, sl st to 3rd ch.
4TH ROUND—4 s, ch 3, 4 s, ch 3, 4 s, ch 3 in each of 7 ch. Wheels are sl st together, and material is buttonholed and wheel sewed in.

No. 250

No. 251

GUEST TOWELS—See Page 14 for Instructions

All pieces in this book where made with No. 40 thread.

ABBREVIATIONS.

Braid—br.	Half Double—h. d. or h. d. c	Shell—sh.
Chain—ch	Loop—l.	Single—s. or s. c.
Cluster—cl.	Mesh or Space—m. or sp.	Skip—sk.
Cross Treble—c. t	Open mesh—o. m	Slip Stitch—sl. st.
Double—d.	Picot—p.	Solid or Closed Mesh—s. m. or c. m.
Double Treble—d. t.	Repeat—*	Treble—t.
Double Triple Treble—d. t. t.	Scallop—scl..	Triangle—tr.

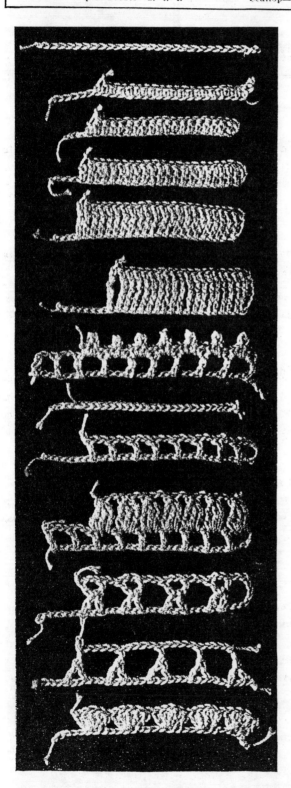

No. 1.

CHAIN—Form loop and always draw thread through loop desired length.

No. 2.

SINGLE CROCHET—Put hook through work, pick up thread, draw back through, now draw thread through both loops.

No. 3.

HALF DOUBLE CROCHET—Thread over needle once, put hook through work, pick up thread, draw back through, thread over needle again, now draw thread through all three loops.

No. 4.

DOUBLE CROCHET—Thread over needle once, put hook through work; pick up thread, draw back through, thread over needle again, draw through 2 loops, thread over needle again, draw through other 2 loops.

No. 5.

TREBLE CROCHET—Same like Double, only start with thread over needle twice, and work off 2 loops each time.

No. 6.

DOUBLE TREBLE CROCHET—Same like Double Crochet, only start with thread over needle 3 times, work off 2 loops at a time.

No. 7.

PICOT—Make a chain of 3 or 4 stitches, sl st to 1 st of chain.

No. 8.

SLIP STITCH—Used mostly in joining the work. Put hook through work and draw thread through work and loop on needle at once.

No. 9.

MESH OR SPACE—One double in stitch, chain 2, skip 2 stitches, one double in next stitch.

No. 10.

CLUSTER—Work 3 or 4 trebles in space, keeping last loop of each treble on needle, now thread over needle, once, and draw through all loops at once.

No. 11.

CROSS TREBLE—Thread over needle, twice, work off ½, skip 2 stitches, 1 double in next stitch, now work up other part of treble, chain 2, 1 double in middle of double.

No. 12.

TRIANGLE—Thread over needle twice, work off ½, skip 2 stitches, 1 double in next stitch, now work up other part of treble, chain 4, sk 2 stitches to start next triangle.

No. 13.

SHELL—Work 5 doubles into 1 stitch or space to make a shell.

4

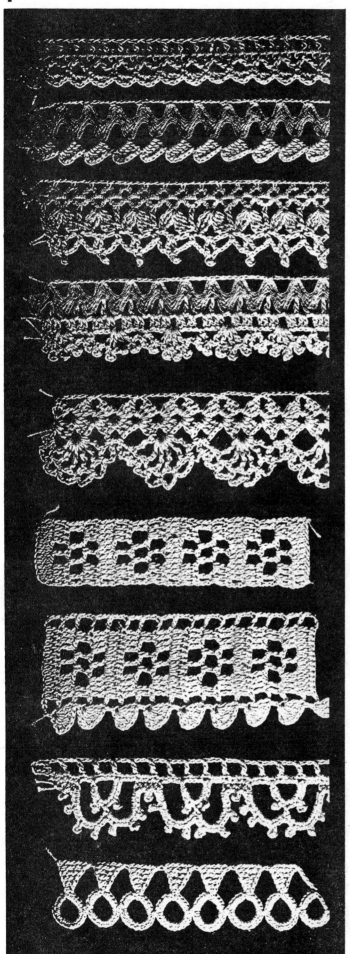

No. 200.

UPPER EDGE—1 d in br, ch 1, 1 d in br.
LOWER 1ST. EDGE—1 d in br, ch 3, sk 2 1 of br, 1 d in br, ch 3, 1 d in same 1 of br.
2ND ROW—1 s, 1 h d c, 1 d, 1 h d c, 1 s in 3 ch.

No. 201.

UPPER EDGE—1 s in br, ch 4, 1 s in br.
LOWER EDGE—sl st to br., 1 d in next scl, ch 3, 5 d over d, 1 d in next scl, ch 3, 5 d over d.

No. 202.

UPPER EDGE—sl st to br., ch 2, sl st to br.
LOWER EDGE—1ST. ROW—1 cl of 3 t in br, ch 3, 1 cl of 3 t in same 1 of br., 1 t in next 1 of br.
2ND. ROW—1 s in t, ch 3, 1 d, 1 p, 1 d in 3 ch., ch 3, 1 s in t.

No. 203.

UPPER EDGE—1 s in br, ch 4, 1 s in br.
LOWER EDGE—1ST. ROW—1 d in br, ch 2, 1 s in point of br, ch 2, 1 d.
2ND ROW—2 d in 2 ch, 2 d in next 2 ch, ch 1, 2 d in 2 ch, 2 d in next 2 ch.
3RD ROW—1 s in 1 ch., ch 1, 1 p, ch 1, sk 4 d, 1 d, * 1 p, 1 d; repeat from * twice, ch 1, 1 p, sk 4 d, ch 1, 1 s in 1 ch.

No. 204.

CHAIN 6—1ST ROW—2 d in 4th ch, ch 3, 3 d in next ch.
2ND ROW—ch 3, 3 d, ch 3, 3 d in 3 ch.
3RD ROW—ch 3., 3 d, ch 3, 3 d in 3 ch, * ch 2, 1 t; repeat from * 5 times, ch 2, sl st to 1 st ch.
4TH ROW—* ch 5, 1 s in 2 ch; repeat from * 6 times, ch 2, 3 d. ch 3, 3 d in 3 ch.
UPPER EDGE—1 sl st in 3 ch, ch 5, 1 sl st in next 3 ch.

No. 205.

CHAIN 15—1ST ROW—1 d in 4th ch, 12 d in 12 ch.
2ND ROW—ch 3, 3 d in 3 d., ch 2, sk 2 d, 1 d in d, ch 2, 4 d in 4 d.
3RD ROW—ch 3, 1 d in d., ch 2, sk 2 d, 1 d in 2 ch, ch 2, sk 1 d, 1 d in 2 ch, ch 2, sk 2 d, 2 d in 2 d.
4TH ROW—ch 3, 1 d in d, 2 d in 2 ch, ch 2, sk 1 d, 1 d in 2 ch, ch 2, sk 1 d, 2 d in 2 ch, 2 d in 2 d.
5TH ROW—ch 3, 3 d in 3 d, 2 d in 2 ch, 1 d in d, 2 d in 2 ch, 4 d in 4 d.

No. 206.

CHAIN 23—1ST ROW—1 d in 8th ch, 12 d in 12 ch., ch 2, 1 d in last ch.
2ND ROW—ch 3, 6 d in d, ch 2, 4 d in 4 d; work up like No. 205.
Upper part of lace is worked like insertion No. 205, only an extra mesh added at each side.

No. 207.

CHAIN DESIRED LENGTH—1ST ROW—is made in meshes.
2ND ROW—* 3 s in m; repeat from * 3 times, ch 7, sl st back in 5th s, 4 s, 1 p, 4 s, 1 p, 4 s in 7 ch., * 3 s in next m; repeat from * 4 times, ch 7, sl st back in 5th s.
3RD ROW—4 s in 4 s., ch 10, sl st to scl., ch 10, sk 1 m, 4 s in 4 s.
4TH ROW—2 s in 2 of 4 s, 1 p, 2 s in other 2 of 4 s., * 3 s, 1 p; repeat from * twice, 3 s over 10 ch; repeat.

No. 208.

CHAIN 18—sl st in 12th ch, 20 s in ring, 1 s in ch, 1 h d in next ch, 1 d in next ch, 1 t in next ch, 1 d t in next ch, 1 t t in next ch.

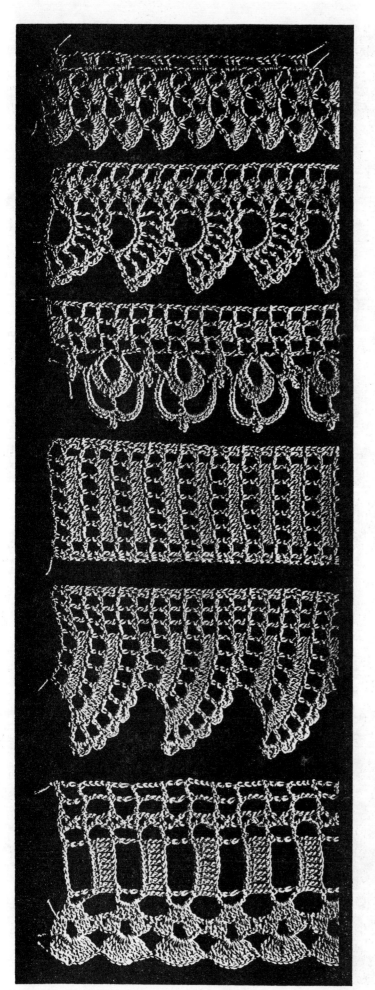

No. 209.

CHAIN 10—1ST. ROW—1 d, ch 3, 1 d in 6th ch., **ch 2**, sk 2 ch, 1 d, ch 3, 1 d in 3rd ch.
2ND ROW—ch 3, 8 d in 3 ch., ch 1, sk 2 ch, 5 d in 3 d.
3RD ROW—ch 5, 1 d, ch 3, 1 d in 3rd d., ch 2, sk 2 d, 1 ch, 2 d., 1 d, ch 3, 1 d in 3rd d.
UPPER EDGE—1ST ROW—1 s in 5 ch, ch 4, 1 s in next 5 ch.
2ND ROW—3 d in 4 ch, ch 3, 3 d in 4 ch.

No. 210.

CHAIN 17—1ST. ROW—2 d in 8th ch, ch 2, 2 d in next ch, ch 2, sk 2 ch, 1 t, ch 7, 1 s in end of ch.
2ND ROW—12 s in 7 ch, 1 s in 1 t, ch 2., 2 d, ch 2, 2 d in 2 ch., ch 2, 1 d in d.
3RD ROW—ch 5., 2 d, ch 2, 2 d in 2 ch., ch 2, 1t in 1 s *, ch 2, sk 1 s, 1 t in 1 s; repeat from * 5 times.
4TH ROW—* ch 3, 1 s in 2 ch; repeat from * 5 times, ch 3, 1 s in t., ch 2, 2 d, ch 2, 2 d in 2 ch., ch 2, 1 d in d.

No. 211.

CHAIN 14—1ST. ROW—1 d in 8th ch, 3 d in 3 ch, ch 2, sk 2 ch, 1 d in ch.
2ND ROW—3 o m.
3RD ROW—1 o m, 1 s m, 1 o m, ch 10, join.
4TH ROW—2 s, 2 h d c, 10 d, 2 h d c, 2 s in ring., 3 o m.
5TH ROW—Like 3rd.
6TH ROW—Like 2nd.
7TH ROW—Like 3rd.
LOWER EDGE—1ST ROW—2 d in d., ch 2, 1 sl st in 2nd h d c, ch 10, 1 d in 6th d, ch 10, sl st in 1 st h d c, ch 2, 2 d in d.
2ND ROW—1 p, 2 s over 2 ch, 14 s over 10 ch, 1 p, 14 s over 10 ch, 2 s over 2 ch, 1 p.

No. 212.

CHAIN 26—1ST ROW—1 d in 4th ch. * ch 2, sk 2 ch, 1 d; repeat from * 5 times, ch 2, sk 2 ch, 2 d in next 2 ch.
2ND ROW—ch 3, 1 d in d, ch 2, sk 2 ch, * 1 d in d, 2 d over 2 ch; repeat from * 4 times, 1 d in d, ch 2, sk 2 ch, 2 d in 2 d.
3RD ROW—ch 3, 1 d in d, ch 2, sk 2 ch, 1 d in d., * ch 2, sk 2 d, 1 d; repeat from * 4 times, ch 2, sk 2 c, 2 d in 2 d.

No. 213.

CHAIN 22—1ST ROW—1 d in 4th ch, * ch 2, sk 2 ch, 1 d; repeat from * 5 times.
2ND ROW—ch 3, 6 d in 2 ch, 1 d in d, * 3 d in 2 ch, 1 d in d; repeat from * once, 3 o m, 2 d in 2 d.
3RD ROW—ch 3, 1 d in d, 3 o m., * ch 2, sk 2 d, 1 d; repeat from * 4 times.
4TH ROW—ch 3, 6 d in 2 ch, 1 d in d, * 3 d in 2 ch, 1 d in d; repeat from * 3 times, 3 o m, 2 d in 2 d
5TH ROW—Like 3rd to end of row.
6TH ROW—* 1 s, 1 h d c, 1 d, 1 h d c, 1 s in 2 ch; repeat from * 6 times, 1 s, 1 h d c, 2 d in 2 ch, 1 d in d, 3 o m, 2 d in 2 d.

No. 214.

CHAIN 25—1ST ROW—1 t in 9th ch, ch 2, sk 2 ch, 1 c t, ch 2, sk 2, 1 t, 9 t in 9 ch.
2ND ROW—ch 7, 1 t in t, ch 8, sk 8 t, 1 t in t, ch 2, sk 2 ch, 1 ct, * ch 2, sk 2 ch, 1 t; repeat from * once.
LOWER EDGE—1ST ROW—5 d in 7 ch, ch 5, 5 d in next 7 ch.
2ND ROW—2 d in d, 1 d in d, ch 5, sk 1 d, 1 d in d, 2 d in d., ch 2, 1 s over 5 ch, ch 2., 2 d in d, 1 d in d, ch 5, sk 1 d, 1 d in d, 2 d in d.
3RD ROW—10 t in 5 ch; repeat.

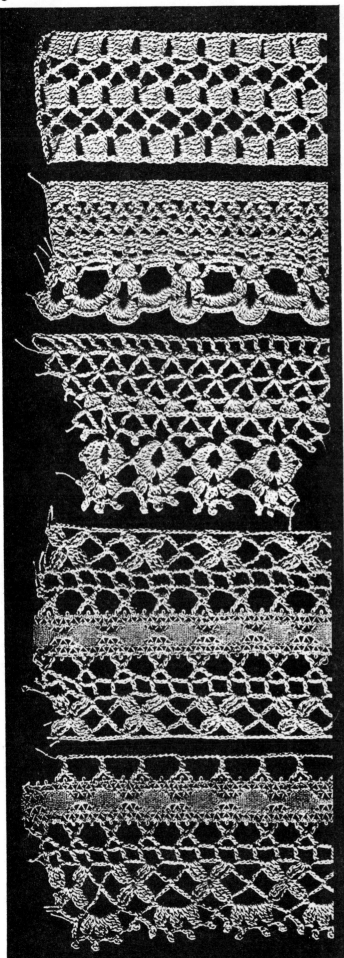

No. 215.

CHAIN 30—1ST ROW—1 s in 8th ch, * ch 5, sk 4 ch, 1 s in ch: repeat from * 3 times.
2ND ROW—ch 4, 5 t in 5 ch., * ch 3, 1 s over 5 ch, ch 3, 5 t in 5 ch; repeat from * once, 1 t.
3RD ROW—ch 5, sk 5 t, 1 s in t, * ch 5, 1 s in t; repeat from *.

No. 216.

UPPER EDGE CHAIN 16—1ST ROW—1 d in 4th ch, 2 d in 2 ch., sk 2 ch, 1 d, ch 1, 1 d in 3rd ch., ch 2, 1 d, ch 1, 1 d in next ch., sk 2 ch, 4 d in 4 ch.
2ND ROW—4 d in 4 d, 1 d, ch 1, 1 d, ch 2, 1 d, ch 1, 1 d in 2 ch., 4 d in 4 d.
LOWER EDGE—1ST ROW—3 s over each d.
2ND ROW—1 s in s, ch 2, sk 2 s, 5 d in s, ch 2, 1 s in s., ch 5, sk 5 s, 1 s in s.
3RD ROW—2 d in d, 1 d in d, ch 5, sk 1 d, 1 d in d, 2 d in d, ch 5.
4TH ROW—10 ds in each 5 ch.

No. 217.

CHAIN DESIRED LENGTH—1ST ROW—is made in meshes.
2ND ROW—3 s in each m.
3RD ROW—1 t in s, sk 5 s, 1 t in 6th s, ch 4, 1 t in same s.
4TH ROW—1 t in 2 t, ch 4, 1 t in same 2 t., sk 4 ch, 1 t, ch 4, 1 t in 2 t.
5TH ROW—4 d in 2 t, ch 1, 4 d in next 2 t.
6TH ROW—1 t in 1 ch, ch 9, sl st in 7th ch., 1 s, 1 h d c, 3 d, ch 3, 5 d, ch 3, 5 d, ch 3, 3 d, 1 h d c, 1 s in ring of 7 ch., ch 2, 1 t in same 1 ch., sk 4 d, 1 t, ch 2, 1 p, ch 2, 1 t in next 1 ch.
7TH ROW—1 d in d, 2 d in d, ch 1, 1 p, ch 1, 2 d, 1 p, 1 d in 3 ch, ch 1, 1 p, ch 1, 2 d in d, 1 d in d, ch 2.

No. 218.

UPPER EDGE—1ST ROW—Work c t in br, ch 3 between each c t.
2ND ROW—1 d, ch 3, 1 d in each c t, ch 3.
3RD ROW—1 s in sp., ch 4, 1 cl of 2 t in same sp., sk 1 sp, 1 cl of 2 t, ch 4, 1 s in next sp., ch 7, sk 1 sp.
4TH ROW—1 cl of 2 t, ch 4, 1 s, ch 4, 1 cl of 2 t on the 2 cl in 3rd row., ch 4, 1 s in 7 ch, ch 4.
5TH ROW—1 s in cl, ch 6, 1 s in cl, ch 6, 1 s in cl.
LOWER EDGE—same.

No. 219.

LOWER EDGE—1st 5 rows like No. 218.
6TH ROW—1 s in 6 ch, ch 2, 1 p, ch 1, 1 cl of 3 t, * ch 1, 1 p, ch 1, 1 cl of 3 t; repeat from * once in 6 ch., ch 1, 1 p, ch 2, 1 s in 6 ch.
UPPER EDGE—1 tr in br, ch 6, 1 tr in br.

No. 220.

CHAIN DESIRED LENGTH.
1ST ROW—1 d, sk 1 ch, ch 1, 1 d.
FOR WHEEL—CHAIN 8, JOIN—1ST ROUND—ch 4, 1 d, * ch 1, 1 d; repeat from * 11 times, ch 1, join.
2ND ROW—3 ch 4, sk 1 d, 1 s in 1 ch; repeat from * 12 times.
Wheels are sl st to-gether.
2ND UPPER ROW—1 s in 1 ch, ch 5, sk 1 d, 1 s in 1 ch, ch 2, 1 s in upper part of wheel, ch 2, sk 1 d, 1 s in 1 ch.

No. 221.

CHAIN 33—1ST ROW—1 s in second ch, 2 s in next 2 ch, * ch 4, sk 3 ch, 1 d, ch 4, sk 3 ch, 3 s in 3 ch; repeat from * twice.
2ND ROW—ch 8, sk 2 ch, 1 s in ch, 1 s in d, 1 s in ch., * ch 4, sk 3 ch, 1 s, 1 d in s, ch 4, sk 3 ch, 1 s in s, 1 s in d, 1 s in s; repeat from * once, ch 4, 1 d in s.
3RD ROW—ch 5, 7 d in 2nd s., * ch 5, sk 4 ch, 1 d and 4 ch, 7 d in 2nd s; repeat from * once, ch 3, 1 d.
4TH ROW—ch 8, sk 2 d, * 3 s in 3 d, ch 4, 1 d over 5 ch, ch 4; repeat from * once., 1 s in 3rd d, 1 s in each of next 2 d, ch 4, 1 d.
5TH ROW—ch 7, sk 4 ch, 1 s., * 1 d in s, ch 4, sk 3 ch, 1 s in 1 ch, 1 s in 1 d, 1 s in 1 ch, ch 4; repeat from * once, sk 3 ch, 1 s, 1 d in 2nd s., ch 4, 1 d in 5th ch.
6TH ROW—ch 9, sk 1 d, 1 s., 7 d in s., ch 5, sk 1 d, 1 s., 7 d in 2nd s., ch 6, 1 d in 4th ch.

No. 222.

UPPER EDGE—1ST. ROW—3 1 cl of 3 t in br, ch 5; repeat from * twice, 1 cl in br.
2ND ROW—1 cl in 5 ch, ch 5, 1 cl in next 5 ch, ch 5, 1 cl in same 5 ch, ch 5, 1 cl in next 5 ch, 1 cl in next 5 ch.
3RD ROW—1 s in 5 ch, ch 5, 1 s in next 5 ch.
4TH ROW—1 s in 5 ch, ch 2, 1 s in next 5 ch.
LOWER EDGE—1ST ROW—Same like upper 1st row.
2ND ROW—1 cl in 5 ch, ch 3, 1 cl in next 5 ch, ch 3; * 1 cl, ch 3; repeat from * twice in same 5 ch, 1 cl in next 5 ch.
3RD ROW—1 s in 3 ch *, ch 5, sk 1 cl, 1 s in 3 ch; repeat from * twice, ch 5, sk 2 cl, 1 s in 3 ch.
4TH ROW—7 s in each 5 ch.

No. 223.

CHAIN DESIRED LENGTH.
1ST ROW—1 d in each ch.
2ND ROW—1 d in d, ch 2, sk 2 d, 1 d in d.
3RD ROW—1 d in d, ch 9, sk 3 m, 1 d in d.
4TH ROW—1 d in each of 1 ch, 1 d and 1 ch., ch 7, sk 7 ch., 1 d in each of 1 ch, 1 d and 1 ch.
5TH ROW—1 d in ch, 3 d in 3 d, 1 d in ch., ch 5, sk 5 ch.
6TH ROW—1 d in ch, 5 d in 5 d, 1 d in ch., ch 3, sk 3 ch.
7TH ROW—1 d in ch, 3 d in 3 d, ch 1, sk 1 d, 3 d in 3 d, 1 d in 1 ch, ch 1.
8TH, 9TH, 10TH, 11TH ROWS are worked opposite way.
12TH ROW—1 d in each ch.
13TH ROW—1 s in d, ch 3, 1 p, ch 3, sk 4 d, 1 s in d.

No. 224.

UPPER EDGE—1 d in br, ch 2, 1 d in br.
LOWER EDGE—1ST ROW—1 d in br, 1 d in br, ch 3, 1 d in br, 1 d in br., ch 7, sk 3 1 of br.
2ND ROW—3 d, ch 2, 3 d in 3 ch., ch 7.
3RD ROW—sk 1 d., 1 d in d, 1 d in next d, 2 d in 2 ch, ch 2, 2 d in 2 ch,. * 1 d in d; repeat from * once, ch 6.
OTHER ROWS are worked the same only increasing 1 d on each side and decreasing 1 ch in each row.
9TH ROW—1 s in d, ch 5, sk 2 d, 1 s in d.

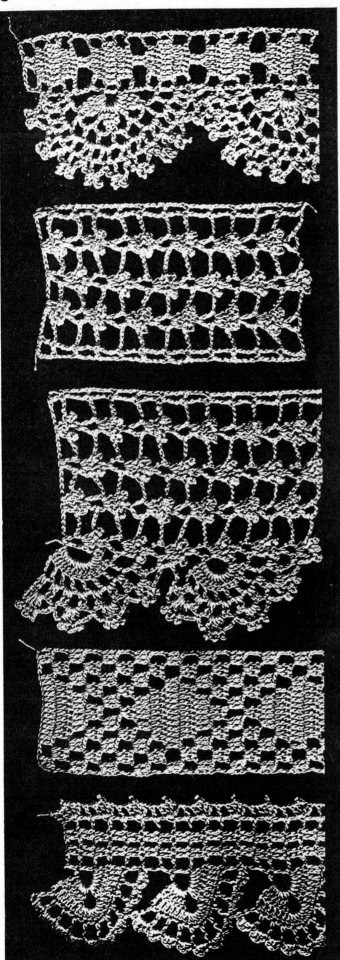

No. 225.

CHAIN 20—1ST ROW—1 d in 13th ch, 1 d in next ch., ch 5, 1 d in last ch.
2ND ROW—ch 4, sk 2 ch, 2 d in 2 ch, 2 d in 2 d, 2 d in 2 ch., ch 2, 1 d.
3RD ROW—ch 4, sk 1 ch, 1 d in 1 ch, 6 d in 6 d, 1 d in 1 ch., ch 1, sk 1 ch, 1 d.
4TH ROW—ch 5, sk 1 ch, 1 d., 6 d in 6 d, ch 2, sk 1 d, 1 ch., 1 d in d.
5TH ROW—ch 7, sk 2 ch, 2 d., 2 d in 2 d., ch 4, sk 2 d, 2 ch., 1 d in d.
6TH ROW—Like 2nd.
7TH ROW—ch 7, 1 d in d, continue like 3rd row.
8TH ROW—Like 4th.
9TH ROW—Like 5th row.
10TH ROW—Like 6th, continue on 6th—* ch 3, 1 cl, ch 3, 1 t in 7 ch; repeat from * twice, sl st to 3rd row.
11TH ROW—ch 5, * 1 d in 3 ch, ch 3, 1 d in cl, ch 3, 1 d in 3 ch; repeat from * twice, ch 3, 1 d in d., upper part like before.
12TH ROW—Like 4th row, continue—* ch 2, 1 d, ch 2, 1 d in 3 ch; repeat from * 9 times, sl st to 1st row.
13TH ROW—ch 3, 1 p, sk 2 d, * 1 d in 2 ch, 1 p, ch 3, sk 1 d, 1 s in 2 ch., ch 3, 1 p, sk 1 d; repeat from * along scl, ch 3, 1 d in d, continue like 5th row.

No. 226.

CHAIN 28—1ST ROW—1 t in 5th ch, ch 4, sk 4 ch., * 1 d, 1 p; repeat from * twice in 1 ch, 1 p, ch 4, sk 4 ch., 1 d, ch 3, 1 d, in 1 ch., ch 4, sk 4 ch., * 1 d, 1 p; repeat from * twice in 1 ch, 1 p, ch 4, sk 4 ch, 1 t in 1 ch, ch 1, sk 1 ch, 1 t in 1 ch.
2ND ROW—ch 5, 1 t in 1 t, ch 4, 1 d, ch 3, 1 d in 2nd p., ch 4, * 1 d, 1 p; repeat from * twice, 1 d in 3 ch., ch 4, 1 d, ch 3, 1 d in 2nd p., ch 4, 1 t in t, ch 1, 1 t in t.

No. 227.

CHAIN 28—1ST ROW—Upper part like No. 226, continue on 1st row—ch 4, sk 4 ch, 1 d, ch 5, sl st to end of ch.
2ND ROW—ch 9., * 1 d, 1 p; repeat from * twice, 1 d in 1 of 5 ch, continue up like No. 226, 2nd row, from ch 4, 1 d, ch 3, 1 d in 2nd p on.
3RD ROW—Upper part like 1st row—continue, ch 2, 15 d in 9 ch.
4TH ROW—ch 5, * sk 1 d, 1 d in d, ch 2; repeat from * 6 times, continue like 2nd row.
5TH ROW—Like 1st—continue, ch 3, 2 d in 2 ch, * ch 2, sk 1 d, 2 d in 2 ch; repeat from * 6 times.
6TH ROW—ch 3, sk 2 d., * 1 d, 1 p; repeat from * twice, 1 d in 2 ch., ch 3, sk 2d, 1 s in 2 ch; repeat 3 times from beginning ch 3, work row up like second.

No. 228.

CHAIN 25—1ST ROW—1 d in 4th ch, 1 d in next ch., ch 2, sk 2 ch, 13 d in 13 ch, ch 2, sk 2 ch, 3 d in 3 ch.
2ND ROW—ch 5, sk 3 d, 3 d in 2 ch, ch 2, sk 1 d, 10 d in 10 d, ch 2, 3d in 2 ch, ch 2, 1 d at end.
3RD ROW—ch 3, 2 d in 2 ch, ch 2, sk 3 d, 3 d in 2 ch, ch 2, sk 1 d, 7 d in 7 d, ch 2, 3 d in 2 ch, ch 2, sk 3 d, 3 d in 2 ch.
4TH ROW—ch 5, sk 3 d, 3 d in 2 ch, ch 2, sk 3 d, 3 d in 2 ch, ch 2, sk 2 d, 3 d in 3 d, * ch 2, 3 d in 2 ch; repeat from * once, ch 2, 1 d.
5TH ROW—ch 3, 2 d in 2 ch, * ch 2, sk 3 d, 3 d in 2 ch; repeated from * 4 times. Other rows are worked the opposite way.

No. 229.

CHAIN 15—1ST ROW—1 d in 8th ch, 1 d in next ch, ch 1, sk 1 ch, 2 d in 2 ch, ch 2, sk 2 ch, 1 d.
2ND ROW—ch 8, 1 d in d, ch 2, 2 d in 2 d, ch 1, 2 d in 2 d, ch 2, 1 d in d.
3RD ROW—Upper part like 2nd row, continue—6 d, ch 3, 6 d in 8 ch.
4TH ROW—ch 3, 1 d in each of 6 d, 8 d in 3 ch, 1 d in each of other ds, work up like before.
5TH ROW—Upper part like before, continue—ch 2, sk 1 d, 1 d in d.
6TH ROW—1 s, 1 h d, 1 d, 1 h d, 1 s in each 2 ch of scl, work up like before.
UPPER EDGE—2 d, 1 p, 2 d in d., ch 1, 1 d in next d, ch 1, 2 d, 1 p, 2 d in next d.

No. 230.

CHAIN 8, JOIN—1ST ROUND—ch 6, 1 s in ring, * ch 4, 1 s; repeat from * 3 times in ring, sl st together.

2ND ROW—1 s, 1 h d, 1 d, 2 t, 1 d, 1 h d, 1 s in 4 ch; repeat all around.

3RD ROW—ch 8, 1 s in t., * ch 5, 1 d, ch 5, 1 s; repeat from * 3 times., ch 5, join.

4TH ROW—1 s, 1 h d, 5 d, 1 h d, 1 s in 5 ch; repeat 7 times.

UPPER EDGE—1ST ROW—1 s in 3rd d, ch 4, 1 s in next 3rd d, ch 4, 1 tr, ch 4.

2ND ROW—1 d in ch, ch 1, sk 1 ch, 1 d in ch.

3RD ROW—1 d in 1 d, * 1 p, 1 d in 1 ch, 1 d in d; repeat from *.

No. 231.

UPPER EDGE—1 d in br, ch 1, 1 d in br.

LOWER EDGE—1ST ROW—1 s in br, ch 5, sk 1 l of br, 1 s in br.

2ND ROW—sl st to 3rd of 5 ch, ch 4, 1 cl of 2 t in 3rd ch., * 1 cl of 3 t in next 3rd ch, 1 cl of 2 t in next 3rd ch, ch 4, sl st to same 3rd ch., ch 4, 1 cl of 2 t in same 3rd ch; repeat from *.

3RD ROW—1 s in cl, 3 p, sk 1 cl, 1 s in next cl., ch 9.

4TH ROW—* 1 d in 5th of 9 ch, 1 p: repeat from * twice, 1 d., ch 2, 1 s in 2nd p, ch 2.

No. 232.

CHAIN 23—1ST ROW—1 s in 10th ch., ch 3, 9 d in 1 of 10 ch, ch 12, sl st in 10th ch, ch 3, 10 d in 10 d., ch 4, 1 d in 5th ch, 1 d in 3rd ch., ch 2, 1 p, ch 3, 1 d in 4th ch.

2ND ROW—ch 5, 1 p, ch 2, 1 s, ch 2, 1 p, ch 2, 1 s in 1 st d, ch 2, 1 p, ch 6, 1 s in last d.

3RD ROW—ch 6, 1 s in 4th ch., ch 3, 1 p, ch 5, sk 2 p, 1 s in s., ch 2, 1 p, ch 2, 1 d.

4TH ROW—ch 6, 1 s in s., ch 3, 9 d in 6 ch, ch 3, 9 d in 9 d., ch 3, 1 s in 5 ch, ch 2, 1 p, ch 4., 12 d in 5 ch.

5TH ROW—ch 3, 11 ds in 11 ds., ch 3, 1 s over 4 ch., ch 2, 1 p, ch 4, 1 s in d., ch 2, 1 p, ch 4, 1 s in last d.

6TH ROW—ch 2, 1 p, ch 4, 1 s in 4 ch., ch 2, 1 p, ch 4, 1 s in s., ch 6, * 1 d in d, ch 1; repeat from * 11 times, catch with s in 1 of 10 ch.

7TH ROW—* ch 2, 2 p, 1 d in 1 ch, 1 p, ch 2, sk 1 d, 1 s in 1 ch; repeat from * 5 times, 1 s in last of d., ch 5, 1 sl st in 5th ch., ch 3, 9 d in 5 ch., ch 3, 9 ds in 9 ds, ch 3, 1 s in 3rd ch., ch 2, 1 p, ch 6, 1 s.

No. 233.

CHAIN 20—1ST ROW—3 d in 6th ch, ch 2, 3 d in next ch., ch 2, sk 2 ch, 1 s, ch 3, 1 s in same ch., ch 5, sk 3 ch., 1 s, ch 3, 1 s in 3rd ch., ch 2, sk 2 ch, 3 d in ch, ch 2, 3 d in next ch., 1 d in last ch.

2ND ROW—ch 3, 3 d, ch 2, 3 d in 2 ch., ch 5, 1 s, ch 3, 1 s in 3rd ch., ch 5, 3 d, ch 2, 3 d in 2 ch., 1 d in d.

3RD ROW—ch 3, 3 d, ch 2, 3 d in 2 ch., ch 2, 1 s, ch 3, 1 s in 3rd ch., ch 5, 1 s, ch 3, 1 s in 3rd ch., ch 2, 3 d, ch 2, 3 d in 2 ch., 1 d in d.

No. 234.

CHAIN 20—1ST ROW—Like No. 233.

2ND ROW—Like No. 233, continue from last 3 d., ch 2, 1 d in 5 ch.

3RD ROW—ch 5, 1 d in 1 st d, ch 2., 3 d, ch 2, 3 d in 2 d, work up like first row. Other rows are worked likewise, only increasing 1 m in scl in each row and making 2 s m in 7 and 8th row.

10TH ROW—1 s in o m, ch 5, sk 1 d, 1 s in o m.

11TH ROW—ch 1, 1 p, ch 1, 1 s in 5 ch.

10

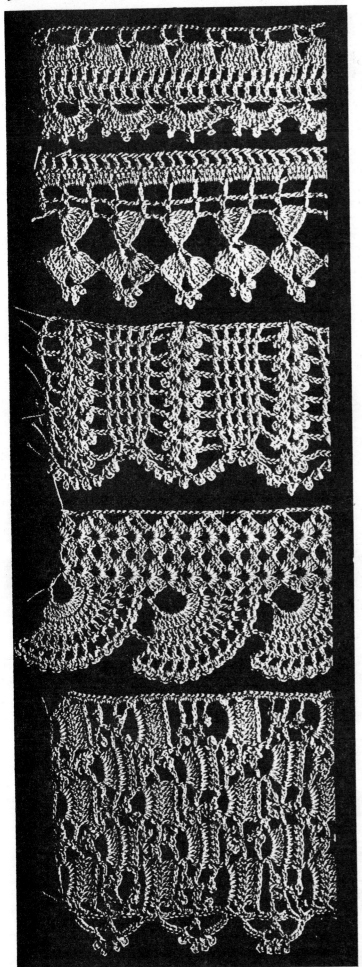

No. 235.

CHAIN DESIRED LENGTH—1ST ROW—1 d in ch, *
ch 2, sk 2 ch, 1 d in ch., ch 4, sk 4 ch, 1 d in
ch; repeat from *.
2ND ROW—8 t in 4 ch., sk 1 d, 2 ch and 1 d., 8 t in
next 4 ch.
3RD ROW—1 d in t, ch 1, sk 1 t, 1 d in t.
4TH ROW—1 d in 1 ch, ch 1, sk 1 d, 1 d in next 1 ch.
5TH ROW—1 s in 1 ch., * ch 7, sk 3 d, 1 s in 1 ch;
repeat from *.
6TH ROW—* 3 d, 1 p; repeat from * twice, 3 d in
7 ch., 1 s in next 7 ch., * 3 d, 1 p; repeat from *
twice, 3 d in next 7 ch.

No. 236.

MIDDLE PART IS MADE FIRST.
CHAIN 12—1ST ROW—1 t in 8th ch, ch 2, 1 t in last
ch.
2ND ROW—ch 10, sl st in 6th ch, 6 t in t., ch 2, sk
2 ch, 1 t in t., ch 2, sk 2 ch, 1 t in t.
1ST UPPER EDGE—5 d in each sp.
2ND ROW—1 d in d, ch 1, sk 1 d, 1 d in d.
LOWER EDGE—5 t, 3 p, 5 t in 1 of 6 ch.

No. 237.

CHAIN DESIRED LENGTH
1ST ROW—1 d, 1 p, 1 d in 1 ch., ch 2, 1 d, 1 p, 1 d in
next ch., ch 3, sk 3 ch., 1 d, * ch 1, sk 1 ch., 1 d;
repeat from * 3 times, ch 3, sk 3 ch, 1 d, 1 p,
1 d in ch., ch 2, 1 d, 1 p, 1 d in next ch.
2ND ROW—1 d, 1 p, 1 d, ch 2, 1 d, 1 p, 1 d in 2 ch.,
ch 3, 1 d in d, * ch 1, 1 d in d; repeat from *
3 times, ch 3, 1 d, 1 p, 1 d, ch 2, 1 d, 1 p, 1 d in
2 ch.
3RD, 4TH, 5TH and 6TH ROWS—Same as 2nd.
7TH ROW—1 d, 1 p, 1 d, ch 2, 1 d, 1 p, 1 d in 2 ch.,
ch 5, 1 d in each of 5 d, ch 5, 1 d, 1 p, 1 d, ch 2,
1 d, 1 p, 1 d in 2 ch.
8TH ROW—1 s in 1st d, ch 1, 1 p, ch 1, 1 s in last d.,
4 ps., 1 d, 1 p, 1 d in 2 ch, 4 ps, 1 s in 1st d.

No. 238.

CHAIN 13—1ST ROW—3 d, ch 2, 3 d in 5th ch., sk
3 ch, 3 d, ch 2, 3 d in next ch., ch 5, 1 d in last
ch.
2ND ROW—ch 3, 12 d in 5 ch., * 3 d, ch 2, 3 d in 2
ch; repeat from * once.
3RD ROW—ch 3, * 3 d, ch 2, 3 d in 2 ch; repeat from
* once, 1 d in each d.
4TH ROW—ch 4, 1 d in d, * ch 1, 1 d in next d, repeat from * 11 times, * 3 d, ch 2, 3 d in 2 ch; repeat from * once.
5TH ROW—ch 3, * 3 d, ch 2, 3 d in 2 ch; repeat from
* once, 1 d in d, * ch 2, 1 d in next d; repeat 11
times.
6TH ROW—* 1 s, 2 h d c, 1 s in 2 ch; repeat from *
11 times, ch 4, * 3 d, ch 2, 3 d in 2 ch; repeat
from * once.

No. 239.

CHAIN 35—1ST ROW—1 s in 10th ch., ch 2, 1 p, ch 2,
1 p, ch 2., sk 5 ch, 1 s in 6th ch., ch 5, sk 5 ch, 1 s
in 6th ch., ch 2, 1 p, ch 2, 1 p, ch 2., sk 5 ch, 1 s
in 6th ch., ch 5, sk 5 ch, 1 s in last ch.
2ND ROW—ch 3, 8 ds in 5 ch, * ch 3, sk 1 p, 1 d in
2 ch., ch 2, sk 1 p, 8 ds in 5 ch; repeat from *
once.
3RD ROW—ch 3, 8 d in 8 d., * ch 2, 1 p, ch 2, 1 s
in d., ch 2, 1 p, ch 2, 8 d in 8 d; repeat from *
once.
4TH ROW—ch 5, 1 p, ch 2, 1 p, ch 2, 1 s in last d.,
* ch 5, 1 s in next d, ch 2, 1 p, ch 2, 1 s in last
d: repeat from * once.
5TH ROW—ch 6, sk 1 p, 1 d in 2 ch., ch 3, sk 1 p, *
8 ds in 5 ch., ch 3, sk 1 p, 1 d in 2 ch., ch 3; repeat
from * once, 1 d at end.
6TH ROW—ch 5, 1 p, 1 s in d., * ch 2, 1 p, ch 2, 8
ds in 8 ds., ch 2, 1 p, ch 2, 1 s in d; repeat from
* once.
UPPER EDGE is made of s c, in each sp.
LOWER EDGE—3 s in each sp, 4 times., ch 7, 1 s
back in 6th s, ch 7, 1 s in next 6th s, 6 s in 7
ch, 4 p, 6 s in next 7 ch., 3 s in next 5 sp. Repeat scl.

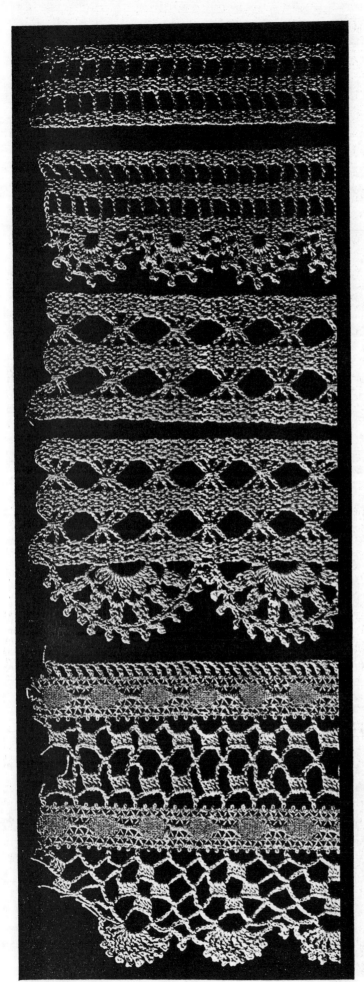

No. 240.

CHAIN 18—1ST ROW—1 d in 4th ch, 1 d in next ch., * ch 4, sk 4 ch, 3 d in 3 ch; repeat from * once.
2ND ROW—ch 3, 2 d in 2 d, * ch 4, sk 4 ch, 3 d in 3 d; repeat from * once.

No. 241.

1ST 3 ROWS like 1 and 2 of No. 240, continue on 3rd row—ch 7.
4TH ROW—3 d in 3 d., * ch 4, sk 4 ch, 3 d in 3 d; repeat from * once.
5TH ROW—ch 3, 2 d in 2 d, * ch 4, sk 4 ch, 3 d in 3 d; repeat from * once, 15 d in 7 ch, sı st to second row, then sl st to 1st row.
6TH ROW—* ch 1, 1 p, ch 1, sk 1 d, 1 d in d; repeat from * 7 times, 2 d in next 2 d, * ch 4, sk 4 ch, 3 d in 3 d; repeat from * once.

No. 242.

CHAIN 26—1ST ROW—1 d in 4th ch, 2 d in next 2 ch, * ch 7, sk 7 ch, 4 d in 4 ch; repeat from * once.
2ND ROW—ch 3, 3 d in 3 d., * ch 7, sk 7 ch, 4 d in 4 d; repeat from * once.
3RD ROW—Like 2nd.
4TH ROW—ch 3, 3 d in 3 d., * ch 3, 1 s over 3 of 7 chains, ch 3, 4 d in 4 d; repeat from * once.

No. 243.

1ST 9 ROWS like No. 242, continue on 9th row—ch 10, sl st to 6th row, now sl st to 5th row.
10TH ROW—ch 3, * 1 cl of 3 t, ch 3; repeat from * 4 times in 10 ch., 4 d in 4 d, work up like before.
11TH & 12TH ROWS—Like 3 and 4.
13TH ROW—like before, continue—* ch 4, 1 cl of 3 t in 3 ch; repeat from * 5 times, ch 3, sl st to 2nd row.
14TH ROW—* ch 1, 1 p, ch 1, 1 s in 4 ch., ch 1, 1 p, ch 1, 1 s in cl; repeat from * 5 times, ch 1, 1 p, ch 1, sl st to d., ch 3, 3 d in 3 d. and finish up like before.

No. 244.

LOWER EDGE—1ST ROW—1 s in br, ch 7, sk 2 l of br, 1 s in br.
2ND ROW—4 d in 7 ch, ch 7, 1 s in next 7 ch, ch 7, 1 s in next 7 ch, ch 7, 4 d in next 7 ch.
3RD LOW—1 s in 7 ch, ch 7, 4 d in next 7 ch, ch 3, 4 d in next 7 ch, ch 7, 1 s in next 7 ch.
4TH ROW—Like 2nd.
5TH ROW—Like 1st.
6TH ROW—1 t, * 1 p, 1 t; repeat from * 7 times in 7 ch, ch 3, 1 s in next 7 ch, ch 3, 1 p, ch 3, 1 s in next 7 ch., ch 3. Middle rows on each side of br are worked like 1st row.
2ND ROW—4 d in 7 ch, ch 7, 4 d in next 7 ch.
Other row same, only caught together with 1 s after crocheting 3 ch.
UPPER EDGE—1 d in br, ch 1, 1 d in br.

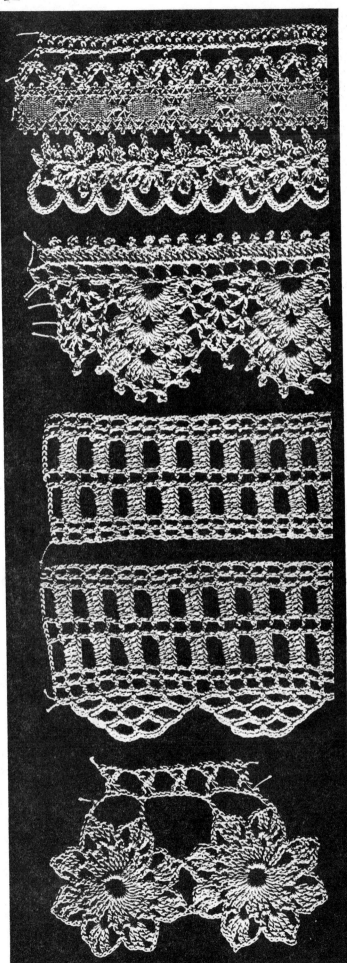

No. 245.

LOWER EDGE—1ST ROW—1 p of 6 ch, ch 4, sl st **in** br, ch 4, sl st to 1 st of 4 ch, 1 p of 6 ch., ch 3.
2ND ROW—sl st to p, 1 p of 6 ch, 1 p of 8 ch, 1 p of 6 ch, sl st to upper p, ch 3.
3RD ROW—sl st to p of 6 ch, ch 7, sl st to p of next 6 ch, sl st to p of next 6 ch.
4TH ROW—12 s over 7 ch.
UPPER EDGE—1 t, ch 4, sl st to br, ch 4, 1 t in same l of br, sk 2 l of br.
2ND ROW—1 d over 2 t, ch 5, 1 d over next 2 t.
3RD ROW—1 d in d, ch 1, sk 1 ch, 1 d in ch.

No. 246.

CHAIN DESIRED LENGTH—1ST ROW—Made **in** meshes.
2ND ROW—1 s in m, ch 3, 1 s in next m, ch 5, 1 s in next m, * ch 3, 1 s in next m; repeat from * twice, ch 7, 1 s in next m, ch 3, 1 s in next m.
3RD ROW—1 d *, ch 2, 1 d; repeat from * twice in 5 ch, sk 3 ch, 1 d in next 3 ch, sk 3 ch, 1 cl **of** 3 t, * ch 2, 1 cl of 3 t; repeat from * once, ch 3, 1 cl of 3 t, * ch 2, 1 cl of 3 t; repeat from * once in 7 ch, sk 3 ch, 1 d in 3 ch.
4TH ROW—1 d, * ch 2, 1 d; repeat from * twice in 2 ch., 1 d in d, sk 2 cl, 1 cl in 2 ch., ch 2, sk 1 cl., 1 cl, ch 2, 1 cl, ch 3, 1 cl, ch 2, 1 cl in 3 ch., ch 2, sk 1 cl, 1 cl in 2 ch., ch 2, 1 d in d.
5TH ROW—1 d, ch 2 , 1 d, ch 2, 1 p, ch 2, 1 d, ch 2, 1 d in 2 ch., 1 d in d, ch 2, * sk 1 cl, 1 cl in 2 ch, ch 1, 1 p, ch 1; repeat from * once, sk next cl, * 1 cl, ch 1, 1 p, ch 1; repeat from * twice in 3 ch., sk 1 cl, 1 cl in 2 ch., ch 1, 1 p, ch 1, 1 cl in next 2 ch., ch 2, 1 d in d.
UPPER EDGE—1 d in d, 1 p, 2 d in m, 1 d in d, 1 **p.**

No. 247.

CHAIN 27—1ST ROW—1d in 5th ch, ch 1, sk 1ch, 1 d in ch, ch 5, sk 5 ch, 1 d in ch, ch 2, sk 2 ch, 1 d in ch, ch 5, sk 5 ch, 1 d in ch, * ch 1, sk 1 ch, 1 d in ch; repeat from * once.
2ND ROW—ch 4, 1 d in d, ch 1, 1 d in d, 5 d over 5 ch, 1 d in d ch 2, sk 2 ch, 1 d in d, 5 d over 5 ch, 1 d **in** d, * ch 1, sk 1 ch, 1 d in d; repeat from * once.

No. 248.

UPPER PART MADE LIKE NO. 247.
LOWER EDGE—3 s in each of 8 sp., * ch 5, sl st to 6th s; repeat from * 3 times., * 7 s over 5 ch; repeat from * twice, 4 s over next 5 ch, turn, * ch 5, sl st to next scl; repeat from * twice, turn, * 7 s over 5 ch; repeat from * once, 4 s over next 5 ch, turn, * ch 5, sl st to next scl; repeat from * once, * 7 s over 5 ch; repeat from * once, * 3 s in next scl; repeat from * once, 3 s in **each** of next 8 sp before starting next scl.

No. 249.

CHAIN ~~10~~, JOIN—1ST ROUND—ch 4, 1 t in ring, * ch 3, 2 t in ring; repeat from * ~~14~~ times, ch 3, sl **st** together.
2ND ROUND—1 s in 3 ch, ch 3, 2 t in 3 ch., ch 3, 2 t in 3 ch., ch 3, 1 s in next 3 ch.
UPPER EDGE—1ST ROW—1 d in 3 ch, ch 9, 1 d **in** next 3 ch, ch 11, 1 d in next 3 ch.
2ND ROW—is made in ct.

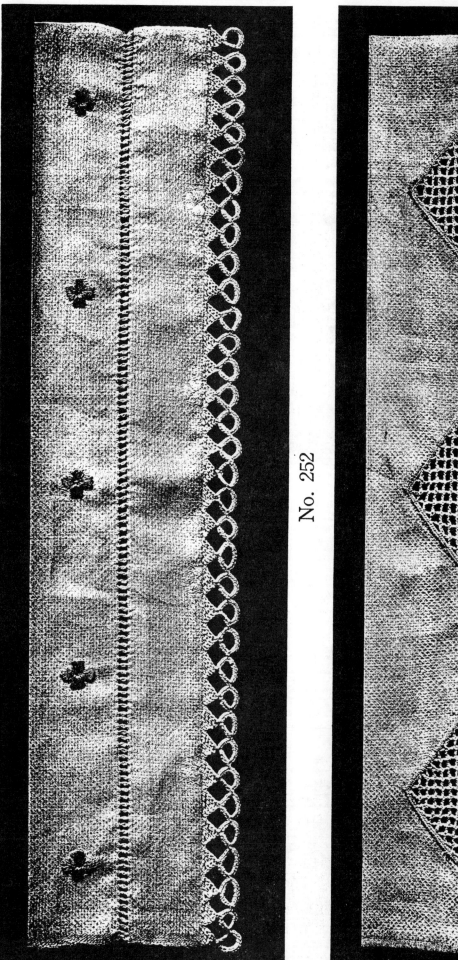

No. 252

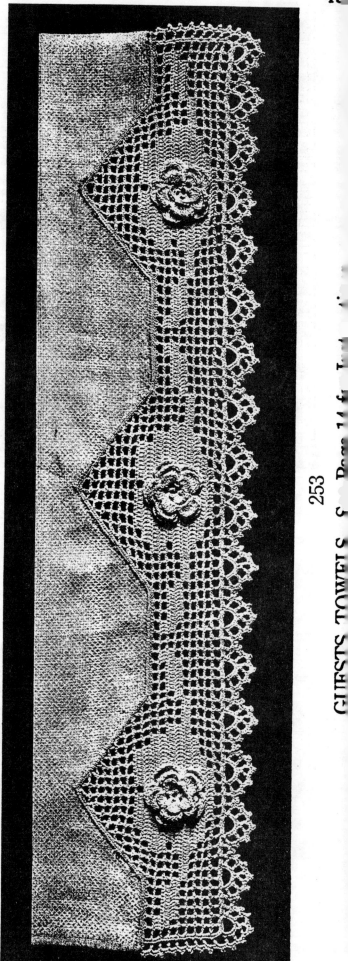

253

GUESTS TOWELS

13

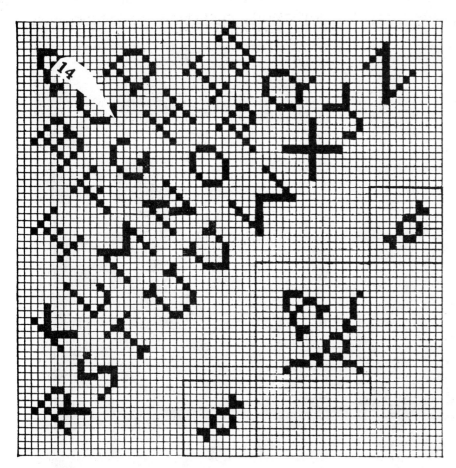

No. 254

GUEST TOWELS.

No. 250.

FOR MEDALLION follow block pattern given in No. 254 on this page, then crochet 3 s in each mesh till you get to between squares, work 2 s in next m, ch 5, sl st to next m of 1 st square, 3 s, 1 p, 3 s over 5 ch; 3 s in each of next 2 m, ch 8, sl st to 1st square, 12 s over 8 ch, 3 s in each of next m till you get to corners where you put in 7 s.

2ND ROUND—4 d, 1 p, all around, work 2 d in each of 3 s at the corners.

FOR EDGE—Scallop material and fold back once, work s all along.

2ND ROW—d s.

3RD ROW—1 s between scl, ch 3, 1 s in d, ch 3, 2 d, ch 3, 2 d in d, continue like illustration all along.

4TH ROW—1 s in s between scl, ch 3, 1 d in s, ch 3, 2 d, ch 1, 1 p, ch 1, 2 d in 3 ch., ch 3, 1 d in d, ch 3., 3 t, ch 1, 1 p, ch 1, 3 t in 3 ch.

No. 251.

MAKE 2 ROWS IN SPACES.

Work 3 s in each of 4 sp., ch 10, * 1 p of 4 ch; repeat from 4 twice, ch 2, sl st to 2nd d, ch 2, sl st to 1 st p, 3 p, ch 2, sl st to 2nd ch., ch 8, sl st to 2nd d, turn, and work 1 s, 1 h d, 1 d, 1 p, * 3 d, 1 p; repeat from * twice, 1 d, 1 h d, 1 s in 8 ch, other side same way, then work 3 s in each of 7 sp before starting next scl.

No. 252.

See No. 208.

No. 253.

Follow block pattern No. 256 given on this page, then work 3 s in each m, 7 s at corner, 3 s in next m, * ch 9, sl st back in 6th s., 6 s, 1 p, 6 s over 9 ch., 3 s in each of next 5 m; repeat from *.

2ND ROW—See illustration, ch 2, 1 d all along but omit 2 ch twice between scls and put in an extra 2 ch and 1 d at point of scl.

3RD ROW—2 s, 1 p, 2 s in each 2 ch.

FOR ROSE—Chain 6, join— ch 6, 1 d in ring * ch 3, 1 d in ring; repeat from * 3 times, ch 3, sl st together.

2ND ROUND—1 s, 1 h d, 4 d, 1 h d, 1 s in each 3 ch.

3RD ROUND—ch 5, sl st under each d of 1 st round; repeat.

4TH ROUND—1 s, 1 h d, 1 d, 4 t, 1 d, 1 h d, 1 s over each 5 ch.

5TH ROUND—Is made like 3rd, only ch 7.

6TH ROUND—Is made like 4th, add 2 more t only. Roses are sewed on afterwards.

No. 255.

INSTRUCTIONS FOR FRONT COVER.

Work for-get-me-nots lengthwise first—ch 8, 1 d in 3rd ch., ch 3, * 2 d, ch 2, sl st in 1st of 3 ch, catching one thread only; repeat from * twice, ch 2, 1 d in same 1st of 3 ch, sl st to 1st d, ch 8 again for your next flower. Petals are sl st together, after crocheting 1st d of next flower.

Work another chain like this for 2nd row of forget-me-not and crochet 1 s in lower petal, ch 5, 1 s in next lower petal on both of the chains.

MEDALLION—ch 8, join.

1ST ROUND—ch 4, 1 cl of 3 t in ring, * ch 8, 1 cl of 4 t; repeat from * twice in ring of 8 ch, ch 8, sl st to-gether.

2ND ROUND—1 p over cl, 12 s over each 8 ch; repeat all around.

MEDALLIONS—are sl st to forget-me-nots after crocheting 6 s of the 12 s in last round and are sl st to every other flowers, also, after crocheting 6 s of the 12 s.

UPPER & LOWER EDGE—4 d in 4 ch, 1 p. See Edging and Insertion Book No. 1 for Lace to match.

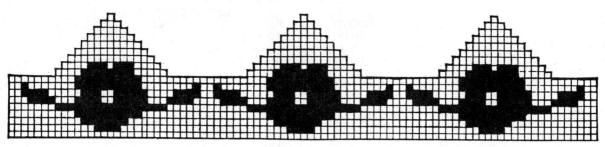

No. 256

HANDKERCHIEF EDGINGS.

No. 105. Ch. 8. Form ring. Ch. 6, 2 sl. st. in ring. Turn. Ch. 6, 2 sl. st. in loop. Turn. Repeat to desired length. **Start Edge—** 4 sl. st. ch. 3, 4 sl. st. in each loop on side.

No. 100. Ch. 11. Join 6. Ch. 4, 1 d. c., 4 ch., 1 d. c., 4 ch., 1 d. c., 4 t. c., 3 times makes one clover. Repeat to desired length.

No. 101. 3 t. c., 2 ch., 3 t. c., 5 ch., Turn. 6 t. c., 3 t. c., 2 ch., 3 t. c. Repeat to desired length.

No. 102. Ch. 5, 1 d. c., ch. 5, 1 d. c. Turn. 9 d. c., 4 d. c., ch. 7, 12 d. c. Turn. Ch. 4, 1 t. c., 2 ch., 7 times. Turn. 2 d. c., 1 p., 7 times. Repeat to desired length.

No. 103. 1 t. c., 3 ch., 5 t. c., 1 t. c., 3 ch., 5 t. c. all around. Repeat to desired length.

No. 104. Draw or Stamp scallops on linen ½ inch wide. Cut out. **1ST ROW—**Work over corner with 3 sl. st. over scallop with 14 sl. st. **2ND ROW—**7 d. c. with 2 ch. betw. each. Sk. 1 on corner. **3RD ROW—**Over d. c., 1 sl. st., 2 ch., 2 d. c., 3 sl. st. Fasten over on next d. c., sk. 2 corner d. c., 1 ch. to next scallop.

4

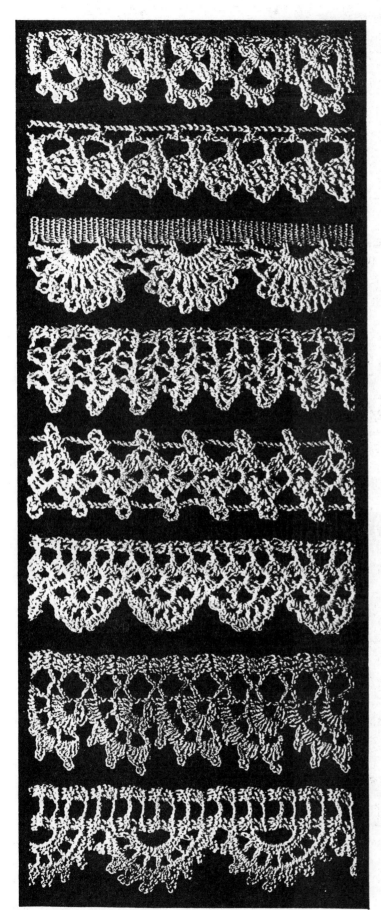

No. 108.
Ch. 10.

1ST ROW—8 d. c. Turn, 8 d. c., Turn, 8 d. c., ch. 3, **2** t. c., 2 t. c., ch. 3. Fasten.
2ND ROW—In d. c., ch. 7, 2 t. c., ch. 3, 1 d. c., ch. 3, 2 t. c., ch. 7. Turn.
3RD ROW—2 d. c., ch. 5, 2 d. c., three times. Repeat.

No. 109.
Ch. 9.

1ST ROW—5 d. t., with 1 ch., between each in 7th st. from hook. Turn.
2ND ROW—Ch. 1, 6 sl. st. over d. t., 2 sl. st. in ch., ch. 6. Turn.
3RD ROW—5 d. t., 1 ch. between each in middle d. t.

No. 110.

1ST ROW—Ch. 5, 1 sl. st. in material.
2ND ROW—1 sl. st. in first 5 ch., ch. 1, 10 d. c. in second 5 ch., ch. 1, 1 sl. st., ch. 5, over next 5 ch. below. Repeat.
3RD ROW—1 sl. st., ch. 2, over 5 ch., 9 d. c., with 6 p. over 10 d. c.

No. 111.
Ch. 12.

1ST ROW—1 d. c. in 4th st. from hook, ch. 2, 1 d. c., ch. 2, 1 d. c. in 4th st. below, sk. 2, 1 d. c., ch. 2, 1 d. c. in one st. below.
2ND ROW—Ch. 5, 5 d. c., with 1 ch., between each, 1 d. c., ch. 2, 1 d. c., over same 2 ch., 2 d. c.

No. 112.
Ch. 9.

1ST ROW—3 d. c., ch. 3, 3 d. c., ch. 5, Turn.
2ND ROW—Same. On side ch. 5, p. in every loop.

No. 113.
Ch. 12.

1ST ROW—3 d. c. in 4th and 5th st. from hook, ch. 3, 3 d. c. in next 3 sts., ch. 2, sk. 2 st. below, 2 d. c. Turn.
2ND ROW—Ch. 3, 1 d. c., (over last 2 d. c.) ch. 2, 3 d. c., ch. 3, 3 d. c. over 3 ch. st. below, ch. 5. Turn.
3RD ROW—3 d. c., ch. 3, 3 d. c., in 3 ch. st., ch. 2, 2 d. c. Turn.
4TH ROW—Ch. 3, 1 d. c., ch. 2, 3 d. c., ch. 3, 3 d. c., ch. 3, 2 d. c. in loop going back, 3 d. c., with 2 ch. between each. Fasten in 1st loop. Turn.
5TH ROW—2 sl. st., 1 d. c., 2 sl. st. in every space over loop.

No. 114.
Ch. 9.

1ST ROW—Ch. 3, 3 t. c., ch. 5, 1 t. c., ch. 3, 1 t. c., Turn.
2ND ROW—10 t. c., ch. 3, 1 d. c., ch. 3, 3 t. c. Turn.
3RD ROW—3 t. c., ch. 5, 1 t. c., ch. 3, 1 t. c. 4 times. Turn.
4TH ROW—1 d. c., 2 t. c., 1 p., 2 t. c. 4 times. Repeat.

No. 115.
Ch. 10.

1ST ROW—2 t. c., ch. 4, 2 t. c., 5 rows wide, ch. 9. Turn
2ND ROW—16 d. c., 2 t. c., ch. 4, 2 t. c. Turn.
3RD ROW—2 t. c., ch. 4, 2 t. c., ch. 2, 1 t. c. 8 times, 1 d. c., 2 t. c., 1 p., 2 t. c., 1 d. c., 8 times. Repeat.

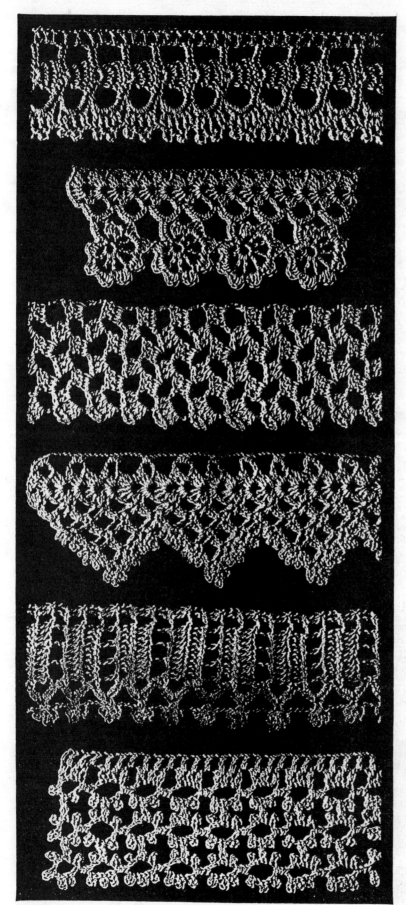

No. 116.
Ch. 16.

1ST ROW—7d. t. in 8th, 9th, 10th, st. from hook, ch. 6, in end of ch. below.
2ND ROW—Turn, 12 sl. st. in loop, 3 sl. st. in first 3 of d. t. below, ch. 1, sk. 1 d. t., 3 sl. st. on next 3 d. t., 3 sl. st. in ch.
3RD ROW—Ch. 7, 7d. t. in the one sl. st. on d. t. below same.
UPPER ROW—1 d. c., ch. 1, Repeat.
LOWER ROW—2 d. c., 2 p., 2 d. c. in every loop.

No. 117.

1ST ROW—Ch. 5, turn, 3 t. c., ch. 3, 3 t. c. Turn
2ND ROW—Ch. 3, 3 t. c., ch. 3, 3 t. c., ch. 5, 10 d. c., 3 t. c., ch. 3, 3 t. c. Turn.
3RD ROW—Ch. 3, 3 t. c., ch. 3, 3 t. c., ch. 5, 5 d. c., ch. 10, Fasten.
4TH ROW—6 t. c., ch. 4, 2 times over needle, 8 times 1 d. c., 3 t. c., 1 d. c., 8 times 5 d. c. in remaining ch., 5 d. c., 3 t. c., ch. 3, 3 t. c. Repeat.

Edging. No. 118.
Ch. 19.

1ST ROW—1 d. c. in the 7th st. from hook, 2 d. c. in the next 2 st., ch. 3, sk. 2 st., 3 d. c. in the next 3 st., ch. 3, sk. 2 st., 3 d. c. in the last 3 st. of 1st row. Turn.
2ND ROW—Ch. 6, 3 d. c. over ch. of 3, ch. 3, 3 d c. over next ch. of 3, ch. 3, 5 d. c. over last ch. Turn.
3RD ROW—Ch. 3, sl. st. bet. 3d and 4th d. c., ch. 6, 3 d. c. over ch. of 3. Repeat 1st and 2nd rows alternately.

No. 119.
Ch. 12. Turn.

1ST ROW—1 d. c. in 7th ch., ch. 3, 1 d. c., ch. 5, 1 d. c., 3 t. c., ch. 3, 3 t. c. Turn.
2ND ROW—Ch. 5, 3 t. c., ch. 3, 3 t. c., ch. 3, 1 d. c., ch. 3, 1 d. c., ch. 5, 3 times in same loop, ch. 5, 1 d. c., ch. 3, 1 d. c., ch. 5, 1 d. c., ch. 5, 1 d. c., ch. 3, 3 t. c., ch. 3, 3 t. c. Turn.
3RD ROW—Ch. 5, 3 t. c., ch. 3, 3 t. c., ch. 3, 1 d. c., ch. 3, 1 d. c., ch. 3, ch. 5 three times, ch. 5, 1 d. c., ch. 3, 1 d. c., ch. 5, 1 d. c., ch. 3, 1 d. c., ch. 5, 1 d. c., ch. 3, 1 d. c., 3 t. c., ch. 3, 3 t. c. Turn.
4TH ROW—Ch. 5, 3 t. c., ch. 3, 3 t. c., ch. 3, 1 d. c., ch. 3, 1 d. c., ch. 5, three times, ch. 3, 1 d. c., ch. 5, three times, ch. 3, 1 d. c., ch. 5, three times. Repeat from beginning.

No. 120.
Ch. 27.

1ST ROW—1 d. c. in 7th st. from hook, 4 o. m., 1 d. c. Turn.
2ND ROW—Ch. 3, 1 o. m., 3 s. m., ch. 6, Turn Form loop.
3RD ROW—3 s. m., 1 o. m., 1 d. c. 1ST FINISH-ING ROW—4 sl. st., ch. 2, 4 sl. st., in 1 sl. st. between every loop.
2ND ROW—3 d. c., ch. 4, p. in every point, ch. 4 to next.

No. 121.
Ch. 5.

1ST ROW—1 d. c., ch. 5, 1 d. c.; ch. 5, 1 d. c., ch. 8, 1 d. c. in 5th ch.
2ND ROW—Ch. 5, Turn, ch. 5, 1 d. c., ch 5, 1 d. c., ch. 5, 1 d. c., 3 d. c. in ch., ch. 5, 1 d. c.
3RD ROW—Ch. 5, 1 d. c., ch. 5, fasten in middle of 2nd ch., ch. 5, 1 d. c., ch. 8, 1 d. c. in 5th ch., ch. 5, 1 d. c. Repeat to any desired width.

6

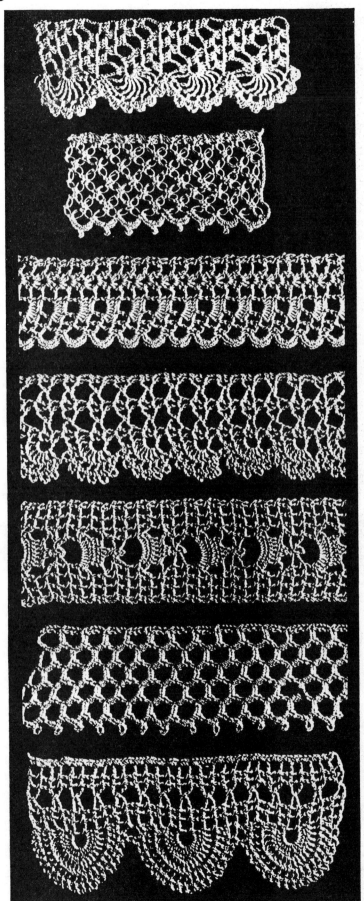

No. 122.
Ch. 18.

1ST ROW—Ch. 7, 3 t. c., ch. 2, 3 t. c., ch. 2, 3 t. c., Turn.
2ND ROW—Ch. 5, 3 t. c., ch. 2, 3 t. c., ch. 5, 3 t. c., ch. 5. Turn.
3RD ROW—3 t. c., ch. 5, 3 t. c., ch. 2, 3 t. c., ch. 5. Turn.
4TH ROW—3 t. c., ch. 5, 3 t. c., ch. 2, 3 t. c., ch. 5. Turn.
5TH ROW—3 t. c., ch. 2, 3 t. c., ch. 5, 3 t. c., ch. 7. Turn.
6TH ROW—3 t. c., ch. 2, 3 t. c., ch. 2, 3 d. tr. c. 8 times.
7TH ROW—Ch. 4, 1 d. c., ch. 4, 1 d. c., 8 times. Repeat to desired length then finish top with 1 d. c., 3 t. c., 1 d. c., 3 t. c.

No. 123.
Ch. 20.

1ST ROW—1 long st., 1 d. c., 1 st. in 7th ch. 3 times.
2ND ROW—1 long st., 1 d. c. three times. Turn.
3RD ROW—Ch. 5, turn, 10 d. c. in ch., 1 long st., 1 d. c., 1 st., 1 d. c. 3 times, ch. 5. Turn.
4TH ROW—10 d. c. in ch. Repeat.

No. 124.
Ch. 20.

1ST ROW—1 d. c., ch. 2, sk. 2, 2 d. c., ch. 3, 2 d. c. (close to last 2 d. c.) ch. 2, 1 d. c., ch. 3, 1 d. c., ch. 2, 1 d. c., ch. 3, 1 d. c., ch. 6. Turn loop.
2ND ROW—1 d. c. over 2 d. below, ch. 2, 7 d. c., ch. 2, 2 d. c., ch. 3, 2 d. c., in 3 ch. below, ch. 2, 2 d. c. Repeat.
EDGE—12 sl. st. in every loop on lower edge.

No. 125.
Ch. 28.

1ST ROW—1 d. c. in 9th st. from hook, ch. 2, 1 d. c. in 10th st., ch. 3, sk. 3, 1 sl. st., ch. 3, 1 d. c., ch. 2, 1 d. c. (Repeat) 2 d. c. Turn.
2ND ROW—Ch. 3, 1 d. c., ch. 5, 1 d. c., ch. 2, 1 d. c., over same. Repeat. In loop 6 d. c., ch. 1 between each turn.
3RD ROW—Between each d. c. below 1 d. c. with p. fasten next loop in p.

No. 126.

1ST ROW—1 d. c. in 4th st. from hook, 3 o. m., ch. 6 over 5, 3 o. m., 2 d. c.
2ND ROW—2 o. m., ch. 3, in last 2 d. c. below 9 d. c., over 6 ch. Repeat.
3RD ROW—2 o. m., ch. 3, 7 d. c., over 9 d. c., ch. 3.
4TH ROW—2 o. m., ch. 2, 1 d. c. in same st. below, ch. 3, 3 d. c., keep on hook, pull loop through.
5TH ROW—3 o. m., ch. 3, 1 p. on pointed d. c. below, ch. 3.

No. 127.
Ch. 35.

1ST ROW—1 d. t. in 8th m. from hook, ch. 5, sk. 5, 1 sl. st. repeat 3 times, ch. 6, 1 sl. st. Turn.
2ND ROW—3 sl. st., 1 p., 4 sl. st., ch. 3, 4 sl. st., 4 sl. st. in next loop, ch. 3, 4 sl. st., repeat to end, 1 sl. st. over d. t.
3RD ROW—Ch. 5, 1 d. t., ch. 5, in 3 ch. below.

No. 128.
Ch. 35.

1ST ROW—1 d. c. in 8th st. from hook, ch. 1, 1 d. c., ch. 3, sk. 3, 1 sl. st., ch. 3, 1 d. c., ch. 1, 1 d. c., ch. 2, 2 d. c.
2ND ROW—Ch. 5, 1 d. c., ch. 1, 1 d. c., ch. 5 (over 3 ch. 1 sl. st. below). Repeat.
3RD and 4TH ROW—Same as second.
5TH ROW—Same, ch. 9, form loop. Turn.
6TH ROW—8 d. c., ch. 2, 8 d. c. in loop.
7TH ROW—8 d. c., ch. 1, between each on d. c. below, 2 d. c. in middle. Repeat.
8TH ROW—1 d. c., ch. 1 between every d. c. below, 2 d. c. in middle. Turn.
9TH ROW—Ch. 3, 1 sl. st. over every d. c. Fasten 2nd loop.

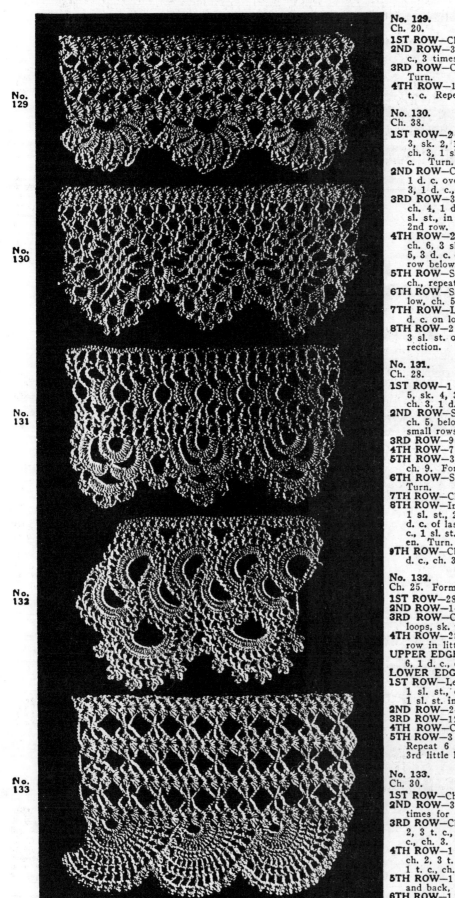

No.
129

No.
130

No.
131

No.
132

No.
133

No. 129.
Ch. 20.
1ST ROW—Ch. 3. Turn.
2ND ROW—3 t. c., ch. 2, 3 t. c., ch. 5, 3 t. c., ch. 2, 3 t. c., 3 times, ch. 3. Repeat 6 times.
3RD ROW—Ch. 10, 1 d. c., in ch., ch. 7, 1 d. c., ch. 4. Turn.
4TH ROW—1 t. c., ch. 2, 1 t. c., ch. 2, 12 t. c. Repeat 6 times.

No. 130.
Ch. 38.
1ST ROW—2 d. c. in 5th ch. from hook, ch. 2, 3 d. c., ch. 3, sk. 2, 1 sl. st., ch. 3, 1 d. c., ch. 4, sk. 4, 1 d. c., ch. 3, 1 sl. st., ch. 3, 1 d. c., ch. 4, 3 d. c., ch. 3, 3 d. c. Turn.
2ND ROW—Ch. 4, 6 d. c., over 3 ch., ch. 12, 3 d. c., ch. 2, 1 d. c. over 1 below, ch. 4, 1 d. c., ch. 3, 1 sl. st., ch. 3, 1 d. c., ch. 4, 1 d. c. Same below.
3RD ROW—3 sl. st., same, ch. 3, 1 sl. st., ch. 3, 1 d. c., ch. 4, 1 d. c., ch. 3, 1 sl. st., ch. 3, 3 d. c., ch. 5, 3 sl. st., in long loop, ch. 5, 3 d. c., ch. 8. Fasten to 2nd row. Turn.
4TH ROW—2 sl. st., 1 p., 2 sl. st., repeat twice, 7 d. c., ch. 6, 3 sl. st., ch. 2 over 3 sl. st. below, 3 sl. st., ch. 5, 3 d. c. over 2 ch. below, ch. 3, 1 sl. st. same as 2nd row below. Turn.
5TH ROW—Same over 2 o. m., 3 d. c., ch. 5, 3 sl. st. over ch., repeat like below, 3 d. c. on loop, ch. 8.
6TH ROW—Same loop, ch. 5, four times, 3 sl. st. on 3 below, ch. 5, 3 d. c. behind same.
7TH ROW—Like below, 5 times 3 sl. st. over 4, ch. 5, 3 d. c. on loop, ch. 8. Turn to middle loop.
8TH ROW—2 sl. st., p., repeat twice, 6 d. c., ch. 5, 4 times 3 sl. st. over 4 below, 3 d. c. Repeat in opposite direction.

No. 131.
Ch. 28.
1ST ROW—1 d. c., ch. 3, 1 d. c. in 8th st. from hook, ch 5, sk. 4, 3 sl. st., ch. 5, sk. 5, 1 d. c., ch. 3, 1 d. c., ch. 3, 1 d. c. Turn.
2ND ROW—Same. Ch. 3, in 5 ch. below, ch. 6 in next, ch. 5, below. (Always the same start and end of these small rows.)
3RD ROW—9 d. c. in 6 ch. (center from below.)
4TH ROW—7 d. c., ch. 3, over 9 d. c.
5TH ROW—3 sl. st., ch. 5, over 7 d. c. after last d. c., ch. 9. Forming loop for small point. Turn.
6TH ROW—Same as 4th Row. 19 d. c. in loop. Fasten. Turn.
7TH ROW—Ch. 11 in middle of loop, ch. 11, fasten on end.
8TH ROW—In 11 ch., 16 d. c., 2 s. c., 1 sl. st. in 2nd ch., 1 sl. st., 2 s. c., 6 d. c., ch. 9. Turn. Fasten in 6th d. c. of last loop. Work 1 sl. st., 1 s. c., 15 d. c., 1 s. c., 1 sl. st. over this ch., 10 d. c. in ch. just left. Fasten. Turn.
9TH ROW—Ch. 3, 3 d. c. with 2 ch. between each in 4th d. c., ch. 3, 1 sl. st., sk. 3. Repeat 6 times over point.

No. 132.
Ch. 25. Form Ring.
1ST ROW—28 d. c. over half of ring, ch. 5. Turn.
2ND ROW—14 d. c. with 2 ch. between each, sk. 1.
3RD ROW—Ch. 4 in space below. This makes 10 little loops, sk. with 11 ch. to corner.
4TH ROW—28 d. c. in these 11 ch. Repeat. Fasten each row in little loops.
UPPER EDGE—Ch. 2, 1 sl. st. in 4 little loops, sk. 1, ch. 6, 1 d. c., ch. 1 over 1 st. row.
LOWER EDGE.
1ST ROW—Leave 2 little loops open from center. In 3rd, 1 sl. st., ch. 11 to 3rd of next scallop. Fasten with 1 sl. st. in 4th little loop, ch. 2.
2ND ROW—24 d. c. Fasten. Turn.
3RD ROW—12 d. c. with 2 ch. between each. Fasten.
4TH ROW—Ch. 4 over every space. Fasten. Turn.
5TH ROW—3 d. p., ch. 2, 1 sl. st., ch. 2 over 2 little loops. Repeat 6 times. Work thread with ch. and sl. st. to 3rd little loop of next scallop.

No. 133.
Ch. 30.
1ST ROW—Ch. 3. Turn.
2ND ROW—3 t. c. in one ch., ch. 2, 3 t. c., ch. 5, four times for four rows.
3RD ROW—Ch. 7 fasten in next 15 t. c. in ch., 3 t. c., ch. 2, 3 t. c., ch. 7, four times and back, 15 t. c. over t. c., ch. 3. Turn.
4TH ROW—1 t. c., ch. 1, 1 t. c., ch. 1, 15 times, 3 t. c., ch. 2, 3 t. c., ch. 5, four times and back, 1 t. c., ch. 1, 1 t. c., ch. 1, 15 times, ch. 3. Turn.
5TH ROW—1 t. c., ch. 2, 1 t. c., ch. 2, ch. 5, four times and back, 1 t. c., ch. 2, 1 t. c., ch. 2, 15 times. Turn.
6TH ROW—1 d. c., 3 t. c., 1 d. c. in each mesh. This completes one scallop. Repeat.

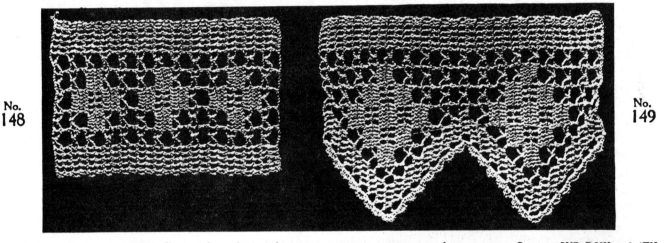

No.
146

No.
147

No. 146. Ch. 34. **1ST ROW**—15 d. c. start in 12th st. from hook, ch. 5, 3 d. c. Turn. **2ND ROW**—Ch. 3, 2 d. c., ch. 3, 1 sl. st. over 5 ch. Ch. 3, 12 d. c., ch. 5, 1 sl. st., ch. 3, 1 sl. st. called p., ch. 5, 1 d. t. in loop between ch. 11. Turn. **3RD ROW**—1 p. over 5 ch. between, ch. 5, 1 p., ch. 5, 3 d. c. Same as 1st row. **4TH ROW**—Same. 6 d. c., ch. 5, 1 p., ch. 5, 3 d. c. over 5 ch. between, ch. 5, 1 p., ch. 5, 1 d. t. in loop between. Ch. 7. Turn. **CENTER ROW**—1 p., 9 d. c. over ch. and 3 d. c. below. Same. 3 d. c. Repeat in opposite direction. **ROW AFTER FINISHED FIRST SCALLOP**—8 d. c., ch. 1, between each, ch. 11. **ROW ON POINTED EDGE**—In loop of 4th row, 5 p. on 6 d. c. In center loop, 9 d. c., 6 p. Connect every 2nd scallop of edging with 3 ch., 1 sl. st. in each of two loops.

No. 147. Ch. 30. **1ST ROW**—2 d. c. in 8th st. from hook. ch. 7, sk. 4, 2 sl. st. Same. 2 d. c. **2ND ROW**—Ch. 3, 1 d. c. (start for every other row) ch. 5, 2 sl. st. Repeat. **3RD ROW**—Ch. 3, 9 d. c., ch. 9, 2 sl. st. in middle of 9 ch. below. Repeat. **5TH ROW**—Ch. 9 for loop, 1 d. c., ch. 4, 2 d. c. same as below. **6TH ROW**—Repeat 2nd Row. 10 d. c., ch. 3, 10 d. c. in loop. Fasten. Ch. 2, fasten again. Turn. **7TH ROW**—10 d. c. over same. 2 d. c., ch. 3, 2 d. c. in point. 2 last rows over point worked separately. 7 d. c., ch. 2, between each. In point 3 d. c., ch. 2, **p.**

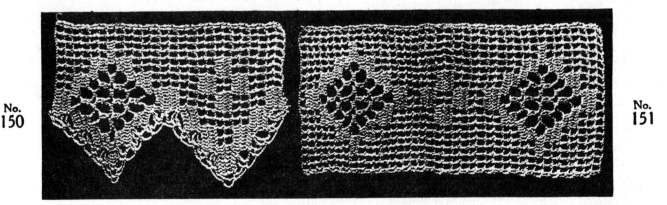

No.
148

No.
149

No. 148. Ch. 60. **1ST ROW**—Ch. 3, 2 d. c., ch. 1, 4 d. c. between each. Start and end for every row. 5 o. m. **2ND ROW and 4TH ROW**—Same as bel. **3RD ROW**—1 s. m. in middle. **5TH ROW**—1 o. m., 1 s. m., ch. 1, 2 d. c., 1 ch. betw. on s. m. bel., 1 s. m., 1 o. m. Repeat.

No. 149. Ch. 50. **1ST ROW**—Ch. 3, 2 d. c., ch. 1, 4 d. c., ch. 1 betw. each. Start for every row on this side. 3 o. m., 5 d. c., ch. 1, betw. each ch. 2, 1 d. c. sk., ch. 1. Turn. **2ND ROW**—Ch. 7, 2 d. c., betw. each. Over 2nd ch. bel., 3 d. c., ch. 1 betw. each, ch. 4 over 3rd ch., 1 d. c., ch. 5. **3RD ROW**—Same. Add on pointed edge 2 ch., 1 d. t. in loop. Ch. 7. Turn. **4TH and 6TH ROWS**—Same as below. **5TH ROW**—3 o. m., 1 s. m., 1 o. m. **7TH ROW**—2 o. m., 1 s. m., ch. 1, 1 d. c., ch. 1 betw. each over s. m., 1 s. m., 1 o. m, **8TH and 9TH ROW**—1 o. m., 1 s. m. same. 1 long d. t. for point, ch. 4. **10TH ROW**—Turn. 1 d. c., ch. 1, over 3rd d. c. below.

No.
150

No.
151

No. 150. First Design. Ch. 38. **1ST ROW**—1 d. c. in 4th st. from hook. 7 d. c., 8 o. m., 1 d. c. **2ND ROW**—Same and ch. 9. **3RD ROW**—Same as 1st Row. Ch. 4 (after 8 d. c.) sk. 4 d. c. bel., 8 d. c., 6 o. m. **4TH ROW**—6 d. c., 5 d. c. on first 4 d. c. bel. ch. 5, 2 d. c., over 4th ch. Ch. 5, 5 d. c over 4, ch. 9. **5TH ROW**—Same. Ch. 5, 3 sl. st. on 5th ch. bel., 3 d. c., ch. 1 betw. each, ch. 4 **o. m.** **6TH ROW**—4 o. m., 5 d. c., ch. 5, 2 d. c., ch. 5, 2 d. c. on 2nd ch. bel. Repeat. **CENTER ROW**—8 d. c., ch. 5, 4 times, 3 sl. st., ch. 2, betw. each on ch. below. Repeat in opposite direction. **Second Design.** **1ST and 2ND ROWS**—8 o. m., 8 d. c., ch. 9, Turn. Same as in 1st Design. **3RD and 4TH ROWS**—10 o. m., 8 d. c., ch. 9. **5TH and 6TH ROWS**—6 o. m., 2 s. m., 4 o. m., 8 d. c. ch. 9. **CENTER ROWS**—4 o .m., 2 s. m., 2 o. m., 2 s. m., 4 o. m., 8 d. c., Ch. 1, Turn, 5 sl. st. over 1st 5 d. c. bel., ch. 2, 2 d. c. on last 2 d. c. bel, 2 s. m. Repeat Opposite Side. **1ST ROW**—1 sl. st. in 1st Row, ch. 3, 1 d. t., ch. 3, 1 d. t. in every cor., 1 sl. st., ch. 3, 1 sl. st. on every little point. **2ND ROW**—Ch. 5 over every d. t. and in every 3rd ch. over point.

No. 151. Ch. 65. **1ST ROW**—1 d. c. in 4th st. from hook, 18 o. m., 1 d. c., ch. 3. **2ND ROW**—1 d. c., 8 o. m., 2 s. m., 8 o. m. **3RD ROW**—Same. **4TH ROW**—6 o. m., 8 d. c., ch. 4, Same. **5TH ROW**—6 o. m., 5 d. c. over 4 d. c., ch. 5, 2 d. c. over 4th ch. **6TH ROW**—4 o. m., 8 d. c., 5 ch., 3 sl. st. over 5th ch. bel., ch. 2, 3 sl. st. over next 5 ch. Repeat. **7TH ROW**—Same as 5th Row—3 times 2 d. c. **CENTER ROW**—2 o. m., 8 d. c., ch. 5, 4 times, 3 sl. st. with 2 ch. between. **Second Design.** **1ST and 2ND ROWS**—8 o. m., 2 s. m., 8 o. m. **3RD and 4TH ROWS**—6 o. m., 2 s. m., 2 o. m., 2 s. m., 6 o. m. **5TH and 6TH ROWS**—Same as 1st and 2nd Rows.

No. 152. Ch. 125. **1ST SINGLE ROW**—Ch. 3, 2 d. c., ch. 3, sk. 2, 1 sl. st., ch. 3, 1 d. c. (start for every row). Repeat 16 times. 3 d. c. Turn. (End of every row). **2ND SINGLE ROW**—Ch. 3, 2 d. c., ch. 5, 1 d. c. until end. **3RD SINGLE ROW**—Same. In 8th, 9th, 10th, o. m., 3 s. m. (6 d. c. over o. m.) **4TH SINGLE ROW**—1 o. m., 6 s. m., 1 o. m., 1 s. m., Repeat always 2 rows alike. **3RD DOUBLE ROW**—1 o. m., 1 s. m., 4 o. m., 1 s. m., 3 o. m. Repeat in opposite direction. **4TH DOUBLE ROW**—1 o. m., 1 s. m., 1 o. m., 2 s. m., 1 o. m., 1 s. m., 3 o. m. **5TH DOUBLE ROW**—1 o. m., 1 s. m., 1 o. m., 1 s. m., 2 o. m., 1 s. m., 3 o. m. **6TH DOUBLE ROW**—1 o. m., 1 s. m., 1 o. m., 4 s. m., 3 o. m. **7TH DOUBLE ROW**—1 o. m., 1 s. m., 6 o. m., 1 s. m. **8TH DOUBLE ROW**—1 o. m., 1 s. m., 5 o. m., 3 s. m. **9TH DOUBLE ROW**—2 o. m., 1 s. m., 4 o. m., 3 s. m. **10TH DOUBLE ROW**—3 o. m., 1 s. m., 2 o. m., 5 s. m. **11TH DOUBLE ROW**—4 o. m., 1 s. m., 1 o. m., 5 s. m. **12TH DOUBLE ROW**—5 o. m., 1 s. m., 1 o. m., 3 s. m. **13TH DOUBLE ROW**—3 o. m., 2 s. m., 1 o. m., 1 s. m., 1 o. m., 1 s. m. **14TH DOUBLE ROW**—2 o. m., 4 s. m., 1 o. m., 1 s. m., 1 o. m. **15TH DOUBLE ROW**—1 o. m., 6 s. m., 1 o. m., 1 s. m. Center Row. Repeat in opposite direction.

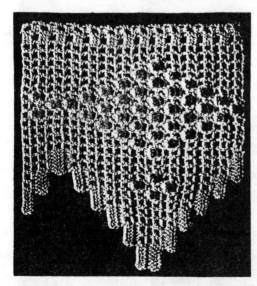

No. 153. Ch. 56.

1ST ROW—7 d. c. start in 4th st. from hook, 15 o. m.

2ND ROW—Ch. 3, 1 s. m., 8 o. m., 5 d. c. in next o. m. Draw the last loop through 1st of 5 d. c. to puff up. 1 d. c. on d. c. between 5 o. m., 7 d. c., ch. 9. Turn.

3RD ROW—9 d. c., 15 o. m., 1 s. m. Turn. (One plain row over every puff st. row.)

4TH ROW—1 s. m., 7 o. m., 1 puff st., 1 o. m., 1 puff st., 6 o. m. Add one puff st. in each of the next three double rows.

4TH DOUBLE ROW—1 s. m., 4 o. m., 5 puff st., 4 o. m., 1 puff st., 5 o. m.

5TH DOUBLE ROW—1 puff st. over 5, 2 over 1.

6TH DOUBLE ROW—1 s. m., 4 o. m., 5 puff st., 4 o. m., 1 puff st., 4 o. m., 7 d. c., ch. 3. Turn.

No. 154. Crochet every wheel separately.

1ST ROW—Ch. 8. Form Ring.

2ND ROW—16 d. c. with 2 ch. between each. Close 1st connecting row, 3 sl. st. in every space from first half of each wheel. For corner in ¼ of wheel.

2ND ROW—Same on other half corner in ¾ of wheel.

3RD ROW—On upper end of each wheel 1 d. t., ch. 6, 1 sl. st., ch. 6, 1 d. t., 1 d. t. in 5th st. of next wheel.

4TH ROW—6 sl. st. over every 6 ch. below. Lower end of wheel. Ch. 7, going back to 2nd with 1 sl. st., ch. 2, 1 sl. st. in 3rd st. below. Repeat 4 times. Corner, 8 times, ch. 3 to next wheel.

Corner Alphabet for Handkerchiefs, Napkins, Etc.

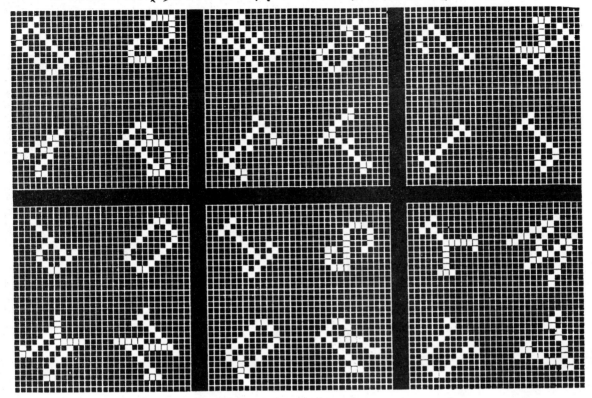

Leave Two or More Open Meshes All Around Closed Meshes of Each Letter.   Can Be Used Either With or
Without Wreath on Cover.

Basket Tidy With Lace Edge

DIRECTIONS

Ch 258, turn. **2nd Row—** 86 solid meshes.

3rd Row—1 solid mesh, 84 open meshes, 1 solid mesh.

4th and 5th Rows—Like 3rd row, then begin and follow design.

Edge—1 row open meshes all around.

2nd Row—Ch 9, * 1, tr tr in 2nd open mesh, ch 4, 3 tr, tr in 2nd open mesh holding the last two stitches of each tr tr on needle and slipping all off at once, ch 4, repeat from *.

3rd Row— * 6 sc over ch of 4, 1 p, 6 sc over each of mesh 3, ch of 4, ch 12, turn, catch back 2 sp, turn, 5 sc over ch just same ch, 1 p, 5 sc in same ch, repeat from *.

This Medallion Can Be Used for Many Other Purposes; Center of a Bed Spread With Bow Knot
Border on Page 6, or as an Insert for Pillow Shams, Dresser Scarfs, Etc.

3

[61]

Handkerchief Edgings

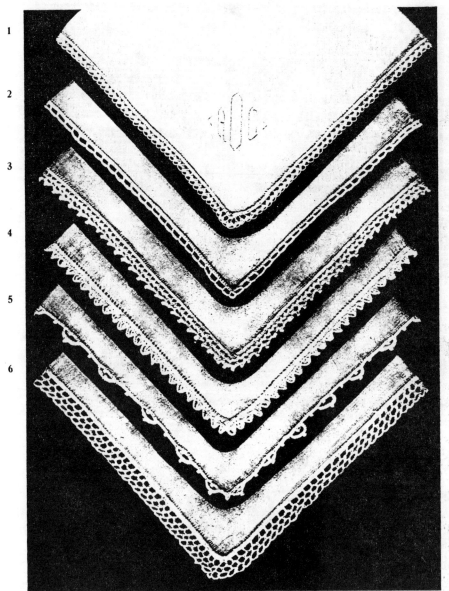

DIRECTIONS

If the material is very sheer, use No. 150 thread and No. 14 steel hook, or No. 100 thread and No. 13 hook. Handkerchief linen 11 inches square.

Handkerchief No. 1—Rolled edge with sc covering, rolled edge all around. Make hairpin trimming No. 1 and whip to edge.

Handkerchief No. 2—Rolled edge, crocheted with a single stitch over the roll for the first row; second row, ch 6, skip 2 sts and make a dc in 3d st; repeat all around.

Handkerchief No. 3—Is made like No. 1, after which it is finished with a row made thus: 2 sc, 1 p, 2 sc in first loop, 1 sc in next loop; repeat all around, filling each loop at the corners.

Handkerchief No. 4—Hemstitched edge, then crochet directly into the edge of the hem. * 1 sc, 1 dc, ch 4 and catch into edge of hem. Repeat all around from *.

Handkerchief No. 5—Rolled edge. * 5 sc over edge, p 6, sc, p 3 sc, ch 8. Turn, catch back into 3d st back of the p; turn, make 5 sc into the loop. 1 p, 5 sc and repeat from *.

Handkerchief No. 6—Is made like No. 2, only it has three rows of crochet, make just like the first, widening at each corner.

Dainty Designs for a Girl's Dresser Cover

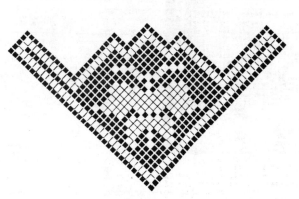

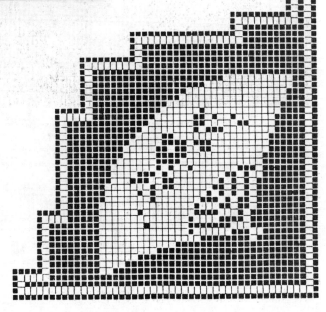

4

Handkerchief Edgings and Corners

All these handkerchiefs are finished with a rolled hem, closely covered with single crochet.

No. 1—Ch 7, sc in 5th st from needle. Repeat around.

No. 2—1st Row—Ch 7, sk 5, sc in next, ch 3, sk 2, sc in next. Repeat around, making 3 ch at corners.

2nd Row—Sl st to 3 ch, sc under ch, 2 dc, p, 2 dc, sc, all under same ch. Ch 4, sl st into center of 7 ch, ch 4. Repeat around.

No. 3—1st Row—Ch 5, sk 2, dc in 3d, repeat.

2nd Row—Sl st to center of ch. Ch 5, dc in center of next ch. * Ch 5, dc in center of next sp. * Repeat around.

3rd Row—Fill ch with 1 sc, 4 dc, 1 sc. Repeat around.

No. 4—1st Row—Ch 3, sk 2, dc in 3d st.

2nd Row—Over ch sl st, 3 sc, sl st. Repeat around.

No. 5—1st Row—Ch 3, sk 2, sl st into 3d st, ch 3, dc in 3d st, repeat around.

2nd Row—Ch 3, p, ch 3, sl st over dc. Repeat around.

No. 6—* Sl st over 2 sts, ch of sc, 3 dc, sc in next st.

No. 7—Turn hem ⅛ in. all around, cover with sc.

2nd Row—1 dc * ch 9, sk 4, 1 dc in next sc. Repeat from *.

3rd Row—* 1 sc over dc, ch 4, 1 sc in center of ch 9, ch 4. Repeat from *.

No. 8—Turn hem ⅛ in. all around, cover hem with sc all around.

2nd Row—* Ch 9, sk 5, 1 sc in next sc, ch 3, sk 2, 1 sc in next sc. Repeat from *.

3rd Row—* 1 sc in center of ch 9, ch 4, 3 sc in ch 3, 1 p, 3 sc in same ch, ch 4. Repeat from *.

No. 9—Turn hem ⅛ in. all around, cover with sc.

2nd Row—Ch 5 * sh 3, 1 dc, in next sc, ch 2. Repeat from *.

3rd Row—* 4 sc in open mesh, 4 sc in next open mesh, 1, 4 sc in each of next two open meshes; 3 dc in next mesh, 3 dc in same mesh. Repeat from *.

No. 10—Turn hem ⅛ in. all around * 10 sc, ch 5, turn back in 4th sc, turn 3 sc around ch, 1 p, 3 sc in same ch, 13 sc over hem, turn. Ch 5, catch back in 2 sc, ch 5, catch in 2 sc, turn. 3 sc around ch, 1 p, 3 sc in same ch, 3 sc in next sh, turn, ch 5, catch by last turn, 3 sc around ch 1, 3 sc in same ch 1, 3 sc. Repeat from *.

DIRECTIONS FOR CORNERS

No. 7—Ch 107, turn. 2nd Row—31 open meshes, make as many rows open meshes as desired, then follow design.

No. 8—Ch 122, turn. 2nd Row—39 open meshes, make as many rows open meshes as desired, then follow design.

No. 9—Ch 134, turn. 2nd Row—43 open meshes, make as many rows open meshes as desired, then follow design.

No. 10—Ch 128, turn. 2nd Row—41 open meshes, make as many rows of open meshes as desired, then follow design.

5

Insertions for Towels, Sheets, Covers, Runners and other Household Linens.

Edgings

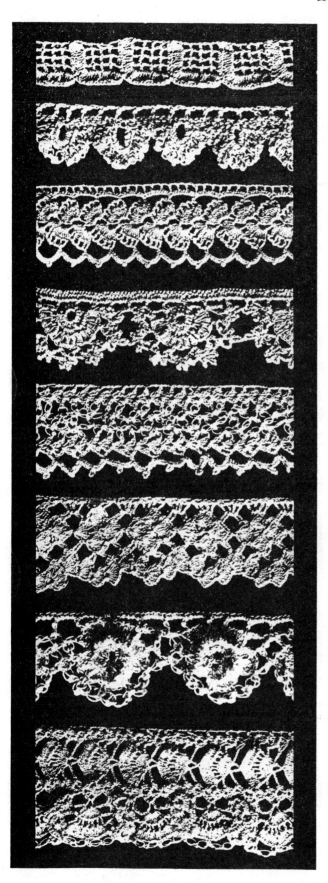

DIRECTIONS

No. 1—For the advanced worker, no directions necessary.

SINGLE ROSE EDGE

MATERIALS—No. 50 thread. No. 11 hook.

No. 2—* Ch 6, join, 15 sc in ring, turn, ch 5, * repeat desired length. For top make a row of sps, 4 sps between each ring. For lower edge, from 1st, make a short knot st. Sc into 3d in ring. Repeat around ring, 6 knot sts around ring, catching last one over the dc of 2nd sp. Repeat around all rings.

DOUBLE FAN LACE

MATERIALS—No. 70 Crochet Cotton. No. 12 hook.

No. 3—Ch 10, join. Repeat into same place. Ch 3, 10 dc over first ring. Ch 4, turn. 1 dc, 1 ch, sk 1, * repeat across. (You will have 7 dc, 6 sps). Make 2nd fan into 2nd ring same way. Ch 5, make a 3d fan in the ch between the first 2 fans, ch 5 and repeat to the desired length, turn, ch 6, sc into 1st st of next fan, repeat across, turn. Cover these ch with sc, and on the top make a row of spaces. For the lower edge, ch 12 between shs. For last row cover chs with 6 sc, p, sc.

ROLL STITCH EDGE

MATERIALS—No. 70 Crochet Cotton. No. 12 hook.

No. 4—Ch 8, join. Cover with sc. Ch 4, miss 4, sl st into 5th st, repeat 4 times.

2nd Row—Ch 3, 5 rolls st into 1st loop, 5 rolls into next loop, 5 rolls into 3d loop, turn. Ch 2, p, ch 2, sc between 2nd and 3d roll. Repeat back to 1st roll, turn. 3 loops of five ch each into 1st ch. Repeat back to last roll. Make a second scallop in same manner, on the last row, fasten the 1st of the 3 loops of 5 ch into the last one of 1st scallops. Join next center same way, fastening loops of 2nd to 6th and 1st to 7th loops. When all are done for top dc in first loop, ch 3 dc between ch and roll, ch 3 dc over ring, ch 3 dc between ch and roll, ch 3 dc between roll and loops, ch 3 dc between 2 scallops. Repeat across last row, 5 dc in each space.

KNOT STITCH

MATERIALS—No. 50 Crochet Cotton. No. 11 hook.

No. 5—Ch 20, turn. 2nd Row—1 tr in 4th st of ch, ch 2, 2 tr in same st. 1 kt st, fasten with sc in 8th st of ch, 2 kt st, fasten with sc in 12th st of ch, 1 kt st and shell at end of ch, turn.

3rd Row—Ch 5, sh in sh, 1 kt st, fasten in kt st of 2nd row, 2 kt sts, fasten in double kt st of 2nd, fasten in double kt st of 2nd row. 1kt st and sh in sh. Ch 1, sc in 3d R L st, top of edge, turn.

4th Row—Ch 5, shell in shell, 3 kt sts, shell in shell, ch 5, turn.

For lower edge. sc in 1st sh. * Ch 12, sc in next sh, repeat from *.

2nd Row—* Sc over ch, 1 p, sc over same ch. Repeat from *.

SHELL LACE

MATERIALS—No. 50 Crochet Cotton. No. 11 hook.

No. 6—Ch 28. 1st Row—Sc into 4th st from needle. 7 loops of 4 ch each into this ch, always fastening with a sl st, except at top, where first and last st is always a sc.

2nd Row—Ch 4, sh of 8 dc under 1st loop at lower edge, ch 8, sk 1 sl st, and fasten into next, sh in next sl st, ch 8, sk 1 sl st and sc into sc at top edge, turn.

3rd Row—Ch 4, sc into same st. Ch 4, sl st into middle of 8 ch. This makes the first of the row of loops of 4 ch each. Make 7 more loops, last one fastens to lower point of shell of bottom, turn.

4th Row—Sh under loop last made, ch 8, sk 1 sl st, fasten into sl st in middle of 8 ch, make sh in sl st at point of sh of former row. Sl st into top of sh. Sh in sl st at last point of sh, ch 4, sc into top edge, turn.

5th Row—Ch 4, sc into same place, 8 loops of 4 ch each, last one fastens into middle of lower sh, turn.

6th Row—Ch 4, sh under middle of sh of former row, sh into the sl st, between two shells, ch 8, sc into top edge, turn.

7th Row—Ch 4, sc into same st. 7 loops as in 1st row. All rows down are loops of 4 ch, shs are made in rows going up. This finishes last scallop. Repeat from 2nd row.

ROSE EDGE

MATERIALS—No. 60 Crochet Cotton. No. 12 hook.

No. 7—Make a Rose with 2 rows of leaves (5 in a row). 1st Row—1 sc 3 dc, 1 sc, 5 times in ring.

2nd Row—1 sc, 1 dc, 6 tc, 1 dc, 1 sc, back of front row. Around lower leaves make 7 kt sts. Across two upper leaves make 3 sps. Repeat desired length.

FAN LACE

MATERIALS—No. 70 Crochet Cotton. No. 12 steel hook.

No. 8—This lace must have the upper part made the length desired, and scallops added.

Ch 16, turn. *Sh of 2 dc, 2 ch, 2 dc, in 6th st from needle. Ch 4, sk 4, dc 3 ch, dc in next, ch 4, sk 4, sh in next, ch 3, turn. Sh in sh, ch 3, 9 dc over the 3 ch, sh in sh, dc back into point of sh of preceding row, ch 3, turn. Sh in sh, 7 dc with 1 ch between dcs in the fan, ch 3, sh in sh, ch 3, turn. Ch 1, 18 dc in fan, ch 1, sh in sh, dc, back into point of sh of former row, ch 3, turn. This finishes the scallop of top. Repeat from * for length desired.

For lower part—Sh in sh, ch 4, dc 3 ch, dc over ch of next sh, ch 4, sh in sh, ch 3, turn. Make the fan just as you did for upper row. When finished make a ch covered with sc down side of scallop, 2 half kt sts across bottom sc over ch between shs up other side of scallop. Repeat.

[65]

Medallions for the Nursery

In Making These Separate Medallions Allow at Least Two Open Meshes Around the Design, But if Space to be Used for Them Permits, Four or Six Open Meshes Make a Bette Effect.

Working Designs for Corners for Handkerchiefs, Napkins Pillows, Scarfs, Etc.

Made from Working Designs on opposite page

Wide Edgings for the Advanced Worker
NO DIRECTIONS NECESSARY

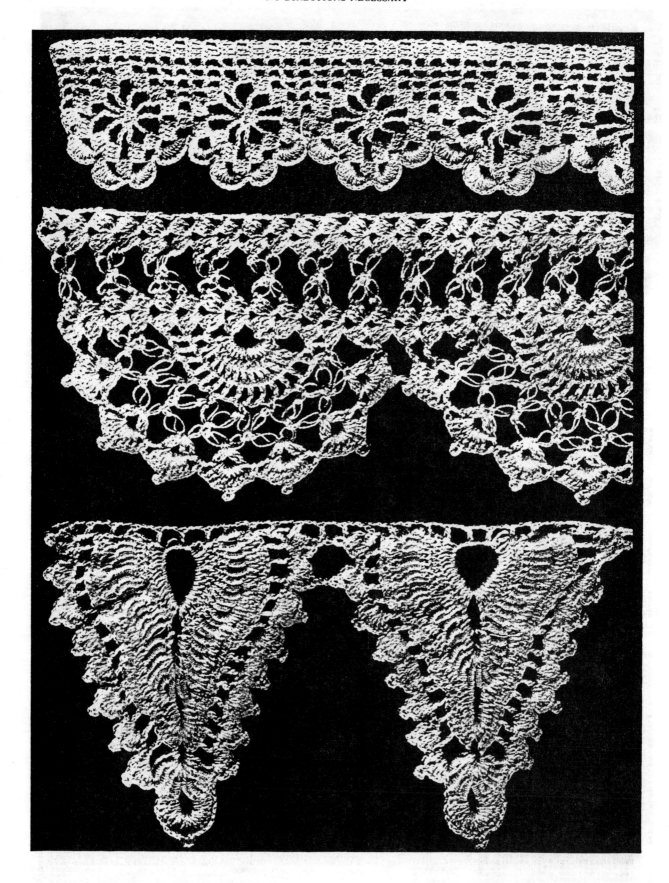

Edgings For Advanced Worker
No Directions Necessary.

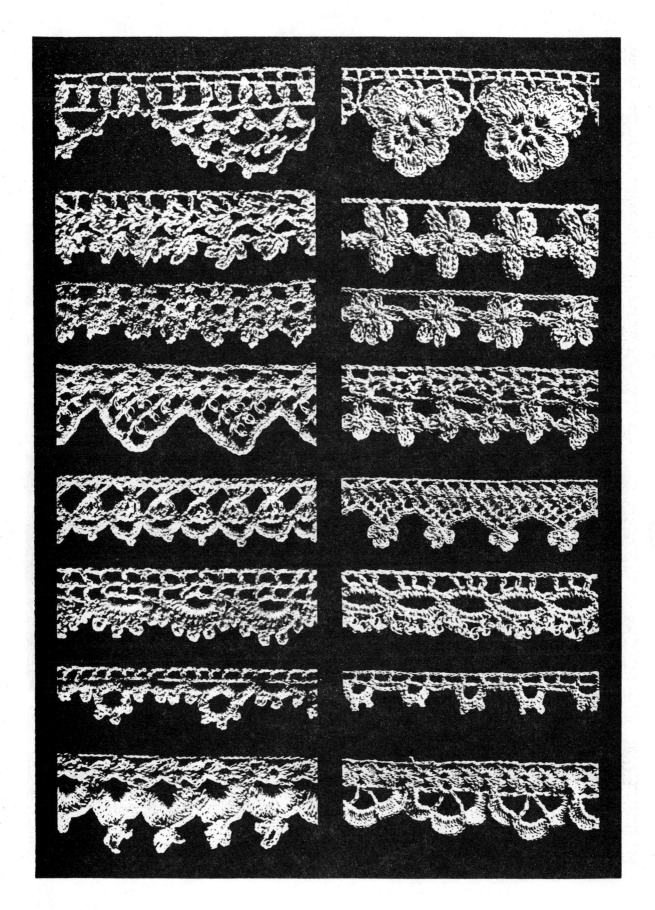

Luncheon Set
APPROPRIATELY DESIGNED IN A VASE OF FLOWERS

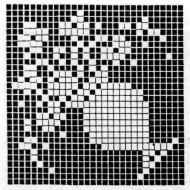

WORKING DESIGN FOR CENTER PIECE

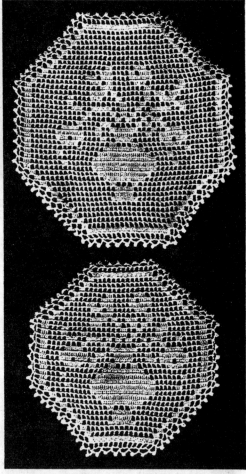

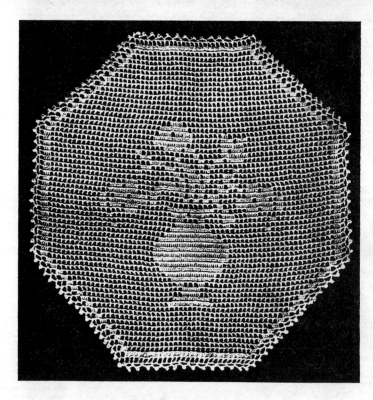

over dc—2 dc in small sp at end of row. Ch 4, turn. In this end loop always make 2 dc—both ways. Follow the working model for the pattern.

When you have completed 32 rows, you will have 66 dc, 1 sp (at the upper side) of 1 ch, 1 dc, ch 4, turn. 2 dc in small sp, 2 dc over 2 dc. * ch 2 sk 1 st, dc over dc. * repeat until have 32 sp. When points are all done, make an edge by * ch 2, p ch 2, sk 1 dc, sl st into next dc. * Repeat around.

DOILEY FOR SERVING PLATE

Largest Size—Ch 91, turn, 1 dc in 8th. 1 dc in each st 81 times. Ch 2, sk 2, 1 dc, turn.

2nd Row—Ch 7 dc in last dc of first row, 2 dc in sp, dc in next dc, 27 open meshes over solid meshes of first row, then follow design.

DOILEY FOR BREAD PLATE

Ch 58, proceed same as large size.

GLASS DOILEY

Ch 46, proceed same as large size.

EDGE

Fasten in open sp. * ch 7, fasten with sc in 3d st of ch, ch 3, 1 sc in next sp, repeat from *.

DIRECTIONS

CENTERPIECE WITH FILET POINTS

MATERIALS—7 balls Crochet Cotton No. 50. Linen center 21 in. in diameter.

On this linen turn a hem 1-8 in. wide; over this hem, 1-8 in. apart, put 3 dc. Make the outer edge as close and firm as possible. It must be done with a very fine hook and fine crochet cotton.

2nd Row—Ch 5, * dc in same st, dc in 3d st, ch 2; repeat from *.

3rd Row—Ch 5, dc under ch of 2 in last row, * dc in next ch of 2, ch 2, dc under same ch; repeat from *. For the circle make twelve points. Ch 71, first row. 3 dc in 5th st from needle, 2 dc over 2 dc. 32 sp of 2 ch, sk 1 st, dc in 2 st, repeat 31 times, ch 4, turn. Ch 1, dc

12

Broad Edgings

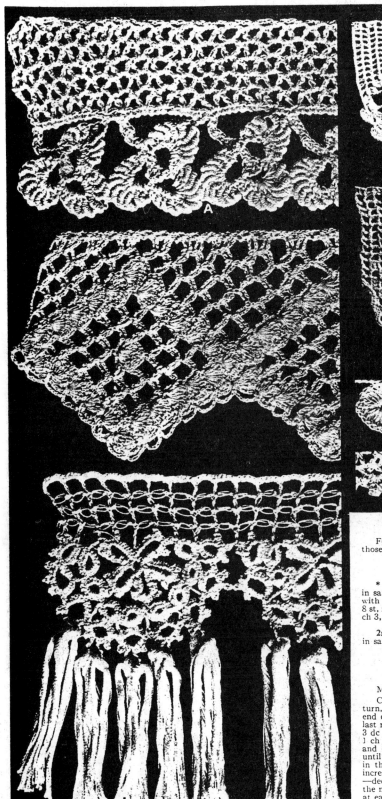

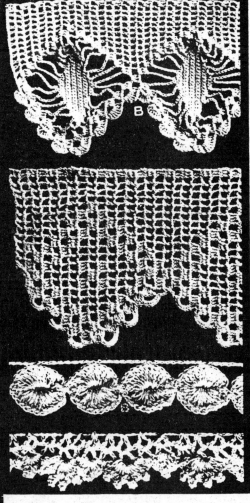

For the advanced worker. No directions necessary, **except** those given for A and B.

EDGE A

* Ch 23, catch back in 7th st, ch 6, catch in same st, ch 6, catch in same st, turn, fill last loop made with 12 roll st, fill next loop with 12 roll st, fill next loop with 12 roll st, 1 sc in each st of ch for 8 st, repeat from * till you have the desired length; for the heading ch 3, * 1 dc in 3d st, ch 3, 1 dc in same st, repeat from *.

2nd Row—Ch 7, 1 dc in first ch, * 1 dc in next ch, ch 3, 1 dc in same ch, repeat from *. Make as many rows as desired.

SPIDER WEB LACE—EDGE B

MATERIALS—No. 30 Crochet Cotton. Hook No. 10.

Ch 32, 4 dc, * ch 1, dc * clear across, 3 dc in last 3 sts. Ch 5 turn, dc over dc. Ch over ch, 3 dc in last sp, ch 20, 3 dc, in the end of 4 dc of first row, ch 4, turn, 3 dc in between last 2 dc of last row, ch 10, 2 sc into middle of 20 ch of preceding row, ch 10, 3 dc into 1st sp, 10 sps, 3 dc in last sp, ch 5, turn. 10 sps (1 dc, 1 ch each , 3 dc in last sp, ch 10, 6 sc, 10 ch, 4 dc in between 3d and 4th dc at end of row. Ch 4, turn. Work in this manner until you have 14 of the 10 chs, 7 on each side of the solid diamond in the center. You decrease the number of sps, one each row, increase the sc of the diamond 2 on each side. Then you reverse —decreasing the sc 2 on each side of the diamond and increasing the number of sps until you have again as at 1st row, 12 sps, 3 dc at each end of row of sps, and 4 dc at end of long chains. When you have the desired length, make a sh of 7 dc in every other sp around the points, fastening with sc in the alternate blks.

13

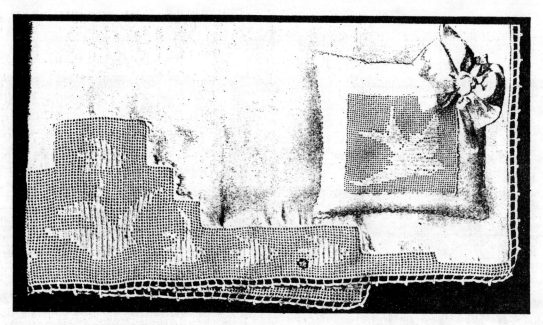

DRESSER SCARF AND PIN CUSHION FROM WORKING DESIGNS ON PAGE 15

Thoroughly Japanese in Design is this Library Table Runner

Working Design for Center Medallion. The Japanese Letters are from the Anne Orr Book on "Filet Designs and Their Appropriate Uses."

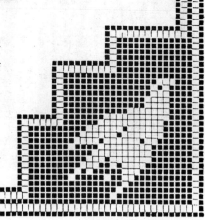

DIRECTIONS FOR FLAG—TABLE RUNNER

A hem ⅛ inch wide all around linen and crochet. Sc close together all around over hem.

2nd Row—Open meshes all around made by making a dc in every alternate sc of first row.

3rd Row—Sl st to center of open mesh * ch 3, sc in next sp, ch 3, sc in next sp. Ch 6 sc in same sp. Repeat from star all around.

CORNER

Ch 158, turn. **2nd Row**—50 open meshes, 1 bk, turn.
3rd Row—Sl st across bk, 1 bk, 49 open meshes, turn, follow design, making each row 1 bk shorter than the preceding one.

CENTER

Ch 149, turn. **2nd Row**—Solid blocks all across. Follow design till flag is finished. For design of letter, see alphabet in Anne Orr Filet Book.

14

[72]

WORKING DESIGNS FOR TABLE COVER ON OPPOSITE PAGE

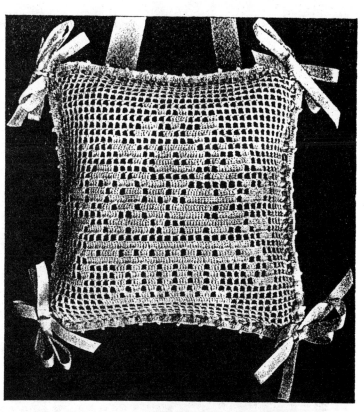

This pincushion is so plain in cut, any worker in filet can copy without directions

BASKET PIN CUSHION

Ch 117, turn. **2nd Row**—39 open meshes, make 4 more open meshes, and follow design.

Edge * 1 dc over dc, 2 dc in open mesh for 3 meshes, 1 p. Repeat from *.

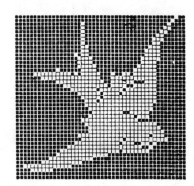

BLUE BIRD MEDALLIONS

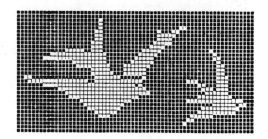

These Designs Can Be Used as Separate Medallions. or the Last Three in a Continuous Border

No. 1

No. 2

No. 3

No. 4

No. 5

No. 6

No. 7

2

CROCHETED EDGINGS.

Explanation of stitches used.

Chain Stitch—ch. s. or c. s.

Single Crochet Stitch—s. c. s.

Double Crochet Stitch—d. c. s. Thread once around the needle.

Treble Crochet Stitch—t. c. s. Thread twice around the needle.

Double Treble Crochet Stitch—d. t. c. s. Thread three times around the needle.

Extra Treble—ex. tr. Thread 4 times around the needle.

Long Treble—L. tr. Thread 5 times around the needle.

Extra Long Treble—ex. L. tr. Thread 6 times around the needle.

Picot Stitch—p. s.

Slip Stitch—sl. st.

( ) repeat all that is included as many times as the following figure indicates.

NO. 1.

For the heading work a chain foundation the length required.

Turn * 1 s. c. s. in the second stitch from needle, 1 s. c. s. in each of the next 2 s., 2 ch. s., miss 2 s. in the foundation, 1 s. c. s. in each of the next 2 stitches, 7 ch. s. repeat from *. This forms the lower part of the lace. Finish off the top of the edging as follows: * 2 d. c. s., 2 ch. s., miss 2 s., repeat from *.

NO. 2.

Row I.—6 ch. s., * 1 p. s., 6 ch. s., 1 p. s., 1 d. c. s., in each of the first 5 ch. s., s. c. s., repeat from *.

Row II.—Edging. * 3 s. c. s., over the loop of 6 ch. s., 3 ch. s., 3 s. c. s. over the same loop, repeat from *.

Row III.—Foundation. 1 d. c. s., 2 ch. s., miss 2 s., repeat all along.

NO. 3.

Row 1.—10 ch. s., 1 d. c. s., in the 6 stitch from the needle, 1 d. c. s. in each of the next 4 stitches. Retain the last stitch of each d. c. s. on the needle until the last d. c. s. is reached. Draw the thread through all the stitches on the needle. 5 ch. s. * 1 d. c. s. over the loop just made, 1 ch. s., repeat from * until there are 6 d. c. s., 1 long t. c. s. This will join the two different scallops together. 10 ch. s., turn 1 s. c. s. in the 4 d. c. s. in last round. 5 ch. s., repeat from the beginning. Foundation.—2 s. c. s., miss 2 s., repeat.

Row II.—1 s. c. s. in every stitch.

NO. 4.

Work chain stitches the length required.

Row I.—3 d. c. s., 2 ch. s., miss 2 s., repeat all along.

Edging.—1 s. c. s. between the d. c. s., just made, 5 ch. s., repeat.

Row II of Edging.—1 s. c. s. over the 5 ch. s., just made 2 d. c. s. over the next loop 2 ch. s., 2 d. c. s., 2 ch. s., 2 d. c. s., 2 ch. s., 2 d. c. s., 1 s. c. s., over the next loop repeat.

Foundation.—1 s. c. s. between the d. c. s. in first row. 5 ch. s., repeat.

NO. 5.

Row I.—9 ch. s. 1 d. c. s. in the 4th stitch from needle, 1 ch. s., 1 d. c. s in same space as last. 2 ch. s., miss 2 s., 1 d. c. s. in next.

Row II.—Turn. 2 ch. s., 1 d. c. s. between the d. c. s. in last row, 1 ch. s., 1 d. c. s. in same space as last. 6 ch. s., 1 s. c. s. at the base of the first d. c. s. made.

Row III.—Turn 2 s. c. s. over the ch. s., just made, 3 ch. s., 2 s. c. s., 3 ch. s., 2 s. c. s., 3 ch. s., 1 s. c. s., 2 ch. s., 1 d. c. s., between the d. c. s. in last row, 1 ch. s., 1 d. c. s. in same space as last 2 ch. s., 1 d. c. s. repeat.

NO. 6.

Work chain stitches the length desired.

Row I.—1 s. c. s. 5 ch. s., miss 3 s., 1 s. c. s., repeat all along.

Row II.—1 s. c. s. over loop of 5 ch. s., just made. 1 d. c. s. in the 3 stitch of the next loop. 7 d. c. s. in the same space. 1 s. c. s. in the 3 stitch of the next loop, repeat.

Foundation.—1 d. c. s. on either side of the s. c. s. in first row. 3 ch. s., miss 2 s., repeat.

NO. 7.

Row I.—6 ch. s., 1 s. c. s. in each stitch, repeat until there are four rows. Continue working thus until the length of edging needed is reached.

Edging.—1 s. c. s. at one of the unattached ends of the square. 3 ch. s., 1 s. c. s. in same space 3 ch. s., 1 s. c. s. at the attached end of square, 1 s. c. s. opposite. 3 ch. s., repeat.

Foundation.—1 s. c. s., on end of square, 4 ch. s., 1 d. c. s., between the squares. 4 ch. s., repeat.

3

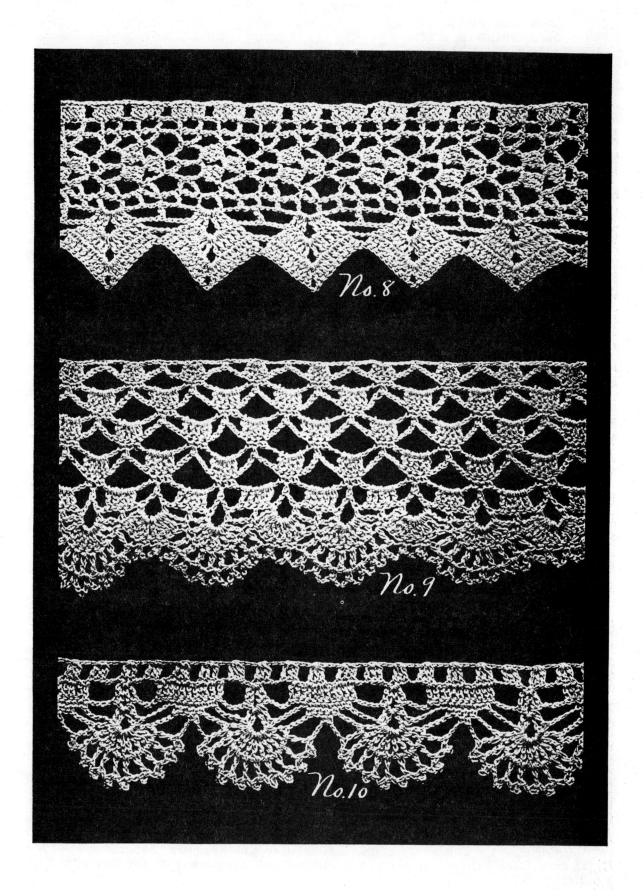

4

NO. 8.

Use T. B. C. Cordonnet 6-fold Crochet Cotton (size 30 was used in the models shown; NUN'S Handy Crochet Hook size 10 was used). Commence with 28 ch. s.

Row I.—1 d. c. s. in seventh ch., from needle, 3 ch. s., miss 3 s., 1 d. c. s. in each of the next 3 s., 2 ch. s., miss 2 ch. s., 1 d. c. s., into each of the next 3 ch. s., 3 ch. s., miss 3, 1 d. c. s. in next, 2 ch. s., miss 2, 1 d. c. s. in next.

Row II.—7 ch. s. to turn work, miss 2 s., 1 d. c. s. in next, 3 ch. s., miss 2 s., 1 s. c. s. in next, 3 ch. s., miss 3 s., 3 d. c. s. in gap, 3 ch. s., miss 3 s., 1 s. c. s. in next, 3 ch. s., miss 2 s., 1 d. c. s., in next d. c. s., 2 ch. s., miss 2 ch. s., 1 d. c. s. in next.

Row III.—7 ch. s. to turn work, miss 2 s., 1 d. c. s., 4 ch. s., 1 s. c. s. in first d. c. s. of next group, 4 ch. s., miss 1 s., 1 s. c. s. in next, 4 ch. s., 1 d. c. s. in next d. c. s., 2 ch. s., miss 2 s., 1 d. c. s. in next.

Row IV.—7 ch. s. to turn work, miss 2 s., 1 d. c. s., 3 ch. s., miss 1 s., 1 s. c. s. in next, 4 ch. s., 1 d. c. s. in next loop, 4 ch. s., 1 s. c. s., in next space, 3 ch. s., miss 1 s., 1 d. c. s., 2 ch. s., miss 2 ch. s., 1 d. c. s. in next. Repeat these four rows until ready for the edging.

Edging.—3 d. c. s. in first space on side of insertion, 3 ch. s., 3 d. c. s. in same space. * 4 ch. s., miss 2 space, 1 d. c. s., miss 2 spaces, 3 d. c. s. in next space, 3 ch. s., 3 d. c. s. in same space, repeat from *.

Row II.—1 d. c. s. in each of the next 3 d. c. s. of last row and 3 d. c. s. in the loop of ch. s., 3 ch. s., 3 d. c. s. in same space, 1 d. c. s. in each of the next 3 d. c. s. of last row, 3 ch. s., repeat.

Row III.—1 d. c. s. in each of the 6 d. c. s. of last row, 3 d. c. s. in loop of ch. s. (9 d. c. s., in all), 3 ch. s., 3 d. c. s. in same space, 1 d. c. s. in each of the next 6 d. c. s. repeat.

For Heading or Foundation.—5 d. c. s., 2 ch. s., miss 1 gap, repeat along entire length. An insertion to match can be made from the first four rows.

NO. 9.

The thread best adapted for this lace is T. B. C. Cordonnet 6-fold Crochet Cotton. Size 20 is recommended. Use size 9, NUN'S Handy Crochet Hook with this size of crochet cotton.

Make chain the length required.

Row I.—Turn 1 d. c. s., in fifth stitch from needle. 4 d. c. s. in same place. * 4 ch. s., miss 3 ch. s., 1 s. c. s., 4 ch. s., miss 3 ch. s., 5 d. c. s. in next stitch, repeat from * all along.

Row II.—Turn. 8 ch. s., 3 s. c. s., in the second, third and fourth d. c. s. in the preceding row. * 8 ch. s., 3 s. c. s. in the second, third and fourth stitches of next group, repeat from *.

Row III.—Turn. 7 ch. s., 5 d. c. s. over the 8 ch. s. of the preceding row. * 4 ch. s., 1 s. c. s. in center s. c. s. of last row. 4 ch. s., 5 d. c. s. over the 8 chain stitches and repeat from *. Repeat these last two rows until the desired width of lace has been made.

Edging.—Turn. 1 s. c. s. in center d. c. s. of last row, 4 ch. s., miss 3 s., 1 s. c. s. * 4 ch. s., miss 5 s., 1 s. c. s., 4 ch. s., miss 3, 1 s. c. s., 4 ch. s., miss 3 s., 1 s. c. s., repeat from * across.

Row II.—Turn. * 8 d. c. s. in loop of ch. s. between groups of d. c. s. in former row. 1 s. c. s. through s. c. s. of last row, repeat from * across.

Row III.—Turn. 1 d. c. s. with 1 ch. s. between, in each of the 8 d. c. s. in last row, miss 3 s., 4 s. c. s. in each of the next 4 s., repeat from the beginning of this row all along. The fourth row consists of picot stitches between the stitches just finished.

5

[77]

NO. 10.

Use T. B. C. Cordonnet 6-fold Crochet Cotton and NUN'S Handy Crochet Hook. Model was made of size 30 crochet cotton with size 10 crochet hook.

Commence with crochet chain the length desired.

Row I.—Turn. 3 d. c. s. in fifth chain from needle, 2 ch. s., miss 3 s., repeat from beginning.

Row II.—Turn. 4 ch. s. * 1 d. c. s. in each of the next eleven stitches, 5 ch. s., miss 6 s., 2 d. c. s. in next, 2 ch. s., 2 d. c. s. in same space as last, 5 ch. s., miss 6 stitches, repeat from *.

Row III.—Turn. 5 ch. s., miss 2 d. c. s. in last row, 1 s. c. s. in each of the next 8 stitches, 5 ch. s., 2 d. c. s. between the d. c. s. in former row. 3 ch. s., 2 d. c. s. in same space, repeat across.

Row IV.—Turn. 1 d. c. s. over chain stitches between the d. c. s. in last row. 1 ch. s. repeat until there are 11 d. c. s. in the same space as first stitch, 4 ch. s., miss 2 s. c. s., 1 s. c. s. in each of the next 5 stitches, 4 ch. s., repeat from beginning of row.

Row V.—Turn. 5 ch. s., * 1 d. c. s. between the d. c. s., just finished, 1 picot stitch, 1 ch. s. repeat in each of the next 10 spaces. 3 ch. s., miss 1 s. c. s., 1 s. c. s. in each of the next 2 stitches, 3 ch. s., repeat from *.

This edging is suitable for towels and pillow cases.

NO. 11.

Use T. B. C. Cordonnet 6-fold Crochet Cotton and NUN'S Handy Crochet Hook. For edging suitable for bed spreads use NUN'S Colonial Twist and size 7 crochet hook.

Commence with a chain of 50 stitches.

Row I.—1 d. c. s. in fifth stitch from needle, 1 d. c. s. in each of the next 2 stitches, 2 ch. s., miss 2, 1 d. c. s., in each of the next four stitches. 2 ch. c., miss 2, 1 d. c. s., in each of the next 22 stitches, 2 ch. s., miss 2 s., 1 d. c. s., 2 ch. s., miss 2 s., 1 d. c. s., in each of the next 4 stitches, 2 ch. s., miss 1 s., 1 d. c. s.

Row II.—5 ch. s., turn. 3 d. c. s. over the 2 ch. s. in first row. 1 d. c. s. in next 2 ch. s., miss 2 s., 1 d. c. s., 2 ch. s., miss 2 s., 1 d. c. s., 2 ch. s., miss 2 s., 1 d. c. s. in each of the next four stitches, 5 gaps, 4 d. c. s., 1 gap, 4 d. c. s., 1 gap, 4 d. c. s.

Row III.—4 ch. s. turn. 1 d. c. s. in each of the next 3 stitches, 1 gap, 4 d. c. s., 1 gap, 1 d. c. s. in each of the next 16 stitches, 1 gap, 4 d. c. s., 4 gaps, 1 d. c. s. in last d. c. s. of former row. 3 d. c. s. over the 2 ch. s. in preceding row. 2 ch. s., 1 d. c. s. in next stitch.

Row IV.—5 ch. s. Turn. 3 d. c. s. over the 2 ch. s. in former row. 1 d. c. s. in next stitch, 5 gaps, 4 d. c. s., 1 gap, 4 d. c. s., 3 gaps, 4 d. c. s., 1 gap, 4 d. c. s., 1 gap, 4 d. c. s.

Row V.—4 ch. s. Turn. 1 d. c. s. in each of the next 3 stitches, 1 gap, 4 d. c. s., 1 gap, 4 d. c. s., 1 gap, 4 d. c. s., 1 gap, 4 d. c. s., 1 gap, 4 d. c. s., 6 d. c. s., 1 d. c. s. in last d. c. s. in last row, 3 d. c. s. in space, 2 ch. s., 1 d. c. s., in next stitch.

Row VI.—5 ch. s. Turn. 3 d. c. s. over chain stitches, 1 d. c. s. in first d. c. s. of last row. 7 gaps, 4 d. c. s., 1 gap, 4 d. c. s., 3 gaps, 4 d. c. s., 1 gap, 4 d. c. s., 1 gap, 4 d. c. s.

Row VII.—4 ch. s. Turn. 1 d. c. s. in each of the next 3 stitches. 1 gap, 4 d. c. s., 1 gap, 1 d. c. s. in each of the next 16 stitches. 1 gap, 4 d. c. s., 8 gaps, 1 d. c. s. in last d. c. s. in former row. 3 d. c. s. in space. 2 ch. s., 1 d. c. s. in next stitch.

Row VIII.—5 ch. s. Turn. 3 d. c. s., 1 d. c. s. in first d. c. s. of last row. 9 gaps, 4 d. c. s., 7 gaps, 4 d. c. s., 1 gap, 4 d. c. s.

Row IX.—4 ch. s. Turn. 1 d. c. s. in each of the next 27 stitches. 1 gap, 4 d. c. s., 1 gap, 1 d. c. s. in each of the next 22 stitches. 2 gaps, 1 d. c. s. in last d. c. s. in former row. Repeat from second row until the desired length of lace has been attained.

6

No.11

No.13

No.12

7

NO. 12.

Use T. B. C. Cordonnet 6-fold Crochet Cotton and ʌuɴ's Handy Crochet Hook. Model was made of size 60 crochet cotton with size 12 crochet hook.

Chain 22 s.

Row I.—1 d. c. s. in 5th stitch from needle. 2 ch. s., miss 2 s., 3 d. c. s. in next stitch, 2 ch. s., 3 d. c. s. in same space as last, 12 ch. s., miss 11 s., 3 d. c. s. in next, 2 ch. s., 3 d. c. s. in same space as last.

Row II.—4 ch. s., 3 d. c. s. between the d. c. s. in last row, 2 ch. s., 3 d. c. s. in same space, 12 ch. s., 3 d. c. s., 2 ch. s., 3 d. c s. in same space. 2 ch. s., miss 2 s., 1 d. c. s., 1 ch. s., miss 1 s., 1 d. c. s. in next.

Row III.—5 ch. s. Turn. Miss 1 s., 1 d. c. s., 2 ch. s., 3 d. c. s., 2 ch. s., 3 d. c. s. in same space as last, 10 ch. s. Turn work. I d. c. s. in the 4 s. from needle 1 d. c. s. in each of the next 6 s. Repeat until there are four rows of d. c. s. This forms the square. 3 d. c. s. between the d. c. s. of former row. 2 ch. s., 3 d. c. s. in same space. Repeat until the ninth row is reached. Work leaf. Finish the tenth row. When the thirteenth row is reached join leaf and work next row. In the fifteenth row finish off the ends of the leaf with groups cf. d. c. s. In the remaining rows finish off the ends of the leaf as the work advances.

NO. 13.

Use size 70 T. B. C. Cordonnet 6-fold Crochet Cotton and size 13 ʌuɴ's Handy Crochet Hook.

This corner is made of small medallions joined together while working the last round.

Two rows of edging are then worked and the foundation stitch is finished off in one row of d. c. s. and one row of s. c. s.

NO. 14.

Model was made of size 70 T. B. C. Cordonnet 6-fold Crochet Cotton, with No. 13 ʌuɴ's Handy Crochet Hook. For bed spreads use ʌuɴ's Colonial Twist and size 7 crochet hook.

For this corner make a foundation chain of 33 stitches.

Fasten chain. 1 d. c. s. through the next ch. s., 1 ch. s., 1 d. c. s. in same stitch as last d. c. s., miss 1 s. Repeat all along until a corner is reached. Widen the corner in every other row by: 1 d. c. s., 1 ch. s., 1 d. c. s., 1 d. c. s., 1 ch. s., 1 d. c. s. in same stitch as last. This lace can be made the width desired and finished off with a simple scallop like the one given in the cut.

NO. 15.

Model was made of size 30 T. B. C. Cordonnet 6-fold Crochet Cotton, with size 10 ʌuɴ's Handy Crochet Hook.

Chain 30 stitches.

Row I.—1 d. c. s. in the 5 stitch from needle, 1 d. c. s. in next. 2 ch. s., miss 2 s., 1 d. c. s., 2 ch. s., miss 2 s., 1 d. c. s., 2 ch. s., miss 2 s., 4 d. c. s., 2 ch. s., miss 2 s., 1 d. c. s., 2 ch. s., miss 2 s., 1 d. c. s., 2 ch. s., miss 2 s., 3 d. c. s.

Row II.—Turn 4 ch. s., 1 d. c. s. in each of the next 2 s., 2 gaps, 4 d. c. s., 1 gap, 4 d. c. s., 2 gaps, 3 d. c. s.

Row III.—Turn. 4 ch. s., 2 d. c. s., 3 gap, 4 d. c. s., 3 gaps, 3 d. c. s., repeat from first row.

Insertion shown on same plate as Nos. 14 and 15 is made of ʌuɴ's Colonial Twist and can be made in either White, Cream or Arabian color.

NO. 16.

Model is made of size 60 T. B. C. Cordonnet 6-fold Crochet Cotton, with size 12 ʌuɴ's Handy Crochet Hook.

Commence with 32 ch. s.

Row I.—3 d. c. s. in fifth stitch from needle, 3 ch. 2., 3 d. c. s. into same space, 3 ch. s., miss 5, 1 d. c. s., 3 ch. s., miss 5 s. 3 d. c. s. in next 3 ch. s., 3 d. c. s in same space, 3 ch. s., miss 5 s., 3 d. c. s. in next 3 ch. s., 3 d. c. s., in same space, 3 ch. s., miss 5 s., 3 d. c. s., in next 3 ch. s., 3 d. c. s,, in same space, 5 ch. s., miss 3 s., 1 d. c. s. in next 5 ch. s., miss 3 s., 1 d. c. s., in next.

(Continued on page 11)

8

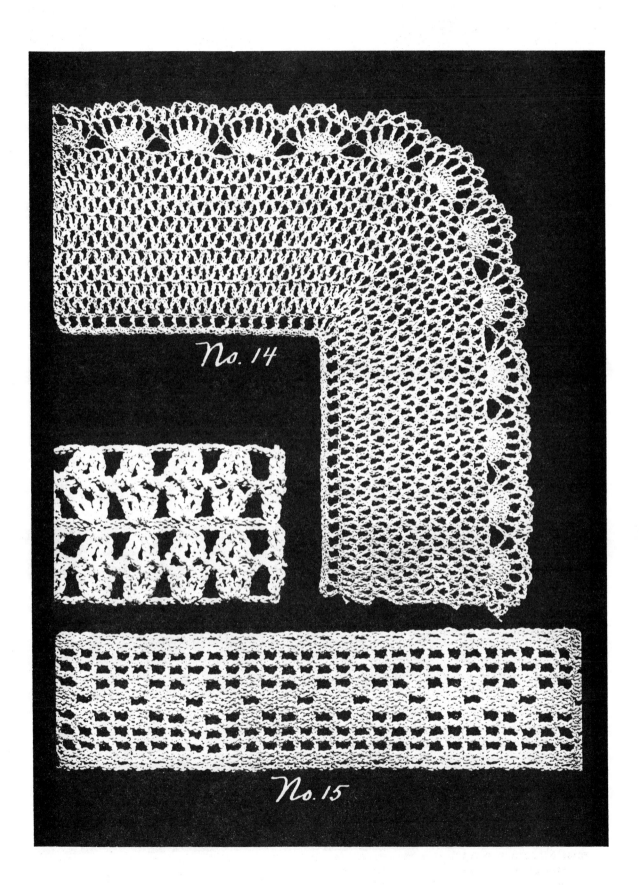

No. 14

No. 15

9

No. 16

No. 17

10

Row II.—6 ch. s., 1 d. c. s. in first loop, 5 ch. s., 1 d. c. s. in next loop, 5 ch. s., 3 d. c. s. into loop between d. c. s., 3 ch. s., 3 d. c. s., in same space, 3 ch. s., 8 long d. c. s., into next loop between the d. c. s. in last row 3 ch. s., 3 d. c. s., into the next loop between the d. c. s., 3 ch. s., 3 d. c. s., in same space 4 ch. s., 1 d. c. s. into first of the next group of d. c. s.

Row III.—3 ch. s., 3 d. c. s. into first loop of ch. s., 3 ch. s., 3 d. c. s., in same space, 2 ch. s., 3 d. c. s., into loop between the 2 groups of d. c. s., 3 ch. s., 3 d. c. s. into same space, 3 ch. s., 1 s. c. s., in first d. c. s. of next group, 4 ch. s., miss 1 s., 1 s. c. s. in next, 4 ch. s., miss 1 s., 1 s. c. s., in next, 4 ch. s., 1 s. c. s. in next, 4 ch. s., 1 s. c. s. in next, 4 ch. s., 1 s. c. s. in next, 3 ch. s., 3 d. c. s. in loop between the 2 groups of d. c. s. 3 ch. s., 3 d. c. s. in same space, 4 ch. s., 1 s. c. s. in next loop, 5 ch. s., 1 s. c. s. in next loop, 5 ch s., 1 s. c. s. in next loop.

Row IV.—6 ch. s. Turn, 1 s. c. s. in first loop, 5 ch. s., 1 s. c. s. in next loop, 5 ch. s., 1 s. c. s. in next loop, 5 ch. s., 3 d. c. s. in loop between d. c. s., 3 ch. s., 3 d. c. s. in same loop, 3 ch. s., 1 s. c. s. into first of 5 loops, 5 ch. s., 1 s. c. s. in next loop, 5 ch. s., 1 s. c. s. in next loop, 5 ch. s., 1 s. c. s. in next loop, 5 ch. s., 1 s. c. s. in next loop, 3 ch. s., 3 d. c. s. in next loop between d. c. s., 3 ch. s., 3 d. c. s. in same loop.

Row V.—5 ch. s. Turn, 3 d. c. s. in loop, 3 ch. s., 3 d. c. s. in same loop, 3 ch. s., 1 s. c. s. into the first of the next 4 loops, 5 ch. s., 1 s. c. s. in next loop, 5 ch. s., 1 s. c. s. in next loop, 5 ch s., 1 s. c. s. in next loop, 3 ch. s., 3 d. c. s. in loop between d. c. s., 3 ch. s., 3 d. c. s. in same loop, 3 ch. s., 1 s. c. s. in next loop, 5 ch. s., 1 s. c. s. in next loop, 5 ch. s., 1 s. c. s. in next loop, 5 ch. s., 1 s. c. s. in next loop.

Row VI.—6 ch. s. Turn. 1 s. c. s. in first loop, 5 ch. s., 1 s. c. s. in next loop, 5 ch. s., 1 s. c. s. in next loop, 5 ch. s., 1 s. c. s. in next loop, 3 ch. s., 3 d. c. s. in loop between d. c. s., 3 ch. s., 3 d. c. s. in same loop, 3 ch. s., 1 s. c. s. in first of the next 3 loops, 5 ch. s., 1 s. c. s. in next loop, 5 ch. s., 1 s. c. s. in next loop, 3 ch. s., 3 d. c. s., in loop between d. c. s., 3 ch. s., 3 d. c. s. in same loop.

Row VII.—5 ch. s. Turn, 3 d. c. s., in loop, 3 ch. s., 3 d. c. s. in same loop, 3 ch. s., 1 s. c. s. in first of next 2 loops, 5 ch. s., 1 s. c. s. in next loop, 3 ch. s., 3 d. c. s. in loop between d. c. s., 3 ch. s., 3 d. c. s. in same loop, 3 ch. s., 1 s. c. s. in first loop, 5 ch. s., 1 s. c. s. in next loop, 5 ch. s., 1 s. c. s. in next loop, 5 ch. s., 1 s. c. s. in next loop.

Row VIII.—6 ch. s. Turn, 1 s. c. s. in loop, 5 ch. s., 1 s. c. s. in next loop, 5 ch. s., 1 s. c. s. in next loop, 5 ch. s., 1 s. c. s. in next loop, 5 ch. s., 1 s. c. s. in next loop, 3 ch. s., 3 d. c. s. in loop between d. c. s., 3 ch. s., 3 d. c. s. in same loop. 3 ch. s., 1 s. c. s. in loop, 3 ch. s., 3 d. c. s. in loop between d. c. s., 3 ch. s., 3 d. c. s. in same loop.

Row IX.—4 ch. s. Turn, 3 d. c. s. in loop, 3 ch. s., 3 d. c. s. in same loop, 2 ch. s., 1 d. c. s. in s. c. s. of last row, 2 ch. s., 3 d. c. s. in loop between d. c. s., 3 ch. s., 3 d. c. s. in same loop, 3 ch. s., miss 1 loop, 3 d. c. s. in next 3 ch. s., 3 d. c. s. in same loop, 3 ch. s., 1 s. c. s. in next loop, 5 ch. s., 1 s. c. s. in next. Repeat. The foundation stitches are the simple d. c. s.

NO. 17.

Model is made of size 60 T. B. C. Cordonnet 6-fold Crochet Cotton, with size 12 NUN'S Handy Crochet Hook.

For the square medallions used in this corner, work according to the following instructions:

Chain 10, join in circle. 4 ch. s. (this will stand for 1 d. c. s.) 5 t. c. s. over circle, 5 ch. s., 6 t. c. s., 5 ch. s., 6 t. c. s., 5 ch. s., 6 t. c. s., 5 ch. s., join.

Row II.—5 s. c. s. over the first five t. c. s., 7 s. c. s. over corner, 6 s. c. s., repeat all around. When working the second square join the first to the second at opposite corners. At a corner in the lace the medallion falls sideways as shown in the cut.

Foundation.—1 s. c. s., in middle stitch of the seven s. c. s., 7 ch. s., miss 3 s., 1 t. c. s., miss 4 s., 1 t. c. s., miss 6 s., 1 t. c. s. (This is worked on the next square) miss 4 s., 1 t. c. s., 7 ch. s., miss 3 s., 1 s. c. s., repeat. The next three rows of the foundation are very simple and can easily be worked from the illustration.

The edging is finished off in scallops made of d. c. s.

11

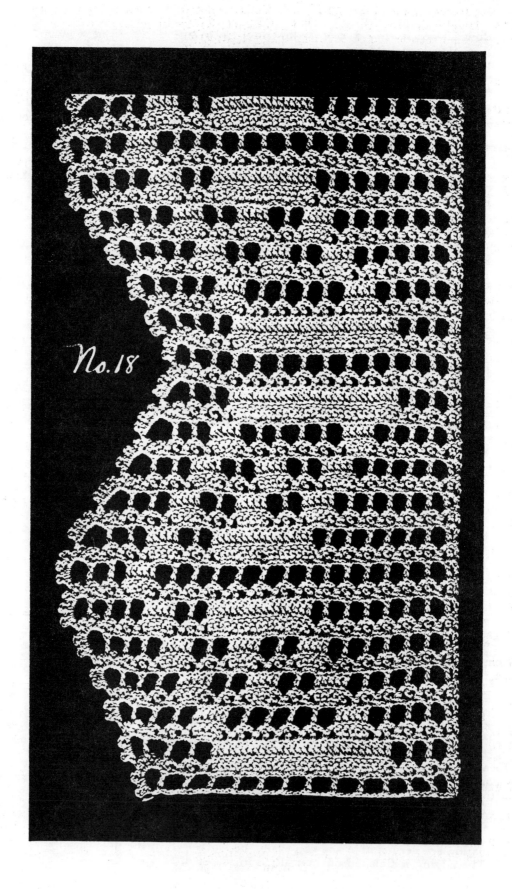

No. 18

12

NO. 18.

Model was made of size 20 T. B. C. Cordonnet 6-fold Crochet Cotton, with size 8 NUN'S Handy Crochet Hook. NUN'S Colonial Twist in white, cream or Arabian color is also recommended for making this pattern.

Commence with a chain of 54 stitches.

Row I.—1 d. c. s. in fifth stitch from needle. * 3 ch. s., miss 3 s., 1 d. c. s., repeat from * until there are 12 gaps, 5 ch. s., 1 s. c. s., in same place as last d. c. s.

Row II.—Turn. 4 picots s., over loop of ch. s. just made. 1 d. c. s. over the next d. c. s. in former row. * 2 ch. s., miss 1 s., 1 s. c. s., 2 ch. s., miss 1 s., 1 d. c. s., repeat from * twice. 29 d. c. s. * 2 ch. s., miss 1 s., 1 s. c. s., 2 ch. s., miss 1 s., 1 d. c. s., repeat from * 3 times   1 d. c. s.

Row III.—4 ch. s. Turn. 1 d. c. s. over d. c. s. in last row * 3 ch. s., miss 5 s., 1 d. c. s., repeat from * 3 times. 29 d. c. s. * 3 ch. s., miss 5 s., 1 d. c. s. repeat from * 3 times. 5 ch. s., 1 s. c. s., between the second and third picot stitch in last row.

Row IV.—Turn. 4 picots s., 1 d. c. s. over d. c. s. in preceding row. * 2 ch. s., miss 1 s., 1 s. c. s., 2 ch. s., miss 1 s., 1 d. c. s. repeat from * twice. 5 d. c. s. * 2 ch. s., miss 1 s., 1 s. c. s., 2 ch. s., miss 1 s., 1 d. c. s., repeat from * 5 times. 5 d. c. s., *2 ch. s., miss 1 s., 1 s. c. s., 2 ch. s., miss 1 s., 1 d. c. s., repeat from * 4 times. 1 d. c. s.

Row V.—4 ch. s. Turn. 1 d. c. s. * 3 ch. s., miss 5 s., 1 d. c. s., repeat from * 4 times. 5 d. c. s. (3 ch. s., miss 5 s., 1 d. c. s. In every other row, will be now called gaps.) 5 gaps, 5 d. c. s., 3 gaps, 5 ch. s., 1 s. c. s. between the second and third picot stitches of last row.

Row VI.—Turn. 4 picots s., 1 d. c. s. over d. c. s. in former row * 2 ch. s., miss 1 s., 1 s. c. s. 2 ch. s., miss 1 s., 1 d. c. s., repeat from * twice. 5 d. c. s., * 2 ch. s., miss 1 s., 1 s. c. s., 2 ch. s., miss 1 s., 1 d. c. s., repeat from * twice. 5 d. c. s., * 2 ch. s., miss 1 s., 1 s. c. s., 2 ch. s., miss 1 s., 1 d. c. s. repeat from * twice. 5 d. c. s., * 2 ch. s., miss 1 s., 1 s. c. s., 2 ch. s., miss 1 s., 1 d. c. s., repeat from * 5 times. 1 d. c. s.

Row VII.—4 ch. s. Turn. 1 d. c. s. in next. 5 gaps, 5 d. c. s., 2 gaps, 5 d. c. s., 2 gaps, 5 d. c. s., 3 gaps, 5 ch. s., 1 s. c. s. between the second and third picot of last row.

Row VIII.—Turn. 4 picot stitches. 1 d. c. s. over first d. c. s. in last row. * 2 ch. s., miss 1 s., 1 s. c. s., 2 ch. s., miss 1s, 1 d. c. s., repeat from * twice. 5 d. c. s., * 2 ch. s., miss 1 s., 1 s. c. s., 2 ch. s., miss 1 s., 1 d. c. s., repeat from * twice. 5 d. c. s. * 2 ch. s., miss 1 s., 1 s. c. s., 2 ch. s., miss 1 s., 1 d. c. s., repeat from * twice. 5 d. c. s., *2 ch. s., miss 1 s., 1 s. c. s., 2 ch. s., miss 1 s., 1 d. c. s., repeat from * 6 times. 1 d. c. s.

Row IX.—4 ch. s. Turn. 1 d. c. s. in next. 6 gaps, 5 d. c. s., 2 gaps, 5 d. c. s., 2 gaps, 5 d. c. s., 3 gaps, 5 ch. s., 1 s. c. s. between the second and third picots.

Row X.—Turn. 4 picots s., 1 d. c. s. * 2 ch. s., miss 1 s., 1 s. c. s., 2 ch. s., miss 1 s., 1 d. c. s., repeat from * twice. 5 d. c. s., * 2 ch. s., miss 1 s., 1 s. c. s., 2 ch. s., miss 1 s., 1 d. c. s., repeat from * twice. 17 d. c. s., * 2 ch. s., miss 1 s., 1 s. c. s., 2 ch. s., miss 1 s., 1 d. c. s. repeat from * 7 times. 1 d. c. s.

Row XI.—4 ch. s. Turn. 1 d. c. s. in next. 7 gaps. 17 d. c. s., 2 gaps, 5 d. c. s., 3 gaps, 5 ch. s. 1 s. c. s. between second and third picot stitch.

Row XII.—Turn. 4 picots, 1 d. c. s. over d. c. s. * 2 ch. s., miss 1 s., 1 s. c. s., 2 ch. s., miss 1 s., 1 d. c. s., repeat from * twice. 5 d. c. s., * 2 ch. s., miss 1 s., 1 s. c. s., 2 ch. s., miss 1 s., 1 d. c. s., repeat from * 14 times. 1 d. c. s.

Row XIII.—4 ch. s. Turn. 1 d. c. s. in next. 14 gaps, 5 d. c. s., 2 gaps, 5 ch. s., 1 s. c. s. between the first and second picot.

Row XIV.—Turn. 4 picots stitches, 1 d. c. s. over d. c. s. * 2 ch. s., miss 1 s., 1 s. c. s., 2 ch. s., miss 1 s., 1 d. c. s., repeat from * 3 times. 5 d. c. s. * 2 ch. s., miss 1 s., 1 s. c. s., 2 ch. s., miss 1 s., 1 d. c. s., repeat from * twice. 17 d. c. s., * 2 ch. s., miss 1 s., 1 s. c. s., 2 ch. s., miss 1 s., 1 d. c. s. repeat from * 7 times. 1 d. c. s.

Row XV.—4 ch. s. Turn. 1 d. c. s. in next. 7 gaps, 17 d. c. s., 2 gaps, 5 d. c. s., 2 gaps, 5 ch. s., 1 s. c. s. between the first and second picot in last row.

Row XVI.—4 picots s. 1 d. c. s. over d. c. s. * 2 ch. s., miss 1 s., 1 d. c. s., repeat from * 3 times. 5 d. c. s. * 2 ch. s., miss 1 s., 1 s. c. s., 2 ch. s., miss 1 s., 1 d. c. s., repeat from * twice. 5 d. c. s., * 2 ch. s., miss 1 s., 1 s. c. s., 2 ch. s., miss 1 s., 1 d. c. s., repeat from * twice 5 d. c. s., * 2 ch. s., miss 1 s., 1 s. c. s., 2 ch. s., miss 1 s., 1 d. c. s., repeat from * 6 times. 1 d. c. s.

(Continued on page 15)

13

No.19

14

Row XVII.—4 ch. s. Turn. 1 d c. s. in next. 6 gaps, 5 d. c. s., 2 gaps, 5 d. c. s., 2 gaps, 5 d. c. s., 2 gaps., 5 ch. s., 1 s. c. s., between the first and second picot stitch of last row.

Row XVIII.—Turn. 4 picots s., 1 d. c. s., over d. c. s. * 2 ch. s., miss 1 s., 1 s. c. s., 2 ch. s., miss 1 s., 1 d. c. s., repeat from * 3 times. 5 d. c. s., * 2 ch. s., miss 1 s., 1 s. c. s., 2 ch. s., miss 1 s., 1 d. c. s., repeat from * twice. 5 d. c. s. * 2 ch. s., miss 1 s. 1 s. c. s., 2 ch. s., miss 1 s., 1 d. c. s., repeat from * twice. 5 d. c. s. * 2 ch. s., miss 1 s., 1 s. c. s., 2 ch. s., miss 1 s., 1 d. c. s., repeat from * 5 times. 1 d. c. s.

Row XIX.—4 ch. s. Turn. 1 d. c. s. in next. 5 gaps, 5 d. c. s., 2 gaps, 5 d. c. s., 2 gaps, 5 d. c. s., 2 gaps, 5 ch. s., 1 s. c. s. between the first and second picot stitch in last row.

Row XX.—Turn. 4 picot s., 1 d. c. s., over d. c. s. in last row. * 2 ch. s., miss 1 s., 1 s. c. s., 2 ch. s., miss 1 s., 1 d. c. s. repeat from * 3 times. 5 d. c. s. * 2 ch. s., miss 1 s., 1 s. c. s., 2 ch. s., miss 1 s., 1 d. c. s., repeat from * 5 times. 5 d. c. s. * 2 ch s., miss 1 s., 1 s. c. s., 2 ch. s., miss 1 s., 1 d. c. s., repeat from * 4 times. 1 d. c. s.

Row XXI.—4 ch. s. Turn. 1 d. c. s. in next. 4 gaps, 5 d. c. s., 5 gaps, 5 d. c. s., 2 gaps. 5 ch. s., 1 s. c. s. between the first and second picot s. in last row.

Row XXII.—Turn. 4 picot s., 1 d. c. s. over d. c. s. in last row. * 2 ch. s., miss 1 s., 1 s. c. s., 2 ch. s., miss 1 s., 1 d. c. s., repeat from * 3 times. 29 d. c. s., * 2 ch. s., miss 1 s., 1 s. c. s., 2 ch. s., miss 1 s., 1 d. c. s., repeat from * 3 times. 1 d. c. s.

Row XXIII.—4 ch. s. Turn. 1 d. c. s. in next. 3 gaps, 29 d. c. s., 2 gaps, 5 ch. s., 1 s. c. s., between the first and second picot stitch in last row.

Row XXIV.—Turn. 4 picot s., 1 d. s. c., * 2 ch. s., miss 1 s., 1 s. c. s., 2 ch. s., miss 1 s., 1 d. c. s., repeat from * 12 times. 1 d. c. s. repeat from beginning.

NO. 19.

Model made of size 30 T. B. C. Cordonnet 6-fold Crochet Cotton, with size 10 NUNS Handy Crochet Hook. Use size of crochet cotton according to size of medallion wanted.

Chain 10; fasten thread.

Row I.—4 ch. s., 4 d. c. s. over ring. 5 ch. s., 5 d. c. s. over ring, 5 ch. s., 5 d. c. s. over ring. 5 ch. s., 5 d. c. s. over ring. 5 ch. s. 1 slip stitch.

Row II.—4 ch. s., 2 d. c. s., 3 ch. s., miss 3 s., 1 d. c. s., 5 ch. s., 1 d. c. s., in same stitch as last d. c. s. 3 ch. s., miss 3 s., 3 d. c. s., 3 ch. s., miss 3 s., 1 d. c. s., 5 ch. s., 1 d. c. s. in same stitch as last d. c. s. 3 ch. s., miss 3 s., 3 d. c. s., 3 ch. s., miss 3s., 1 d. c. s., 5 ch. s., 1 d. c. s. in same stitch as last d. c. s. 3 ch. s., miss 3 s., 3 d. c. s., 3 ch. s., miss 3 s., 1 d. c. s., 5 ch. s. 1 d. c. s. in same stitch as last d. c. s., 3 ch. s., miss 3 s., 1 slip s. in each of the next 2 s.

Row III.—8 ch. s., miss 4 s., 1 d. c. s., 2 ch. s., 5 d. c. s. over loop. 2 ch. s., 1 d. c. s. over d. c. s. 4 ch. s., miss 4 s., 1 d. c. s., 4 ch. s., miss 4 s., 1 d. c. s., 2 ch. s., 5 d. c. s. over loop. 2 ch. s., 1 d. c. s. over d. c. s. 4 ch. s., miss 4 s., 1 d. c. s., 4 ch. s., miss 4s., 1 d. c. s., 2 ch. s., 5 d. c. s., over loop, 2 ch. s., 1 d. c. s., 4 ch. s., miss 4 s., 1 d. c. s., 4 ch. s., miss 4 s., 1 d. c. s., 2 ch. s., 5 d. c. s., 2 ch. s., 1 d. c. s., 4 ch. s., miss 4 s., 1 slip s., in fifth chain s.

Row IV.—5 ch. s., 1 s. c. s. over d. c. s. in last row. 5 ch. s., 1 s. c. s. over next d. c. s. in last row. 5 ch. s., miss 1 s., 1 s. c. s., 5 ch. s., 1 s. c. s. in same stitch as last. 5 ch. s., miss 1 s., 1 s. c. s., 5 ch. s., miss 2 s., 1 s. c. s., 5 ch. s., miss 4s., 1 s. c. s., 5 ch. s., miss 4 s., 1 s. c. s., 5 ch. s., miss 2 s., 1 s. c. s., 5 ch. s., miss 1 s., 1 s. c. s., 5 ch. s., 1 s. c. s. in same. 5 ch. s., miss 1 s., 1 s. c. s., 5 ch. s., miss 2 s., 1 s. c. s., 5 ch. s., miss 4 s., 1 s. c. s., 5 ch. s., miss 4 s., 1 s. c. s., 5 ch. s., miss 2 s., 1 s. c. s., 5 ch. s., miss 1 s., 1 s. c. s., 5 ch. s., 1 s. c. s. in same space. 5 ch. s., miss 1 s., 1 s. c. s., 5 ch. s., miss 2 s., 1 s. c. s., 5 ch. s., miss 4 s., 1 s. c. s., 5 ch. s., miss 4 s., 1 s. c. s., 5 ch. s., miss 2 s., 1 s. c. s., 5 ch. s., miss 1 s., 1 s. c. s., 5 ch. s., 1 s. c. s. in same space. 5 ch. s., miss 1 s., 1 s. c. s., 5 ch. s., miss 2 s., 1 s. c. s., 5 ch. s., miss 4 s., 1 slip stitch in same space as the s. c. s. in last row.

Row V.—1 slip stitch in third ch. s. in last row. 3 ch. s., 1 s. c. s. over loop of ch. s. in last row. Repeat all around. The sixth row consists of a s. c. s. in every stitch of the preceding row.

Other motifs on the same plate as No. 19 can be very easily made by referring to the illustrations. Size of Crochet Cotton to be used should depend on size of Lace or Medallion desired and the texture of the article with which they are to be used. This also applies to the Edges, Insertions and Fringe shown on the next three pages.

15

16

17

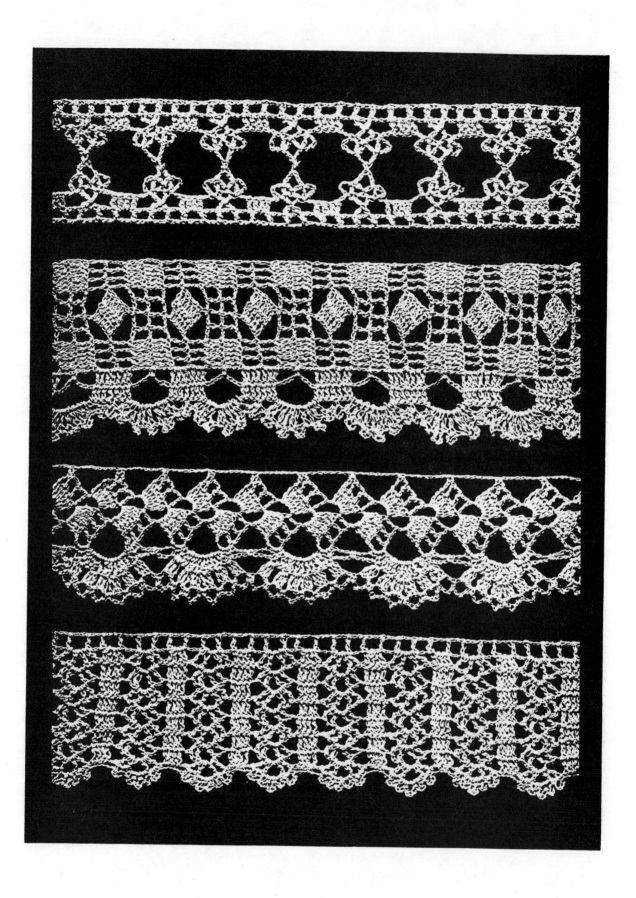

18

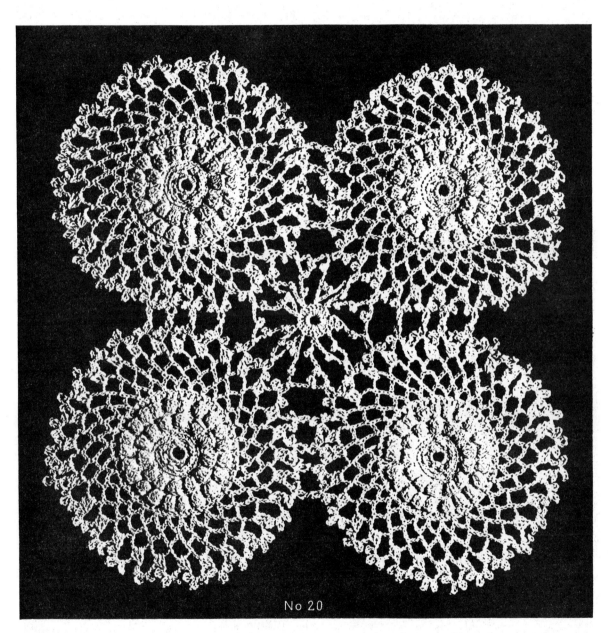

Illustration one-half actual size.

19

NO. 20.

Motif for Bed Spread. Use NUN'S Colonial or NUN'S Crochet Twist in white cream or Arabian color, and size 7 NUN'S Crochet Hook.

Chain 9 and join.

Row I.—Chain 1 and crochet 16 s. c. s. into loop.

Row II.—Chain 6; skip 1; 1 d. c. s.; chain 3; skip 1; 1 d. c. s.; repeat until 8 d. c. s. are made; join with s. c. s.

Row III.—1 chain; 1 s. c. s. in each stitch until 32 s. c. s. are made; join.

Row IV.—1 chain; 1 s. c. s. in each of the next 3 stitches; 2 s. c. s. in the next stitch; 1 s. c. s. into the next 5 stitches; 2 s. c. s. in next stitch; 1 s. c. s. into next 5 stitches; 2 s. c. s. in next stitch; 1 s. c. s. in next 4 stitches; 2 s. c. s. in next stitch; 1 s. c. s. in next 5 stitches; 2 s. c. s. into next stitch; 1 s. c. s. in next 4 stitches; 2 s. c. s. in next stitch; 1 s. c. s. and join.

Row V.—3 chain; 1 d. c. s. in next 2 stitches; 5 d. c. s. in next stitch; join 5th stitch with back of 1st stitch, this forms popcorn stitch. 2 d. c. s. in next 2 stitches; 5 d. c. s. in next stitch; join 5th stitch with back of 1st stitch, forming another popcorn stitch; repeat until 13 popcorn stitches are made.

Row VI.—1 chain; 1 s. c. s. in next 2 stitches; 3 s. c. s. in stitches in back of popcorn stitch; 1 s. c. s. in next 2 stitches; 3 s. c. s. in stitches in back of popcorn stitches; continue until end of row.

Row VII.—This row is made same as 5th row with the exception that you make 21 popcorn stitches instead of 13.

Row VIII.—3 chain; 1 d. c. s. in next stitch; 1 d. c. s. into space back of popcorn stitch; 1 d. c. s. in next 2 stitches; 1 d. c. s. into space back of popcorn stitches; continue until 63 d. c. s. are made.

Row IX.—5 chain; skip 1; 1 s. c. s.; 5 chain, skip 1; repeat until 28 loops are made.

Row X.—6 chain; 1 s. c. s. in 3rd stitch of ninth row. 6 chain; 1 s. c. s. in 3rd stitch of next loop; continue until 28 loops are made.

Row XI.—6 chain; 1 s. c. s. in 3rd stitch of 10th row. 6 chain; 1 s. c. s. in 3rd stitch of next loop; continue until 29 loops are made.

Row XII.—2 chain; 2 d. c. s.; 5 chain and make a picot; 6 chain, make a picot; 5 chain, make a picot; 2 chain; 3 d. c. s. in next loop; 5 chain, make a picot; 6 chain, make a picot; 5 chain, make a picot; 2 chain; 3 d. c. s. in next loop; continue until 29 clusters of picots are made.

After first motif has been made, commence the second and when crocheting last row join to 4 picots on side of first motif as shown in illustration. Third motif is joined to second in same manner. Fourth motif is joined on one side to third motif and on other side to first motif. The open space in center is filled in as follows:

Chain 9 and join; crochet 21 d. s. c. into loop; chain 2, chain 4, make picot; chain 2, chain 4, make picot; chain 2, join to picot of 1st motif with s. c. s. Chain 3, chain 5, make picot; chain 3, join to 2nd motif. Chain 2, chain 4, make picot; chain 2, chain 4, make picot; chain 2, join to center with s. c. s. Chain 3, chain 4, make picot; chain 3, join with s. c. s. to 2nd motif. Chain 3, chain 4, make picot; chain 3, join to center. Chain 2, chain 4, make picot; chain 2, chain 4, make picot; chain 2, join to picot of 2nd motif. Chain 3, chain 5, make picot; chain 3, join to 3rd motif; continue until space is all filled in.

20

No 21

NO. 21.

Motif for Bed Spread.

Use NUN'S Colonial or NUN'S Crochet Twist in white, cream or Arabian color and size 7 NUN'S Crochet Hook.

Chain 9 stitches and join by s. c. s.

Row I.—3 ch. s., 1 d. c. s. over loop until there are 27 d. c. s. in all.

Row II.—8 ch. s., miss 2 s., 1 d. c. s., 5 ch. s., miss 2 s., repeat until there are 9 d. c. s. in all. Join with s. c. s., 1 s. s. in each of the next 3 s.

Row III.—3 ch. s., 1 d. c. s. in same space; 7 ch. s., 2 d. c. s. in same space as last, miss 5 s, 2 d. c. s., 7 ch. s., 2 d. c. s. in same space as last; repeat until row is finished; join with s. c. s.

Row IV.—1 s. c. s. over group of ch. s., 11 d. c. s., 1 s. c. s., repeat around row. Join with s. c. s.

Row V.—11 ch. s., 1 s. c. s. over the center d. c. s. in next group; repeat all along row.

21

Row VI.—1 s. c. s. in each of the ch. s. made in the preceding row. Join with s. c. s.

Row VII.—6 ch. s., miss 2 s., 1 d. c. s., 3 ch. s., miss 2 s., 1 d. c. s.; repeat until there are 36 d. c. s. Join with s. c. s.

Row VIII.—1 d. c. s. in each of the ch. s. in the preceding row. Join with s. c. s.

Row IX.—5 ch. s., miss 2 s., 1 s. c. s.; repeat until there are nine gaps; 1 s. c. s. in each of the next ten stitches, 9 gaps; 10 s. c. s., 9 gaps; 10 s. c. s., 9 gaps.

Row X.—13 s. c. s., 8 gaps; 16 s. c. s., 8 gaps; 16 s. c. s., 8 gaps; 16 s. c. s., 8 gaps.

Row XI.—19 s. c. s., 7 gaps; 22 s. c. s., 7 gaps; 22 s. c. s., 7 gaps; 22 s. c. s., 7 gaps.

Row XII.—25 s. c. s., 6 gaps; 28 s. c. s., 6 gaps; 28 s. c. s., 6 gaps; 28 s. c. s., 6 gaps.

Row XIII.—31 s. c. s., 5 gaps; 34 s. c. s., 5 gaps; 34 s. c. s., 5 gaps; 34 s. c. s., 5 gaps.

Repeat after the above instruction until there are 58 s. c. s. and one gap in last row.

To make Bed Spread—Join the Motifs with strips of Nos. 6761 or 6838 Bed Spread Linens, No. 6715 Plain Scrim Insertion or Nos. 13117 to 13120 Embroidered Scrim Insertions.

Edge for Bed Spread, Motif No. 21 illustrated on page 21.

22

No. 22. MEDALLION. SIZE WHEN FINISHED, 8 INCHES.
No. 22

Use No. 5 Silver Grey T. B. C. Coton Perle and size 3½ Duchess Steel Crochet Hook.

Chain 6 and join.

Row I.—Ch. 1, 8 s. c. s.

Row II.—Ch. 1, 2 s. c. s., in each st. of last round.

Row III.—Ch. 7, miss 1 s. c. s., 1 d. c. s. in next st. (ch. 4, miss 1 s. c. s., 1 d. c. s. in the next) 6 times. Ch. 4, slip st. in the 3rd ch. s. of loop. 8 spaces in all.

Row IV.—6 s. c. s. in each space of last row, join.

Row V.—Ch. 13, 1 sl. st. in each of 3rd and 4th s. c. s. of next space. Ch. 6, 1 tr. in the st. directly above d. c. s. of 3rd row. Ch. 6, 1 sl. st. in the 3rd and 4th st. in next space, repeat from * all around, ending with 6 ch. 1 sl. st. in 13 ch. loop.

Row VI.—Ch. 1, * 4 s. c. s., p. of 4 ch., 6 s. c. s., on 6 ch., 1 s. c. s., p. over 1st sl. st. of last round, 6 s. c. s., p. 4 s. c. s. on next ch., repeat from * all around.

Row VII.—Ch. 15, 1 d. c. s. between picots on arch of last round, (ch. 12, 1 d. c. s. between picots of next arch), repeat all around. Join last 12 ch. to 3rd st. of 15 ch.

Row VIII.—17 s. c. s. in each space of last round.

Rows IX and X, same as VIII.

Row XI—1 s. c. s. in each of 17 s. c. s. which should bring you above the d. c. s., of 7th row. *ch. 6, sl. st. into last of 17 s. c. s. just made. 3 s. c. s. in loop of chain. (p. 3 s. c. s.) 3 times, 3 s. c. s. in next 3 s. c. s. of Row X, turn, ch. 5, 1 tr. in 2nd s. c. s. between last two picots, ch. 11, 1 tr. between next two p. ch. 5, slip st. in 3rd s. c. s.

23

from loop, this forms foundation for scallop; turn, 5 s. c. s. over 5 ch. 1 s. c. s. in tr., 11 s. c. s., over 11 ch., 1 s. c. s. in tr., 5 s. c. s. over 5 ch., 2 s. c. s. in next 2 s. c. s. of row X, turn. (Ch. 2, miss 1 s. c. s. of last row, 1 d. c. s. in the next) 6 times, ch. 3, miss 1 s. c. s., 1 d. c. s. in next, ch. 3; 1 dc. s. in same s. c. s. with last d. c. s.(ch. 2, miss 1 s. c. s., 1 d. c. s. in the next) 5 times, ch. 2, miss 1 s. c. s. of Row X, 2 s. c. s. in the next 2 s. c. s., turn, (2 s. c. s. over 2 ch., 1 s. c. s. in d. c. s.) 6 times, 3 s. c. s. over next 3 ch. (1 s. c. s. in d. c. s., 2 s. c. s. over 2 ch.) 6 times, 8 s. c. s. in the next 8 s. c. s. of Row X, which should bring you above the next d. c. s. of 7th row.

Repeat all around; then 2 s. c. s. over 2 ch., 1 s. c. s. in d. c. s., ch. 5, 1 sl. st. over last d. c. s. of last scallop, turn 6 s. c. s. over ch. 5, 2 s. c. s. over next 2 ch. of first scallop; 1 s. c. s. in next s. c. s. 2 s. c. s. over next 2 ch. turn; ch. 5, 1 tr. in center s. c. s. of loop just made between scallops. (Ch. 3, 1 tr. in same place) two times, ch. 5, 1 sl. st. in 3rd d. c. s. of last scallop, turn, 3 s. c. s. over ch., p. 2 s. c. s., 1 s. c. s. in tr. 2 s. c. s. over 3 ch. p. over 2nd tr. 2 s. c. s. over 3 ch. ch. 10, turn, sl. st in first treble; this forms loop; turn. Make 12 s. c. s. in loop; then 1 s. c. s. in last treble. 2 s. c. s. over 5 ch. p. 3 s. c. s. over same ch., then finish scallop like the 1st one. After the last scallop is finished, the connecting pattern will have to be crocheted, joining it to the 1st scallop.

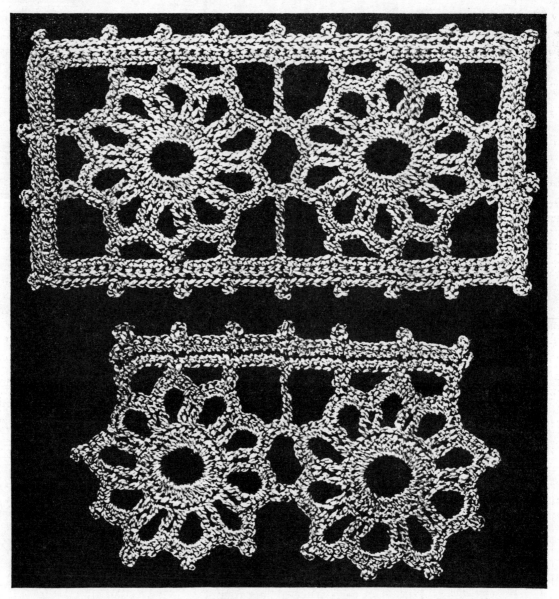

No. 23. INSERTION AND EDGE FOR CUSHION COVER OR SCARF.

No. 23

Use size 5 Silver Grey T. B. C. Coton Perle and No. 3½ Duchess Steel Crochet Hook.

INSERTION—Stars are made first.

24

Commence by chaining 12 and join. Ch. 2 and make 30 d. c. s. into loop, join. Ch. 4 and make 1 d. c. s. Ch. 4; miss 1. Two d. c. s., ch. 4, miss 1; 2 d. c. s. and so on until you have made 20 d. c. s. and 10 spaces. Ch. 1, 1 s. c. s. between the 2 d. c. s.; 4 s. c. s. in space. Ch. 3 and make picot; 3 s. c. s. in same space, 1 s. c. s. between the next d. c. s.; 4 s. c. s. in next space. Ch. 3 and make picot, 3 s. c. s. in same space; and so on all around. This forms a star.

The second star is made same as first one and is joined to 2 picots of first star when making last row.

After making enough stars for length of insertion desired, proceed as follows:

One s. c. s. joined to first picot of star. Ch. 5, and join to 2nd picot, ch. 5 and join to 3rd picot, ch. 5 and make 1 t. c. s. between first and second stars. Ch. 5, join to 1st picot of 2nd star; so on until you get to end picot, then ch. 11 and join 1st picot on side of star. This forms corner. Ch. 5, join to next picot, ch. 11, join to first picot on lower end of star, and so on until you have a row of chains all around stars. Ch. 1 and make 1 s. c. s. in every chain, and so on all around insertion. Make 3 s. c. s. in 6th chain stitch at ends, thus forming the corner. Ch. 1 and make 6 s. c. s., ch. 3 and picot; 6 s. c. s.; ch. 3 and picot, and so on all around both sides of insertion.

EDGE—Stars are made first, same as in the insertion.

Then make 1 s. c. s. in first picot on side of star. Ch. 5, 1 s. c. s. in next picot. Ch. 11 and join to first upper picot of star. Ch. 5, 1 s. c. s. joined to next picot. Ch. 5, 1 s. c. s. joined to 3rd picot; ch. 5, 1 t. c. s. between first and second stars. Ch. 5, 1 s. c. s. joined to first picot of 2nd star and so on to end of stars. Ch. 1, turn and make 1 s. c. s. in every chain stitch to end of chain stitches. Ch. 1, turn; 6 s. c. s., 3 ch. s. and picot; 6 s. c. s., ch. 3 and picot; so on to end of lace.

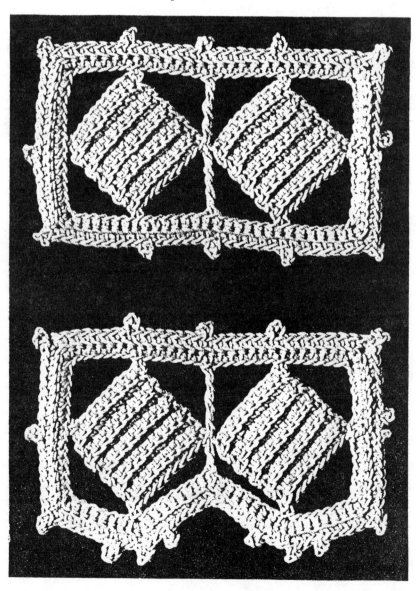

No. 24.   INSERTION AND EDGE FOR CUSHION COVER OR SCARF.

25

[97]

Use NUN'S Colonial Twist in White, Cream or Arabian Color and size 4½ Duchess Steel Crochet Hook.

Insertion.—Squares are made first.

Commence by chaining 11; turn and miss 1 ch. Make 10 s. c. s. in next 10 ch. s.; ch. 1, turn and make 1 s. c. s. in back loop of each stitch of first row. Ch. 1, turn and so on until 10 rows have been made, which forms a square. Ch. 11; turn, miss 1 ch. and make 10 s. c. s. in each ch. s.; ch. 1, turn and make square same as first one. After making enough squares for length of insertion desired, proceed as follows: Ch. 14 and join to corner of square with 1 s. c. s.; ch. 6; make 1 t. c. s. between first and second squares. Ch. 6; 1 s. c. s.; join to corner of second square and so on to end of squares. Then ch. 14; join to second corner of last square. Ch. 14; join to third corner of last square. Ch. 6 and make 1 t. c. s. between squares, same as on other side of insertion. Ch. 6; 1 s. c. s. in corner of next square and so on until you have made a row of chains all around the squares. Ch. 1; turn and make 1 s. c. s. in back loop of the next 6 ch. s. Then make 3 s. c. s. in seventh ch.; this forms corner. 1 s. c. s. in every chain stitch until you reach end of squares. Make 3 s. c. s. in seventh chain, thus forming other corner and so on all around. Ch. 1; turn and make 1 s. c. s. in back loop of each stitch of first row Ch. 4 and make picot. 8 s. c. s. in the next 8 stitches. Ch. 4 and make picot. 8 s. c. s.; ch. 4 and make picot. 7 s. c. s., ch. 4 and make picot; so on all around both sides of insertion.

Edge.—Squares are made first, same as in the insertion.

Then ch. 14 and join to corner of square with s. c. s.; ch. 6; 1 t. c. s. between first and second squares. Ch. 6; 1 s. c. s. on corner of second square and so on until you reach end of squares. Ch. 14 and join to second corner of end square. Ch. 14; join to third corner of square. Ch. 7; 1 d. c. s. between first and second squares. Ch. 7; 1 s. c. s. on corner of second square and so on to end of squares. Then all around with s. c. s. as in the insertion. In crocheting last row around, picots are made same distance apart on top row as in the insertion. Then make picot on corner as follows: 6 s. c. s., 1 picot; 2 s. c. s., 1 picot; 2 s. c. s., 1 picot; 6 s. c. s. and miss 1 s.; 6 s. c. s., 1 picot; 2 s. c. s., 1 picot; 2 s. c. s., 1 picot, and so on to end. The cluster of picots form scallop.

FINISHED TABLE COVER. For details see No. 25 on page 27.

26

No. 25.

EDGE AND MEDAL-
LION for Table Cover
and Scarf. Illustrations
are exact size. Use No. 5
Ecru T. B. C. COTON
PERLE and size 4½
Duchess Steel Crochet
Hook.

EDGE.

After the desired length
of chain stitches have
been made, make 1 d. c. s.
in each chain stitch, then
chain 5. 1 d. c. s. in 4th
d. c. s. Make a picot of
4 chain stitches. Chain 2,
1 d. c. s. in 8th d. c. s.
Chain 12, join 1 chain and
make 5 s. c. s. in loop of
chain. 1 picot, 5 s. c. s.
Cluster of 3 picots. 5 s.
c. s. 1 picot. 5 s. c. s.
Close ring and make 3
chain stitches. 1 d. c. s.,
1 picot. Chain 3, 1 d. c. s.
Chain 15 and join. 5 s. c.
s. Chain 1 and join to
picot of first ring or scallop. 5 s. c. s. Cluster of
3 picots. 5 s. c. s. 1 picot.
5 s. c. s.; this finishes second scallop. Continue full
length of chain or all
around the article to be
finished.

MEDALLION.

Commence in the center. Chain 15 and join; 3 s. c. s. in loop of chain. Chain 1. Make picot of
4 chain; chain 1, 1 picot; chain 1, 1 picot; chain 12 and join. Chain 2, 5 d. c. s. in loop of chain. 1
picot. 6 d. c. s. Cluster of 3 picots. 6 d. c. s. 1 picot. 6 d. c. s. Chain 1. 1 picot. 1 s. c. s. between
picots on other side. Chain 1. 1 picot. 1 s. c. s. Chain 1. 1 picot. 1 s. c. s.; then make 5 s. c. s. in
center ring. Repeat until 11 points or outer rings have been made as shown in illustration.

27

No. 26. INSERTION FOR SCARF.

Illustration above is exact size. Illustration at left shows finished effect of Scarf. Use No. 5 Ecru T. B. C. Coton Perle and size 4½ Duchess Steel Crochet Hook.

SQUARES ARE MADE FIRST.

Chain 10 and join. Ch. 3, 5 t.; ch. 5, 6 t.; ch. 5, 6 t.; ch. 5, 6 t.; ch. 5 and join. Ch. 2 and make s. c. s. all around. This finishes 1st square. Make second square and join to first when making last row.

After the desired number of squares have been made, make 1 s. c. s. at corner of end square. Ch. 8, 1 t., above 2nd treble. 1 t. in 5th t. Ch. 8; 1 s. c. s. on corner of square. Ch. 8; 1 t. in 2nd t. 1 t. in 5th t. 1 t. in 2nd t. of 2nd square. 1 t. in 5th t. Ch. 8; 1 s. c. s. on corner of 2nd square. So on around both sides of squares.

1 s. c. s., ch. 6, 1 t. in next t. Ch. 2, 1 t. in same. Ch. 10; 3 s. c. s. above next s. c. s. Ch. 6; 1 t. Ch. 2; 1 t. and so on up to 5th or center square; then ch. 4; 1 s. c. s. in loop of chain. Ch. 6; 1 s. c. s. in next loop of chain. Ch. 4, 1 t.; ch. 2; 1 t., turn; ch. 2; 1 s. c. s. in t. Ch. 3, 2 t.; ch. 3, 2 t.; ch. 3, 2 t. in loop of chain. This forms scallop. Ch. 3; 1 s. c. s. in next treble. Ch. 2; 1 s. c. s. in next treble; turn. Ch. 3, 2 t. in next space; ch. 2, 2 t. in same space; 4 t. in next space. Ch. 1, 2 t. in next space; ch. 2, 2 t. in same space; ch. 1, 4 t. in next space; 2 t. in next space; ch. 2, 2 t. in same space; ch. 3, 1 s. c. s. in t. Ch. 6, 3 s. c. s. Ch. 6, 1 t. in next s. c. s., ch. 2; 1 t. in same space. Continue all around both sides of squares, making 10 chains instead of 6 at corners; then make 7 d. c. s., ch. 4, and make picot. 7 d. c. s., 1 picot; 7 d. c. s., 1 picot; 7 d. c. s., 1 picot; all around both sides. This finishes Insertion.

28

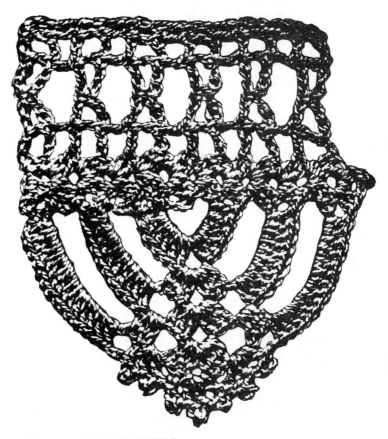

No. 27. SCARF ENDS.

Illustration at left shows finished effect. Illustration at right is exact size of one scallop.

For crocheting use No. 3 Ecru T. B. C. Coton Perle and size 3½ Duchess Steel Crochet Hook.

Embroidered parts of this design to be worked solid with size 5 Ecru T. B. C. Coton Perle and outlined with No. 349½ Brown NUN'S Boilproof Embroidery Floss.

Chain 16; turn. 1 d. c. s. in 3rd chain from hook. Ch. 2; skip 2 ch.; make 1 d. c. s., 3 ch.; skip 2 ch., 1 s. c. s., 3 ch.; 1 d. c. s., 2 ch.; skip 2 ch. 2 d. c. s. in next ch. 2 ch., 2 d. c. s. in same stitch. Ch. 3; turn and make 2 d. c. s. in space between fan. 2 ch.; 2 d. c. s. in same space. 2 ch.; 1 d. c. s. 5 ch.; 1 d. c. s. in d. c. s. of previous row. 2 ch.; 2 d. c. s., 2 ch.; turn; repeat until 7 rows have been made; then chain 8 and catch in end stitch of 5th row. Ch. 1; 1 s. c. s. in end stitch of 4th row. 6 d. c. s. in loop of chain. Ch. 3; 6 d. c. s. in same loop. 2 d. c. s. in center of fan of 7th row. Ch. 2; 2 d. c. s. in same space. Ch. 2; 1 d. c. s. in d. c. s. of previous row. Ch. 5; 1 d. c. s. Ch. 2; 2 d. c. s. Ch. 3 and turn; 1 d. c. s., ch. 2; 1 d. c. s., 3 ch.; 1 s. c. s. in 3rd chain of previous row. Ch. 3; 1 d. c. s., ch. 2; 2 d. c. s. in space of fan. Ch. 2; 2 d. c. s. in same space. Ch. 8; 3 d. c. s. in space of scallop. Ch. 3; 3 d. c. s. in same space. Ch. 8 and join to end stitch of 3rd row. Ch. 1; 1 s. c. s. in end stitch of 2nd row. Turn and make 10 d. c. s. in loop of chain. 2 ch.; 3 d. c. s. in space of scallop. Ch. 3; 3 d. c. s. in same space. Ch. 2; 10 d. c. s. in loop of chain. 2 d. c. s. in center of fan of 9th row. Ch. 2; 2 d. c. s. in same space. Ch. 2; 1 d. c. s. in d. c. s. of previous row. Ch. 5; 1 d. c. s. Ch. 2; 2 d. c. s.; ch. 3 and turn. 1 d. c. s., ch. 2; 1 d. c. s., ch. 3. 1 s. c. s. in 3rd chain of previous row. Ch. 3; 1 d. c. s., ch. 2; 2 d. c. s. in space of fan. Ch. 2; 2 d. c. s. in same space. Ch. 10; 3 d. c. s. in space. Ch. 2; 3 d. c. s. in center of scallop. Ch. 2; 3 d. c. s. in same space. Ch. 2; 3 d. c. s. in next space. Ch. 10 and join to first row. Turn and make 15 d. c. s. in loop of chain. Ch. 2; 1 d. c. s. in next space. Make picot of 3 ch. 1 d. c. s., 1 picot, 1 d. c. s. in same space. 1 d. c. s. in space of scallop. 1 picot, 1 d. c. s.; 1 picot, 1 d. c. s.; 1 picot, 1 d. c. s. in same space. 1 d. c. s. in next space. 1 picot, 1 d. c. s.; 1 picot, 1 d. c. s. in same space. Ch. 2; 15 d. c. s.; 2 d. c. s. in space of fan of 11th row. This completes one scallop; continue width of scarf.

29

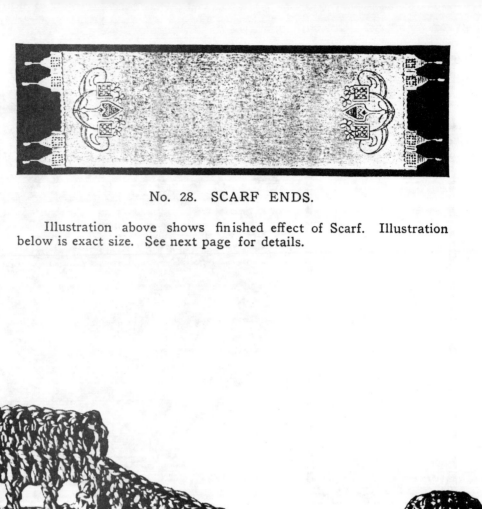

No. 28. SCARF ENDS.

Illustration above shows finished effect of Scarf. Illustration below is exact size. See next page for details.

30

No. 28. SCARF ENDS.

For crocheting use No. 3 Silver Grey T. B. C. Coton Perle and size 3½ Duchess Steel Crochet Hook. Embroidered parts of this design to be worked solid with No. 5 Silver Grey T. B. C. Coton Perle, Color 322 Delft Blue ɴᴜɴ'ꜱ   Boilproof Embroidery Floss and Color 322 ɴᴜɴ'ꜱ   New Art and Craft Silk. Outline with Color 320 Delft Blue ɴᴜɴ'ꜱ   Boilproof Embroidery Floss.

Upper part of pointed scallop is made first. Chain 16.

Row I.—1 d. c. s. in 4th stitch from hook. 1 d. c. s. in each of the next 12 stitches; turn.

Row II.—Chain 3; 3 d. c. s. in the first d. c. s.; this forms scallop. 1 d. c. s. in each of the next 12 d. c. s.; turn.

Row III.—Chain 5; 1 d. c. s. in 3rd d. c. s., ch. 2; 1 d. c. s. in 3rd d. c. s., ch. 2; 1 d. c. s. in 3rd d. c. s.; so on until you have made 4 spaces. Turn.

Row IV.—Chain 3; 3 d. c. s. in 1st d. c. s., ch. 2; 1 d. c. s. in next d. c. s. Now a dot stitch is made as follows: Chain 3, thread over hook and pull a loop through 1st ch. as long as the 3 chain stitches made. Repeat this 4 times. Thread over hook and draw through all loops; ch. 1; this closes dot and is called eye of dot. Thread over hook and make a dot in the next d. c. s. Chain 3 and make dot in the eye of last dot. 1 d. c. s. in the next d. c. s. Ch. 2; 1 d. c. s. in 3rd chain from end.

.Row V.—Chain 5; 1 d. c. s. in 2nd d. c. s. Ch. 2; 1 dot in the center of where the three dots come together. Ch. 2; 1 d. c. s. in next d. c. s. Ch. 2; 1 d. c. s. in next d. c. s.

Row VI.—Chain 3; 3 d. c. s. in 1st d. c. s., ch. 2; 1 d. c. s. in d. c. s. of previous row. Ch. 2; 1 d. c. s. and so on until 4 d. c. s. have been made.

Now make the point: Ch. 1; 2 s. c. s. in each space, 1 d. c. s. in each d. c. s., turn; skip end stitch and make 1 s. c. s. in every s. c. s. made. Repeat back and forth, skipping end stitch of each row until you have reduced the amount of stitches to one.

Ball is made next:

Chain 3; 6 s. c. s. in 2nd chain. 2 s. c. s. in each of the 6 s. c. s.; then 1 s. c. s. in each stitch until 35 s. c. s. have been made. Stuff with cotton. Make 1 s. c. s. in every 2nd stitch until ball is closed. Chain 10 and join to point or scallop with slip stitch. Make 1 slip stitch up the side of point in each row of stitches. 1 s. c. s. in 1st space; ? d. c. s. in same space. 1 d. c. s. in next d. c. s., 2 d. c. s. in space, 1 d. c. s. in next . s. and so on to end of spaces.

This finishes 1st pointed scallop. Repeat first part of instructions and make 2nd scallop. The narrow piece between the ends is made as follows: Make 3 d. c. s. in 3rd d. c. s., turn. Chain 3; 2 d. c. s in 1st d. c. s. 1 d. c. s. in next d. c. s., turn. Chain 3 and repeat until 13 rows have been made; then join to other end when making 14th row.

31

No. 29. CENTERPIECE. SIZE WHEN FINISHED, 22½ INCHES.

No. 29

Use size 10 Linen Color T. B. C. Cordonnet Special Crochet Cotton and No. 3½ Duchess Steel Crochet Hook.

Chain 44.—Turn.

Row I.—1 d. c. s. in third chain from needle. One ch. s., one d. c. s. in second chain; 1 ch. s., 1 d. c. s. in same chain; 2 ch. s., one d. c. s. in fourth chain; 2 ch. s. and 1 d. c. s. in same chain; 2 ch. s. and 5 d. c. s. in next five chains. Two ch. s., 1 d. c. s. in fourth chain; 2 ch. s., 1 d. c. s. in same chain; 2 ch. s., 1 d. c. s. in fourth chain. Two ch. s. and 1 d. c. s. in same chain. Continue until you have seven shells.

Row II.—Turn. 5 ch. s., 1 d. c. s. in shell. 3 ch. s., 1 d. c. s. in same shell. 3 ch. s., 1 d. c. s. in same shell. 1 d. c. s. in second shell. 3 ch. s., 1 d. c. s. in same shell, 3 ch. s. and 1 d. c. s. in same shell. 3 ch. s., 1 d. c. s. in same shell. Continue until all seven shells are alike. 1 ch. s., 1 d. c. s. in first stitch; 2 d. c. s. in next stitch, 1 d. c. s. in next, 2 d. c. s. in next, 1 d. c. s. in next. 1 ch. s., 1 d. c. s. in shell, 3 ch. s. and 1 d. c. s. in same. 3 ch. s., 1 d. c. s. in same. 3 ch. s. and 1 d. c. s. in same. 1 ch. s., 1 d. c. s. in next stitch. 1 ch. s. and 1 d. c. s. in next stitch. 1 d. c. s. in ch. s.

Row III.—Turn. 2 ch. s., 1 d. c. s. in second d. c. s., 1 ch. s., 1 d. c. s. in next stitch, 1 ch. s., 1 d. c. s. in next stitch, 2 ch. s., 1 d. c. s. in center of shell. 2 ch. s., 1 d. c. s. in same. 2 ch. s., 1 d. c. s. in first stitch, 2 d. c. s. in next stitch, 3 d. c. s. in next 3 stitches. 2 d. c. s. in next stitch, 1 d. c. s. in next stitch, 2 ch. s., 1 d. c. s. in center of shell, 2 ch. s., 1 d. c. s. in same, 2 ch. s., 1 d. c. s. in center of next shell, 2 ch. s., 1 d. c. s. in same. Repeat until seven shells are made.

Row IV.—Turn. 5 ch. s., 1 d. c. s. in shell, 3 ch. s., 1 d. c. s. in same. 3 ch. s., 1 d. c. s. in same, 1 d. c. s. in next shell, 3 ch. s., 1 d. c. s. in same. 3 ch. s., 1 d. c. s

32

in same. 3 ch. s., 1 d. c. s. in same, 1 d. c. s. in next shell. Continue until seven shells are made. 1 ch. s., 1 d. c. s. in first stitch, 2 d. c. s. in second, 5 d. c. s. in next 5 stitches; 2 d. c. s. in next stitch, 1 d. c. s. in last stitch. 1 ch. s., 1 d. c. s. in shell. 3 ch. s., 1 d. c. s. in same. 3 ch. s., 1 d. c. s. in same, 3 ch. s., 1 d. c. s. in same. 1 ch. s., 1 d. c. s. in next stitch. 1 ch. s., 1 d. c. s. in next. 1 ch. s. and 2 d. c. s. in next two. Turn and repeat, increasing the number of d. c. s. as in the four rows until you have 31 d. c. s. and 7 shells each way.

For Second Scallop.—Turn. 2 ch. s., 1 d. c. s., in 2nd d. c. s., 1 ch. s., 1 d. c. s. in next, 1 ch. s., 1 d. c. s. in next, 2 ch. s., 1 d. c. s. in shell. 2 ch. s., 1 d. c. s. in same. 2 ch. s. and 5 d. c. s. in next 5 stitches. 2 ch. s., 1 d. c. s. in 4th stitch. 2 ch. s., 1 d. c. s. in same. 2 ch. s. and 1 d. c. s. in 4th stitch. 2 ch. s. and 1 d. c. s. in same. Continue until the 6th shell is reached, then have the last 2 shells in 3rd stitch and continue same as No. 1 scallop.

No. 30. CROCHETED CLUNY LACE CENTERPIECE. SIZE WHEN FINISHED, 18 INCHES.

33

No. 30

Use No. 5 Silver Grey T. B. C. Coton Perle and size 3½ Duchess Steel Crochet Hook.

Make Serpentine Border or Insertion first. Commence by making a chain of 12, turn and make 1 d. c. s. in 6th st. from hook. Ch. 2; skip 2; 1 d. c. s. in next st. Make 2 more spaces (4 in all). Ch. 5, turn and repeat until you have made 12 rows of 4 spaces each.

Ch. 5, turn and make 8 spaces on side of squares just made. Ch. 5, turn and repeat until you have made 8 rows of 4 squares each; then ch. 5 and make 8 rows on other side of the 8 rows just made; this forms Serpentine border. When required length has been made, join, and s. c. s. all around on both edges of squares.

Start from point at inner edge of Serpentine border; ch. 8, 1 tr. in next s. c. s.; ch. 4, skip 1 space; 1 tr. in next s. c. s.; ch. 5, skip 2 spaces, 2 tr. in the next 2 s. c. s. Skip 5 spaces, 2 tr. in the next 2 s. c. s.; ch. 5, skip 2 spaces. 2 tr. in the next 2 s. c. s. Ch. 4, 1 tr. in s. c. s. on point. Ch. 5, 1 tr. in same stitch, repeat this all around.

Next Row.—S. c. s. all around from point to point.

Next Row.—3 s. c. s. on point, then ch. 8; 2 ex. tr. between points above 4 tr. of preceding row. Ch. 8, 3 s. c. s. on next point, ch. 8, and repeat all around; then make 3 rows of s. c. s. all around. This finishes inner edge.

Outer Edge.—Start at point and make 3 sets of L. tr.; 4 L. tr. in each set, 6 ch. between each set.

Ch. 4, and make 2 ex. L. tr. in s. c. s. between points. Ch. 6, 2 ex. L. tr. in same space. Ch. 4 and make 3 sets of L. tr. on next point, repeat all around.

Next Row.—S. c. s. all around.

Next Row.—Over the center set of L. tr. at point, make 2 sets of L. tr. 5 ch. between each set. Ch. 7, make 4 L. tr. above next set of L. tr.; ch. 3, skip 5 or 6 s. c. s.; 2 ex. tr. in next s. c. s. Ch. 7, 2 ex. tr. in the next 2 s. c. s.; these 2 sets of ex. tr. should be in center just above ex. L. tr. of preceding row.

Next Row.—S. c. s. all around.

Next Row.—Or last time around, s. c. s. all around making a picot of 4 ch. st. at each point and 2 between points.

34

No. 31.   CROCHETED CLUNY LACE DOILY.   SIZE WHEN FINISHED, 6½ INCHES.

35

Use No. 50 or 60 white T. B. C. Cordonnet Special Crochet Cotton and No. 5½ or 6 Duchess Steel Crochet Hook.

Cut your linen round, d. c. s. all around, making stitches very close together.

Row I.—Ch. 6, skip 4 d. c. s. and make 1 tr. ch. 7; skip 3 d. c. s. 1 tr. skip 3 d. c. s. 1 tr. ch. 7; skip 3 d. c. s. 1 tr. skip 3 d. c. s. 1 tr. this forms 3 sets of spokes. Ch. 18, skip 6 d. c. s. sl. st. in next st. turn on this loop of ch. make 11 d. c. s. push these st. close together and make 1 sl. st. to fasten stitches. Ch. 12, skip 6th sl. st. in next st. turn and make 11 d. c. s. same as before, push these stitches close together so as to leave 5 chain between the 2 covered chains. Ch. 8, skip 4 d. c. s. make 1 tr. skip 4 d. c. s. 1 tr.; repeat until you have made 3 sets of spokes same as before, then 2 cover chains, repeat alternately all around.

Row II.—9 s. c. s. in space, 9 s. c. s. in next space. 1 d. c. s. in next ch. st. ch. 2, skip 1 ch. 1 d. c. s. Repeat until you have made 13 spaces, then repeat s. c. s. as before.

Row III.—Same as second row.

Row IV.—Same as second row.

Row V.—6 s. c. s. ch. 3; skip 3 s. c. s. 6 s. c. s. then make 15 spaces, 6 s. c. s. ch. 3; skip 3 s. c. s. 6 s. c. s. repeat spaces and s. c. s. all around.

Row VI.—Ch. 7; 4 tr. in small loop in center of s. c. s. ch. 7; 4 tr. in same space. Ch. 6, and make 15 spaces. ch. 7 and repeat all around.

Row VII.—Ch. 7; 1 L. tr. in last space made. Ch. 3; 2 L. tr. in space between 2 cluster of tr. Ch. 3; 2 L. tr. in same space, ch. 3, and repeat until you have made 4 sets of L. tr. s. Ch. 3, 2 L. tr. in first small square or space. Ch. 13, skip 5 spaces, 1 d. c. s. in next space, 1 d. c. s. in next; ch. 13, skip 5 spaces, 2 L. tr. in last space. Ch. 3; 4 sets of L. tr. s. in space, ch. 3, and repeat all around same as before. At end ch. 1, and make 1 s. c. s. in first space so as to start next row from this space.

Row VIII.—2 tr. in same space, ch. 4; 2 tr. in next space, ch. 4; 2 tr. in next space, ch. 4; 2 tr. in same space, ch. 4; 2 tr. in next space, ch. 4; 2 tr. in next space. Ch. 14; 2 s. c. s. in next small space ch. 14; and repeat all around.

Row IX.—Ch. 5; skip 2 ch. 1 d. c. s. ch. 2; skip 2, 1 d. c. s. ch. 2; skip 2, 1 d. c. s. repeat all around.

Row X.—Ch. 10; skip 1 space, 1 s. c. s. in next space, ch. 10; skip 1 space, 1 s. c. s. in next space; continue all around.

Row XI.—Ch. 3; sl. st. in center of loop in preceding row; ch. 10, sl. st. in next loop at point of scallop, ch. 14 for loop.

The three loops between scallops of preceding row are drawn together making only 1 ch. between each loop.

36

No. 32.   CROCHETED CLUNY LACE DOILY.   SIZE WHEN FINISHED, 8½ INCHES.

37

[109]

Use No. 50 T. B. C. White Cordonnet Special Crochet Cotton and size 6 Duchess Steel Crochet Hook.

Chain desired length and join.

1 d. c. s. in 5th ch. from hook. Ch. 3; 2 d. c. s. in the next 2 st. Ch. 3 and repeat to end; join.

Row II.—Ch. 2 and fasten in first space. Ch. 3; 1 d. c. s. in next space ch. 6; 1 d. c. s. in next space, 1 d. c. s. in next space, bring close to the one just made, ch. 6; 1 d. c. s. in next, 1 d. c. s. in next, repeat all around.

Row III.—Ch. 10, 1 tr. between d. c. s. of preceding row; 1 tr. in space of next d. c. s. ch. 12; 1 L. tr. in space of d. c. s.; 1 L. tr. in next; ch. 14; 1 L. tr. in next space of d. c. s.; 1 L. tr. in next, ch. 12; 1 tr. in next, ch. 10 and make 2 d. c. s. in space of d. c. s. of preceding row. Ch. 4; 2 d. c. s. in next space of d. c. s.; ch. 6, 2 d. c. s. in next space of d. c. s., ch. 4; 2 d. c. s. in space of d. c. s.; then ch. 10 and repeat as from start and join.

Row IV.—1 tr. ch. 2; skip 1 ch. 1 tr. ch. 2 and repeat until you have made 36 spaces. Ch. 8, skip 9 st. and make 1 d. c. s. in next ch. st. skip 1 ch.; 1 d. c. s. in next st. Ch. 8 and make tr. s. across chains as before, repeat to end, join.

Row V.—Ch. 5, 3 tr. in first space, ch. 6; skip 1 space, 1 d. c. s. in next space, ch. 2; and repeat until you have made 30 spaces. Ch. 8, skip 1 space, 4 L. tr. in last space; ch. 5, 4 L. tr. in space of d. c. s. of preceding row. Ch. 5, 4 L. tr. in first space. Skip 1 space then continue the d. c. s. in spaces, join.

Row VI.—Continue the d. c. s. spaces across spaces of previous row. Ch. 6, 4 L. tr. in L. tr.; ch. 6, and repeat until you have made 3 sets of L. tr. Ch. 6; d. c. s. in spaces. Repeat all around and join.

Row VII.—2 s. c. d. in first space, ch. 2, 1 d. c. s. in next space, repeat until you have made 32 spaces. 2 s. c. s. in next space, 7 s. c. s. in loop of chain. 3 s. c. s. in cluster of L. tr. 7 s. c. s. in loop of chain, repeat until you reach first space of d. c. s.; turn s. c. s. back and forth 4 times over s. c. s. just made; ch. 11; skip 3 spaces, 1 ex. tr. in 4th space, skip 1 space, 1 ex. tr. in next space. Sl. st. on L. tr 3 s. c. s. sl. st. on ch.; turn, 5 s. c. s. sl. st. turn; 5 s. c. s. sl. st. and turn, 3 s. c. s. this forms spider. Ch. 10, skip 2 spaces, 1 ex. tr. in 3rd space, skip 1 space, 1 ex. tr. in next space, repeat making spiders until you have made 5 spiders. Ch. 12; and s. c. s. back and forth 4 times over s. c. s. of preceding row same as before, catching in chain of 12.

Row VIII.—Break thread; start at top of s. c. s. band, see illustration, and make 15 s. c. s., skip 9 s. c. s. 1 tr. in next st. Ch. 3; 1 tr. in next st. Ch. 15; tr. on top of spider ch. 4; skip 1 st. 1 tr. on spider, ch. 12, 1 L. tr. on next spider. Ch. 5; skip 1 st.; 1 L. tr. on same spider; ch. 12, 1 L. tr. on next spider. Ch. 5, 1 L. tr. on same; ch. 10, 1 L. tr. on next; ch. 5, 1 L. tr. on same spider; ch. 12, 1 tr. on last spider; ch. 4, skip 1 st.; 1 tr. on same, ch. 15, skip 7, 1 tr. in next st. ch. 3, tr. in next st.; ch. 9, skip 9 s. c. s. and make 15 s. c. s. Repeat to end.

Row IX.—Skip 3 s. c. s. of previous row and make 8 s. c. s. in the next 8 s. c. s.; ch. 1, 1 d. c. s. in the next space, ch. 1; and continue until you have made 58 spaces. Repeat 8 s. c. s. same as from start, then 58 spaces of d. c. s. and so on to end.

Row X.—Make 5 s. c. s.; ch. 2, and make 60 spaces, then 5 s. c. s. and so on all around.

Row XI.—1 s. c. s. in 3rd s. c. s.; ch. 12, skip 3 spaces, 1 d. c. s. in next space, 1 d. c. s. in next space, ch. 10, skip 1 space; 1 d. c. s., 1 d. c. s. in next ch. 10, skip 1 space, 1 d. c. s., 1 d. c. s. in next, continue this all around. Ch. 5 and join to center of ch. of 12. Ch. 11, sl. st. from loop to loop on each scallop, ch. 5 between each scallop from loop to loop. This finishes edge.

38

No. 33. CROCHETED CLUNY LACE DOILY. SIZE WHEN FINISHED, 9 INCHES.

39

Use No. 40 or 50 White T. B. C. Cordonnet Special Crochet Cotton and size 5½ or 6 Duchess Steel Crochet Hook.

This lace can be made to fit any size doilie or centerpiece, and makes a very handsome luncheon set. In the 9-inch size commence by making 268 chain stitches. 1 d. c. s. in 5th ch. from hook. Ch. 2, skip 1 ch, 1 d. c. s., repeat until you have made 133 spaces.

Row II.—Ch. 3, skip 1 space, 1 tr. in next space, ch. 6; 1 tr. in next space. Skip 1 space, 1 tr. in next, ch. 6 and repeat until you have four sets of spokes. Ch. 12; skip 3 spaces, 1 ex. tr. in the 4th space, ch. 6, 1 ex. tr. in same space; ch. 12, and repeat 4 sets of spokes. Then ch. 12, skip 3 spaces, make 1 ex. tr. Ch. 6, 1 ex. tr. in same space. Ch. 12, and repeat same as before. Join to first set of spokes.

Row III.—Ch. 18, sl. st. in 2nd set of spokes. Make a sl. st. on chain just made, then 9 d. c. s. 1 sl. st. on same. Push these stitches close together so they will cover half of the chain made. This forms one solid petal. Ch. 10, sl. st. in 3rd set of spokes. 1 sl. st. on ch. just made, 9 d. c. s. 1 sl. st. on same. Ch. 10, sl. st. in 4th set of spokes. You will find that 1st and last petal are not finished. This is done when making next row. On chain over ex. tr. make 20 spaces of s. c. s. 1 chain between each stitch. Ch. 18, and repeat petals same as from start.

Row IV.—1 sl. st. on ch. of 1st petal; 9 d. c. s. 1 sl. st. on same chain. Ch. 4; 1 s. c. s. in 3rd petal: ch. 4; 1 s. c. s. in chain of unfinished 4th petal. Then 9 d. c. s. on chain of 4th petal, 1 sl. st. on same; 1 s. c. s. in each space 1 ch. between each s. c. s., 1 sl. st. on next unfinished petal 9 d. c. s., 1 sl. st. on same, repeat all around to end, join small space to 1st petal.

Row V.—Break thread, start in 6th space of s. c. s.; ch. 1, 1 s. c. s. in next space, continue until you have made 9 spaces. Ch. 5; skip 1 space, 1 d. c. s. in next space, skip 1 space, 1 d. c. s. in next space. Ch. 18, fasten in 1st loop of 4 ch. above petals. Sl. st. on chain just made, 10 d. c. s. and 1 sl. st. on same chain. Push stitches together, this forms 1st upper petal. Ch. 15; fasten in same loop, cover chain same as first and repeat again in same loop, making 3 petals in the first loop. Make 3 petals in the next loop. Push stitches down on chain so work will look even and will leave 5 chain stitches between each petal. Ch. 7; skip 3 small squares, 1 d. c. s. in next, skip 1 space, 1 d. c. s. in next, ch. 5; skip 2 spaces and make 9 spaces, ch. 5; skip 1 space, 1 d. c. s. in next space, skip 1 space, 1 d. c. s. in next space. Ch. 7 and repeat next 6 petals as before.

Row VI.—1 s. c. s. Ch. 1, 1 s. c. s. and repeat until you have made 8 spaces, ch. 3; 1 tr. in the 2 d. c. s. of preceding row. Ch. and 1 tr. in same space, ch. 7; 2 tr. above 1st solid petal. Ch. 7, 2 tr. above next petal, repeat until you have made 1 set of tr. above each solid petal. Ch. 7; 1 tr. in the 2 d. c. s. of preceding row; ch. 4; 1 tr. in same space, ch. 3 and make 8 spaces of s. c. s. same as before, repeat next same as from start, and so on all around.

Row VII.—Make 7 spaces of s. c. s., 1 ch. between each s. c. s. Ch. 5; and catch in center chain between the 2 tr. of preceding row. Ch. 15; sl. st. in the next 2 tr., repeat until you have made 7 loops of chain. Ch. 5, and make 7 spaces of s. c. s., then repeat loop same as first, and so on all around.

Row VIII.—Make 6 spaces of s. c. s. Ch. 5; 1 d. c. s. in 2nd stitch of 1st loop: ch. 2; skip 1 ch. 1 d. c. s. in next chain, repeat until you have 5 spaces on first loop; skip 3 ch. of first loop and 3 of 2nd; make 1 d. c. s. in 4 ch. of 2nd loop. Ch. 2, skip 1 ch. Repeat until you have made 5 spaces on each loop of scallop. Ch. 5, repeat s. c. s. and so on all around.

Row IX.—Make 5 spaces of s. c. s. Ch. 10; sl. st. in first d. c. space, skip 1 space; 1 d. c. s. in next, continue to s. c. s., then make 5 spaces and repeat same as first.

Row X.—S. c. s. in 3rd space of s. c. s. Ch. 3; skip 4 ch. in loop of preceding row: sl. st. in next st. Ch. 7, skip 2 ch. of same loop, sl. st. in next stitch, ch. 3; skip 3 ch. of same loop and 4 chain of next loop. Sl. st. in next stitch. Continue all around, this finishes edge.

40

No. 34. CROCHETED CLUNY LACE DOILY. SIZE WHEN FINISHED, 11 INCHES.

41

No. 34

Use No. 50 or 60 white T. B. C. Cordonnet Special Crochet Cotton and size 5½ or 6 Duchess Steel Crochet Hook.

Row I.—Chain length desired, join; make 1 tr. ch. 2, skip 1 ch. and make 1 tr. repeat all around chain, join.

Row II.—Ch. 21 to start next row, skip 2 spaces; make 3 tr. in next 3 spaces, 2 ch. between each. tr. ch. 18, skip 2 spaces, 3 trs. in the next 3 spaces, 2 ch. between each tr. repeat to end, join.

Row III.—To prevent breaking thread ch. 6, make 3 d. c. s. in 3 center st. of ch. loop, 2 stitches between each d. c. ch. 9, repeat all around, join.

Row IV.—Ch. 5, make 3 tr. in space. Ch. 4, make 4 trs. in next space. Ch. 5; ch. 4 and make picot; ch. 5 and make 4 tr. in next space, ch. 4, 4 tr. in next space, repeat to end of row.

Row V.—Ch. 5 and fasten back in last p. ch. 7; 3 ex. tr. st. in same picot. 4 ex. tr. in next picot. Ch. 20. 2 tr. in next p. ch. 20, 4 ex. tr. in next p. 4 ex. tr. in next picot, repeat all around; join.

Row VI.—Ch. 7 and make 3 ex. tr. in ex. tr. of preceding row. Ch. 6, repeat in next; ch. 12, skip 13 ch. 1 d. c. s. in next ch.; ch. 2, skip 2 and make 1 d. c. s., repeat until you have made 7 spaces. Ch. 12, and repeat all around, joining last ch. of 12 in ex. tr.

Row. VII.—Ch. 8, make 3 tr. in ex. tr. of preceding row, ch. 4; 4 tr. on loop of ch.; ch. 4; 4 tr. in same loop. Ch. 4; 4 tr. in ex. tr. of preceding row. Ch. 8; 1 d. c. s. in next 6 spaces. Ch. 8 and repeat; join.

Row VIII.—Ch. 6; make 3 tr. in tr. of preceding row. Ch. 4, make 4 tr. in loop of ch.; ch. 4, then 4 tr. s. in tr. s. repeat until there are 7 sets of tr.; ch. 6, 1 d. c. s. in the next 5 spaces, repeat all around.

Row IX.—Ch. 12; slp. st. in next cluster of trebles. Ch. 12 and repeat until you have made 6 loops of ch. st. Ch. 12, skip 2 d. c. s. slp. st. in 3rd d. c. s. ch. 12; slp. st. in next cluster of tr. s. ch. 12; and repeat; ch. 3 and catch in 3rd ch. of loop.

Row X.—Ch. 10, skip 3 ch. slp. st. in 4 ch., ch. 3; slp. s. in 4th ch. of next loop. Ch. 10, skip 3 ch., slp. s. in next st. of same loop, repeat until you have made 6 loops. Skip 6 st. slp. s. in next st., ch. 4; skip 6 ch. of next loop. Slp. s. in next st., ch. 6, skip 6 ch. in loop of next scallop, slp. st. in next ch. Repeat all around, this finishes edge.

42

No. 35. CROCHETED CLUNY EDGE FOR TOWEL.

Use No. 40 or 50 T. B. C. Cordonnet Special Crochet Cotton and size 5½ Duchess Steel Crochet Hook.

Row 1.—Commence chaining the desired length, turn, and make 2 d. c. s.; ch. 1; skip 1 ch.; 2 d. c. s., 1 ch.; so on to end of row, turn.

Row II.—Ch. 10, skip one space and make 3 L tr. s. in next space; ch. 1, skip 1 space; 3 L tr. s. in next space; ch. 6, skip 1 space, 2 d. c. s. in next, ch. 6, skip 1 space and make 2 tr. s. in next d. c. s.; ch. 6, skip 1 space, 2 d. c. s. in next space, repeat to end of row finishing with 3 L tr. s., turn.

Row III.—Ch. 4, 1 d. c. s. in 2nd L tr.; ch. 7, 3 d. c. s. in 3 ch. next to 2 tr.; 2 d. c. s. in tr. 3 d. c. s. in the next 3 ch. Ch. 10, 1 tr. in L. tr. of preceding row. Ch. 2, 1 tr. in next L. tr.; ch. 10, then 7 d. c. s. in chains as before, continue to end.

Row IV.—Ch. 7, turn; 1 d. c. s. in first tr.; ch. 3, 1 d. c. s. in next tr.; ch. 7; make 2 d. c. s. in 6th and 7th d. c. s. of preceding row. 1 d. c. s. in d. c. s., 5 s. c. s. in 5 d. c. s.; 1 d. c. s. in d. c. s., then 2 d. c. s. in next 2 ch. st., ch. 7; 1 d. c. s. in 2nd tr.; ch. 3; 1 d. c. s. in next, repeat to end.

Row V.—Ch. 5, turn; 1 d. c. s. on d. c. s. on preceding row; ch. 3, 1 d. c. s. in next d. c. s.; ch. 7, 1 d. c. s. in 6th and 7th ch. st. of preceding row; 1 d. c. s. in next d. c. s., 9 s. c. s.; 3 d. c. s. in st. of preceding row. Ch. 7, 1 d. c. s. in d. c. s., ch. 3; 1 d. c. s. in next d. c. s., repeat across, turn.

Row VI.—Ch. 3, make 14 d. c. s. in the next 14 stitches, ch. 4, skip 7 st. and make 2 tr. s. in 8th st. Ch. 4, skip 8 st. and make 18 d. c. s. in next 18 st. Ch. 4; and repeat to end of row, turn.

Row VII.—Make six loops, a ch. of 12 in each loop. These are made in the d. c. of previous row. Ch. 6, 1 slp. st. in next tr. Ch. 6, 1 slp. st. in next d. c. s., continue the loops to end of row.

Row VIII.—Ch. 3, slp. st. in 4th ch. of loop. Ch. 8, skip 2 ch. slp. st. in next ch. Ch. 3, join to next loop, repeat to last loop on scallop, then ch. 2, slp. st. in 1st loop between scallop, ch. 2; slp. st. in next loop. Ch. 2 slp. st. in 5th st. of next loop, ch. 8, skip 2 ch. and slp. st. to next ch. of same loop continue to end. This finishes the edge of lace.

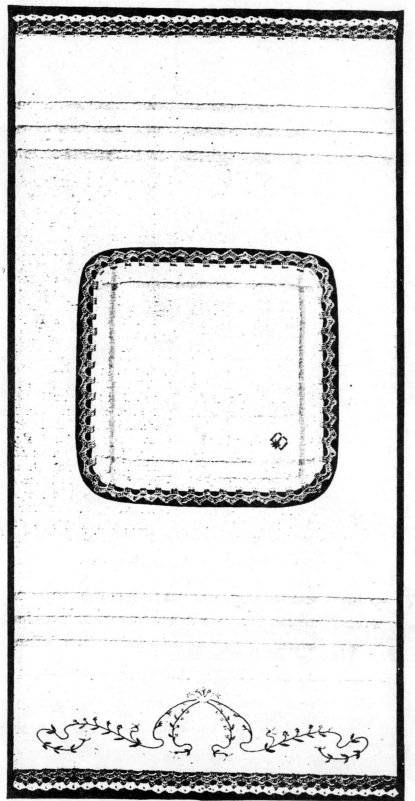

No. 36.

EDGE FOR TOWEL AND WASH CLOTH.

Use No. 5 T. B. C. Coton Perle and size 3½ Duchess Steel Crochet Hook.

Row I.—Begin by making 4 d. c. s. into hem of towel; ch. 6, skip space the length of 5 ch. st. and make 4 d. c. s. in towel, ch. 5; 4 d. c. s., repeat to end of towel.

Row II.—4 d. c. s. in loop of chain. Ch. 3; 4 d. c. s. in same space. 4 d. c. s. in next space, ch. 3; 4 d. c. s. in same space. 4 d. c. s. in next space, ch. 3; 4 d. c. s. in same space, continue to end.

Row III.—4 d. c. s. in center of shell, ch. 6; 4 d. c. s. in center of next shell. Ch. 6; and continue to end.

Row IV.—Is made same as second row. A pretty effect is obtained by making first three rows of a color and fourth row of white T. B. C. Coton Perle.

Edge for Wash Cloth is made by using first two rows of above instructions.

No. 36.   EDGE FOR TOWEL AND WASH CLOTH.

44

No. 37. EDGE FOR SHAMPOO OR COMBING JACKET.

No. 37

Use size 5 T. B. C. Coton Perle and No. 3½ Duchess Steel Crochet Hook.

After having turned a narrow hem on all raw edges to be crocheted, proceed as follows: Make 1 d. c. s. in hem, ½ inch from first stitch, 1 d. c. s., 1 picot of 3 ch. 3 d. c. s. in loop, 1 d. c. s. in hem, 1 p. 3 d. c. s. in loop, so on all around the jacket. D. c. s. in hem to be about ½ inch apart.

To make frog: Ch. 11; 1 s. c. s. in 2nd ch. from hook; 1 s. c. s. in the next 9 ch. st. Ch. 2 and make 1 s. c. s. in 8 stitches on the other side of the chain st. Ch. 2; turn, skip 1 s. c. s., make 1 s. c. s. in the next 7 s. c. s., 1 s. c. s. in loop of ch.; ch. 2, 1 s. c. s. in same space, 1 s. c. s. in the next 7 s. c. s. Ch. 2; turn and continue until you have made 10 rows, this forms leaf shaped ornament. Make two ornaments for jacket. Make a loop of 23 s. c. s. for buttoning.

To Make Button.—Cover a wooden mold with ribbon same color as crochet thread; use a brass ring a little smaller than mold and crochet on same as follows: Make enough s. c. s. on ring to cover, then 1 s. c. s. in each s. c. s. Continue until you have made a little more than half to cover button, then skip every other stitch, this shapes to form mold.

To Make Girdle or Belt.—Ch. 6; turn, 1 d. c. s. in 3rd ch. from hook, 1 d. c. s. in the next 2 ch. st. Ch. 3 turn 1 d. c. s. in the next 3 d. c. s. Ch. 3, turn; 1 d. c. s. in the next 4 st., ch. 3, turn, and repeat until girdle is width of 12 d. c. s. Continue until you have desired length, decreasing number of stitches at other end same as first. Finish ends with a tassel.

45

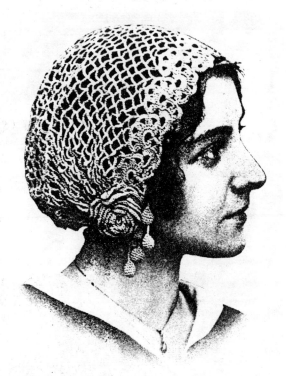

No. 38. AUTO OR BOUDOIR CAP.

No. 38

Use size 30 Ecru T. B. C. Cordonnet Special Crochet Cotton, No. 4½ Duchess Steel Crochet Hook and proceed as follows:

Band is made first.

Ch. 12 and join, ch. 3, turn and make 14 d. s. c. into ring, ch. 3, turn, 3 d. c. s. in first 3 d. c. s. of previous row. Ch. 3, 1 d. c. s. in each of next 3 d. c. s. Ch. 3 and repeat until there are 4 spaces and 5 clusters of 3 d. c. s. Turn,* 1 s. c. s. in second d. c. s., 5 s. c. s. in space of 3 ch. 1 s. c. s. in second d. c. s., 5 s. c. s. in space of 3 ch. Repeat from * until all spaces are filled, ch. 8 and join over last 3 d. c. s. This forms first fan. Make second fan same as first to end of second row; fasten in center of first fan. Last row like last row of first fan. After the second fan all others should be fastened between the first and second scallops of the last fan on the same side of the work. Make 18 double fans and join. Front of cap is made first. Start over joined section, ch. 10, catch in each space over 11 double fans, catch in first stitch of twelfth fan, turn; ch. 5, catch in center of chain of 10, then chain 10, catch in center of next chain of 10 of previous row and so on to end of row. Turn, ch. 5, catch in center of chain of 10, then chain 10, catch in center of each chain of 10 loops of previous row; continue back and forth in this manner, catching in each chain of 10 and in each stitch of first and thirteenth fans until 41 rows are made. This leaves 5 open fans in the back. Ch. 5, catch in chain of 10. Ch. 5, catch in space of fan, ch. 5, catch in chain of 10, ch. 5, catch in space of fan, continue over 2 fans. In the third fan catch the chains in each stitch and in the next 2 fans catch the chains in spaces.

ROSES.

Make Irish crochet roses as follows and sew over fullness on each side of cap. Chain 7 and join 1st row—10 d. c. s. 2nd row—5 ch., 1 t. c. s. in 1 d. c. s., 2 ch., 1 t. c. s. in next d. c. s., repeat. 3rd row—7 ch., miss 1, 1 d. c. s. and repeat. 4th row— 1 d. c. s., 7 t. c. s., 1 d. c. s. in 7 ch. 5th row—chain 9, 1 d. c. s. in d. c. s. between each leaf; repeat. 6th row—1 d. c. s., 9 t. c. s., 1 d. c. s. in 9 ch. and repeat. 7th row—chain 11, 1 d. c. s. in d. c. s., repeat. 8th row—1 d. c. s., 11 t. c. s., 1 d. c. s. in 11 chain, repeat. 9th row—chain 11, 1 d. c. s. in d. c. s., repeat. 10th row—1 d. c. s., 3 t. c. s., 4 d. t. c. s., 3 t. c. s., 1 d. c. s. in ch. 11, repeat. 11th row—chain 5; miss 2; 1 d. c. s. and repeat.

PENDANTS.

Chain 6 and join; make s. c. s. around until there are 70 of them in all; fill with cotton and narrow off. Ch. 12, catch back in 6th stitch and make 2nd pendant. Ch. 6 and break thread. Make 3 pendants for each side of cap.

46

No. 39. CROCHETED BAG FOR GATE TOP.

Use NIJN'S New Arts & Crafts Crochet and Knitting Silk and size 3½ Duchess Steel Crochet Hook.

Ch. 5 and join; make 18 d. c. s., ch. 1 and make 10 rows of s .c. s. Ch. 5; skip 2 and make 1 s. c. s. Ch. 5, skip 2 s. c. s.; make 1 s. c. s.; so on all around. This forms row of loops; ch. 5; 1 s. c. s. in loop; ch. 5, 1 s. c. s. in next loop, repeat until you have made 11 rows of ch. loops. Ch. 6; 1 s. c. s. in next loop. 6 ch. 1 s. c. s. in next loop and so on all around.

1st Row of Shell—3 s. c. s. in loop; 3 d. c. s. in next loop, ch. 2; 3 d. c. s. in same loop; 3 s. c. s. in next loop. 3 d. c. s. in next, ch. 2; 3 d. c. s. in same loop, so on all around. This forms row of shells.

2nd Row of Shell—Ch. 5 and make 3 d .c. s. in center of shell. Ch. 2; 3 d. c. s. in same space, ch. 3; 1 t. c. s. in 2nd s. c. s.; ch. 3, 3 d. c. s. in center of shell, ch. 2; 3 d. c. s. in same space, ch. 3; 1 t. c. s. and so on all around.

3rd Row of Shell—Ch. 4, 1 s. c. s. in space, 1 s. c. s. in next space, ch. 4; 3 d. c. s. in next shell, ch. 2; 3 d. c. s. in same space, ch. 4; 1 s. c. s. in space, 1 s. c. s. in next space, so on all around.

Next row—1 t. c. s. in space, before finishing 2nd half of treble stitch, thread around hook and in next space, finish 2nd half of both trebles together: ch. 4; 1 s. c. s. in center of shell, ch. 4, 2 trebles; ch. 4; 1 s. c. s., so on all around; then ch. 5; 1 s. c. s. in loop, ch. 5; 1 s. c. s. in next loop. .Ch. 5; and repeat until you have made 9 rows of loops. This finishes bag.

Make a tassel the size desired and draw loop or stem of same through a wooden mold, then crochet over mold: Ch. 5 and join; make 10 s. c. s., 1 s. c. s. in each s. c. s. Repeat until you have made a little more than half to cover mold, then skip every other stitch until you have shaped same to fit mold.

Cord or Handle—3 strands of silk each 5 yards long are twisted, then doubled. Cord is twisted and doubled 3 times.

47

Just a word

In choosing the pieces shown in this book I have endeavored to present a more elaborate assortment, believing that the demand is more among the experienced workers.

For those who are learning the art, and at this time there are many, I suggest the making of the Filet pieces as a start, where one needs but the chain and the double crochet. There are nevertheless many simple edgings and insertions that the beginner can readily master.

The illustrations show all articles (that are not otherwise noted), just four-fifths actual size. In other words add one fourth to the length and width of any picture and it will be the finished size in the thread mentioned. By this rule one is enabled to judge before engaging in the work the effect that would be obtained in a lighter or heavier thread.

For the benefit of all the every detail is given in the instructions, and these have been very carefully re-read to eliminate error.

Anna Valeire

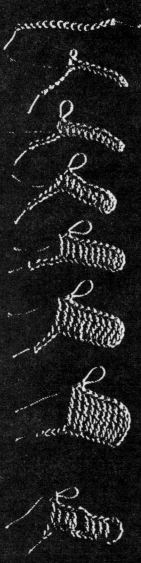

1.–Ch.–CHAIN. Make a slip knot. Draw thread thro loop. Continue to draw thro loops.

2.–s.sl.st.–SINGLE SLIP STITCH. Form chains, put hook in last chain and draw thread thro. Pull loop just made thro first loop.

3.–sl.st.–SLIP STITCH. Form chains, put hook in last chain and draw thread thro. Put thread over the hook and draw thro both stitches.

4.–sc.–SINGLE CROCHET. Form ch. with thread once around hook, bring into ch. and pull loop through. Twist thread around hook again and pull thro the three loops at one time.

5.–dc.DOUBLE CROCHET. With a st. (stitch) on the hook, and thread over the hook, put hook thro the work, draw thro making 3 sts. on the hook, with thread over draw thro 2 sts., with thread over draw thro last 2 stitches.

6.–dt.–DOUBLE TREBLE. With a st. on the hook and thread over the hook twice; draw thro 3 times.

7.–tt.–TRIPLE TREBLE. Stitch on the hook, and thread three times over hook; draw thro four times.

8.–om.–OPEN MESH. Form ch. on the turn take 1 dc. in 6th st. from hook. Then ch 2 and a dc. in 3rd. ch below. Repeating.

8a.–sm.–SOLID MESH. 4 treble crochets in 4 chains. Where they alternate—open and solid meshes, note there are only 2 chains untouched. When two solid meshes adjoin, use 7 t. c. the center one counting for each side of it. Three together, use 10 t. c.; adjoining meshes always adding only 3.

9.–p.–PICOT. sk. (Skip) 3 chs. and make a sl. st.. Ch. 4 and catch back into first ch. thread over hook once, draw thro both loops. Make 3 or 4 sl. st. or number desired, between picots and continue to desired length.

10.–sh.–SHELL STITCH. 5dc. into one chain. Repeat, sk. 3 chs.

11.–pt.st.–PETAL STITCH. Form ch. work 3 dc. in chs. having last loop of each on hook, draw a loop thro the three on hook, and make 5chs.

12.–X.st.–CROSS STITCH. Form chain, wind thread over hook twice draw thread thro, making 4 st. on the hook, draw thro 2.keep 2 on the hook, skip 2 chs., then 1 dc. in next. work off the 2 st. on hook, add 2 chs. 1 dc. in middle of dc. just made. ch 2, and repeat—thread over hook twice.

13.–lac. LACET. In a ch of 7 sts; – 1 dc.ch3,sk2, 1 sl.st. in 4th ch.–Ch3, sk2.1 dc in 7th ch. This forms the "K".–Coming back, –1dc over same, ch5.1 dc over same.

14.–kn.st.–KNOT STITCH. Form chain. Make a stitch, draw out the loop on hook one quarter to one third inch. Make a ch., that is take up thread and draw through this loop to fasten. Then take up thread and draw with another long loop thro stitch on hook. Fasten again with one stitch and with another one in long chain, skip 5. Take one st. on hook, long loop, fasten, then 2 st. between the two doubles, on knots in last row. Make 2 Knot st. and repeat.

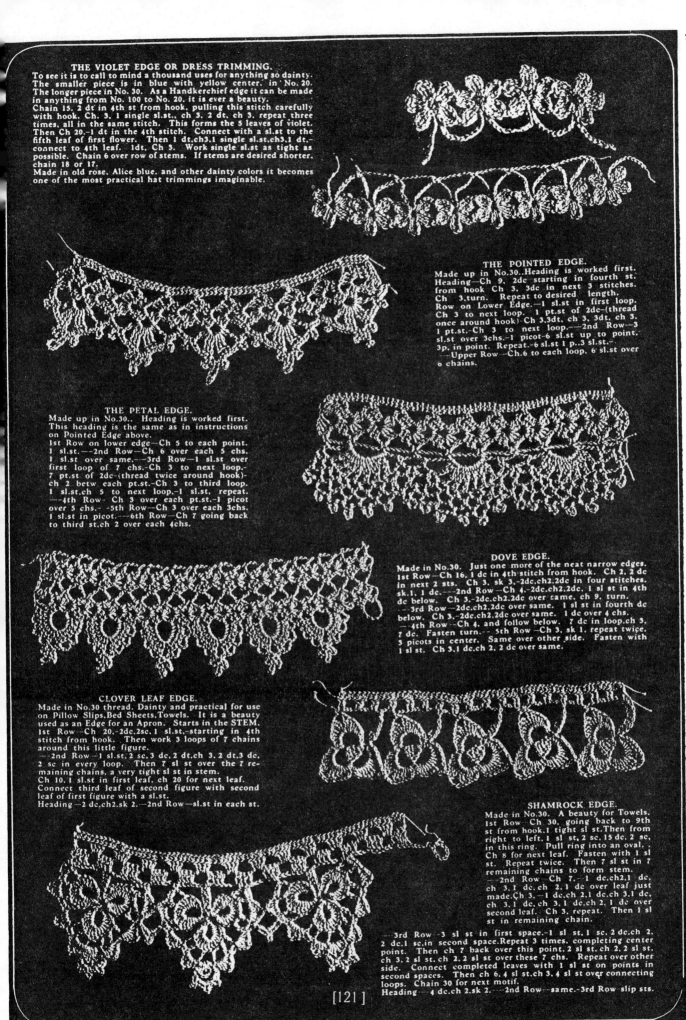

THE VIOLET EDGE OR DRESS TRIMMING.

To see it is to call to mind a thousand uses for anything so dainty. The smaller piece is in blue with yellow center. in No. 20. The longer piece in No. 30. As a Handkerchief edge it can be made in anything from No. 100 to No. 20, it is ever a beauty.
Chain 15. 2 dt in 4th st from hook, pulling this stitch carefully with hook. Ch. 3, 1 single Ch.st., ch 3, 2 dt, ch 3. repeat three times, all in the same stitch. This forms the 5 leaves of violet. Then Ch 20.-1 dt in the 4th stitch. Connect with a sl.st to the fifth leaf of first flower. Then 1 dt,ch3.1 single sl.st.ch3.1 dt.- connect to 4th leaf. 1dt. Ch 3. Work single sl.st as tight as possible. Chain 6 over row of stems. If stems are desired shorter. chain 18 or 17.
Made in old rose. Alice blue. and other dainty colors it becomes one of the most practical hat trimmings imaginable.

THE POINTED EDGE.

Made up in No.30..Heading is worked first. Heading—Ch 9, 2dc starting in fourth st. from hook Ch 3, 3dc in next 3 stitches. Ch 3.turn. Repeat to desired length. Row on Lower Edge.—1 sl.st in first loop. Ch 3 to next loop. 1 pt.st of 2dc-(thread once around hook)-Ch 3.3dt, ch 3, 3dt, ch 3, 1 pt.st.-Ch 3 to next loop.—2nd Row—3 sl.st over 3chs.-1 picot-6 sl.st up to point. 3p. in point. Repeat.-6 sl.st 1 p..3 sl.st.- —Upper Row—Ch.6 to each loop. 6 sl.st over 6 chains.

THE PETAL EDGE.

Made up in No.30.. Heading is worked first. This heading is the same as in instructions on Pointed Edge above.
1st Row on lower edge—Ch 5 to each point. 1 sl.st.—2nd Row—Ch 6 over each 5 chs. 1 sl.st over same.—3rd Row—1 sl.st over first loop of 7 chs.-Ch 3 to next loop.- 7 pt.st of 2dc-(thread twice around hook)- ch 2 betw each pt.st.-Ch 3 to third loop. 1 sl.st.ch 5 to next loop,-1 sl.st. repeat. —4th Row— Ch 3 over each pt.st.-1 picot over 5 chs.- -5th Row— Ch 3 over each 3chs. 1 sl.st in picot.—6th Row—Ch 7 going back to third st.ch 2 over each 4chs.

DOVE EDGE.

Made in No.30. Just one more of the neat narrow edges. 1st Row—Ch 16, 1 dc in 4th stitch from hook. Ch 2, 2 dc in next 2 sts. Ch 3. sk 3.-2dc.ch2.2dc in four stitches. sk.1, 1 dc.---2nd Row—Ch 4.-2dc.ch2.2dc. 1 sl st in 4th dc below. Ch 3.-2dc.ch2.2dc over same, ch 9, turn. —3rd Row—2dc.ch2.2dc over same. 1 sl st in fourth dc below. Ch 3.-2dc.ch2.2dc over same. 1 dc over 4 chs. —4th Row—Ch 4, and follow below. 7 dc in loop.ch 5, 7 dc. Fasten turn.- - 5th Row—Ch 3, sk 1, repeat twice. 5 picots in center. Same over other side. Fasten with 1 sl st. Ch 3,1 dc,ch 2, 2 dc over same.

CLOVER LEAF EDGE.

Made in No.30 thread. Dainty and practical for use on Pillow Slips,Bed Sheets,Towels. It is a beauty used as an Edge for an Apron. Starts in the STEM. 1st Row—Ch 20,-2dc.2sc, 1 sl.st,-starting in 4th stitch from hook. Then work 3 loops of 7 chains around this little figure.
—2nd Row—1 sl.st, 2 sc, 3 dc. 2 dt.ch 3, 2 dt.3 dc. 2 sc in every loop. Then 7 sl st over the 7 remaining chains, a very tight sl st in stem. Ch 10, 1 sl.st in first leaf, ch 20 for next leaf. Connect third leaf of second figure with second leaf of first figure with a sl.st.
Heading—2 dc,ch2.sk 2.—2nd Row—sl.st in each st.

SHAMROCK EDGE.

Made in No.30. A beauty for Towels. 1st Row—Ch 30, going back to 9th st from hook.1 tight sl st.Then from right to left, 1 sl st, 2 sc. 15 dc. 2 sc, in this ring. Pull ring into an oval, . Ch 8 for next leaf. Fasten with 1 sl st. Repeat twice. Then 7 sl st in 7 remaining chains to form stem.
—2nd Row—Ch 7,- 1 dc,ch2,1 dc, ch 3,1 dc.ch 2,1 dc over leaf just made.Ch 3.—1 dc.ch 2,1 dc.ch 3,1 dc, ch 3,1 dc, ch 3,1 dc.ch 2, 1 dc over second leaf. Ch 3, repeat. Then 1 sl st in remaining chain.
—3rd Row—3 sl st in first space.-1 sl st,1 sc, 2 dc.ch 2, 2 dc,2 sc.in second space.Repeat 3 times, completing center point. Then ch 7 back over this point, 2 sl st, ch 2, 2 sl st, ch 3, 2 sl st, ch 2, 2 sl st over these 7 chs. Repeat over other side. Connect completed leaves with 1 sl st on points in second spaces. Then ch 6, 4 sl st,ch 3, 4 sl st over connecting loops. Chain 30 for next motif.
Heading—4 dc,ch 2.sk 2.---2nd Row--same.-3rd Row-slip sts.

[121]

3

A MILE IN TWO MINUTES EDGE.

Made in No.30 thread. Just the thing to use a Draw string or ribbon on Lingerie.

1st Row.—Ch 14,—1 dc,ch2,1dc in fifth stitch from hook. Ch 3, sk 2, 1 sl.st. Ch 5, sk 2,—1 dc,ch2,1dc in last stitch. Ch 5, turn.

—2nd Row—1 dc,ch2,1 dc over same. Ch 5,-1 dc,ch2,1 dc over same. Ch 1, 1 dc over 4chs below. Ch 4, turn.

Finishing Row— 6 sl.st over each 5 chs.below.

NARROW CURTAIN EDGE.

1st Row—Ch 12, 3 om, ch 4, turn.—2nd Row— 2 om,1 sm, turn-ch 5.—3rd Row—2 om, 1 sm. Then ch 4,-4dc in same space. Ch 3, turn. 4th Row-4dc,ch3,4dc over last 4 chs. 2 om, 1 sm.

PETAL CURTAIN EDGE.

1st Row—Ch 16,2 dc start in 5th st from hook. Ch 2, 2 dc in next 2 sts. sk 1, 1 dc, 2 om ch 4, turn.—2nd Row—2 om, 1 dc over same.-2dc,ch2, 2dc over 2 chs.-1 dc,ch 3, turn.

—3rd Row—2dc,ch2,2dc over same. 1 dc.-1 om 1 sm, ch 4.-4 dc in same space. Ch 3,turn.

—4th Row—4dc,ch3,4dc over last 4 chs. 2 om, dc over same.-2dc,ch2,2dc,1 dc.

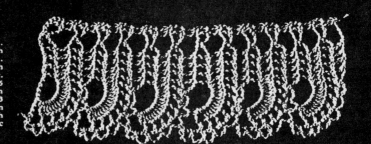

NARROW HALF-ARCH EDGE.

1st Row—Ch 25, 1 dc in 4th st from hook. Ch 3, sk 2, 1 sl.st. sk 2.Ch 3.-Then 4dc with 1 ch betw each. Ch 7, sk 5.1 sl.st, Ch 3. Turn.

—2nd Row—14 dc over 7 chs.—Ch 1, 4dc with 1 ch betw each over same. Ch 5, 2 dc.

—3rd Row— Ch 3, 1 dc, Ch 3, 1 sl.st over 5 chs below. Ch 3, -4dc as in previous row.Then 7dc with 2chs betw each over 14 dc. Sk 1, ch 3 fasten in the remaining ch. Ch 4, turn

—4th Row— Ch 4 over each 2 chs. 4dc with 1 ch betw each over same. Ch 5, 2dc

CHURCH WINDOW EDGE.

Made in No.30 thread. For Curtains it is exceptionally nice. Dainty for Towels or Lingerie.

1st Row—Ch 10, 4dc,start in 4th st from hook.Ch 2, sk 2, 1 dc. Thus forming 1 open and 1 solid mesh. Ch 5.turn.

—2nd Row— 2 om. Ch 3,turn.

—3rd Row—1 s m. 1 o m.

—4th Row--Ch 9, 1 dc over 1st dc below. 2 om,ch 3.turn.

—5th Row—1,sm,1 om,then 10 dc in loop of 9 chs. Ch 3, 10 dc. Fasten with 1 sl.st. Turn.

—6th Row—10 dc over same. 2dc,ch3,2dc over 3chs. 10 dc. 2 om.—7th Row—1 sm, 1 om, 6dc with 2chs betw each over 10 dc.-1 dc,ch3,1 dc over 3chs. repeat over other side of loop. fasten turn. 1 picot over each dc.-1 sl.st over last dc. Ch5 2 om. Connect last and first picots between motifs.

WAVELET INSERTION.

Made in No. 30 thread.

1st Row -Ch 40, 1 dc in 4th st from hook. Ch 2, sk 2, sk 2,—1 dc,1 p,1 dc in next st. Sk 4, ch 4, 9 dc. Ch 4, sk 4, 1 dc,1 p,1 dc in next st. Ch 3, sk 3, 2dc,ch2,2dc.turn.

—2nd Row--Ch 3,- 1 dc,ch 2,2dc over same. Ch 2, 1 dc,1 p,1 dc in one st below. Ch 2, 1 sl.st in picot. Ch 2,15dc—(over 3chs,9dc,& 3chs)- Ch 2,-1 dc,1 p,1 dc.-Ch 2, 1 sl.st in picot. Ch.2, 2dc over same. Ch 2, 2 dc.

—3rd Row—Ch 3,1 dc, ch 2, 2dc over same Ch 2,-1 dc, 1 p, 1 dc over 2 chs. Ch 3, 1 sl. st in picot.Ch4, 9 dc over same. Ch 4,-1 dc. 1 p,1 dc over 2,.1 sl.st in picot. Ch 2, 2dc. ch 2, 2dc. turn.—4th Row— Ch 3, 1 dc. ch 2, 2dc over same. Ch 2,- 1 dc, 1 p, 1 dc over 2 chs. Ch 3, 1 sl.st in picot. Ch 5, 3dc in middle on 9 dc below. Ch 5, 1 dc, 1 p. 1 dc in one stitch. Ch 3, 1 sl.st in picot. Ch 2,2dc over same. Ch 2, 2dc.

WAVELET EDGE AND INSERTION TO MATCH

Made in No. 30 thread..Ch 35, 1 dc in4th st from hook.Ch 2, sk 2, 2dc in next 2 sts.sk 2, ch 2,-1 dc,1p,1dc in next st.Sk 3, ch 3. Then 9dc in next 9 sts. Sk 2, ch 3, 1 sl.st., sk 3, ch 3, 1 dc,1 p,1 dc in last stitch.

—2nd Row—Ch 6, turn. 1 sl.st in picot. Ch 3 15 dc (over 3chs,9dc,3chs)-Ch 2, 1 p, 1 dc Ch 2,1 sl.st in picot. Ch 2, 2dc, ch 2, 2dc.

—3rd Row— Ch 3, 1 dc,ch 2, 2dc.ch 2,-1 dc, 1 p,1 dc over 2 chs.-Ch 3, 1 sl.st in picot. Ch 4, 9dc over same. Ch 4, sk 3chs,-1 dc, 1 p, 1 dc. 4th Row— Ch 11, turn.1 dc,1 p,1 dc in 8th st from hook, this forms ring for working scallop. Ch 2, 1 sl.st in picot.-Ch 2,-1 dc, 1 p,1 dc in one st of 4 chs below. Ch 5,-3dc over middle of 9 dc below. Ch 5,-1 dc, 1 p,1 dc Ch 3, 1 sl.st in p. Ch 2, and follow by —5th Row—Same as first.

Lower Edge - 1st Row- 1 sl.st. in small loop. Ch 3, 15dc in large loop. Ch 3,repeat.—2nd Row- 1 sl.st over same.Ch 1, 15dc with 1 ch betw each over same. Ch 1.—3rd Row- Ch 3, over each dc, 1 sl.st between each dc.

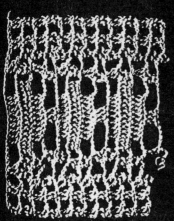

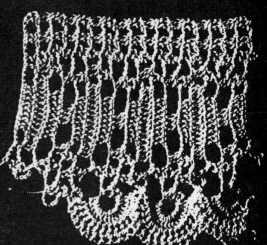

[122]

BEEHIVE EDGE.
Made in No.30 thread. Simple and serviceable in many ways.
1st Row—2chs, 1 dc in linen.
2nd Row—11 sl.st over first 4 spaces.Ch 4, sk 2 spaces. 1 dc,ch3,1dc in one dc below. Sk 2 spaces. Repeat.
—3rd Row —9 sl.st over 11 sl st. Ch 4,1 dc in same below. Ch 1. 1dc.3chs.1dc over 3 chs below.Ch 1,1 dc,Ch 4, repeat.
—4th Row—7 sl st over 9 sl. st,ch 4.–6dc, that is,1 dc in each one below ch1, and 2dc over the 3 chs in center.–ch 3.
—5th Row–5 sl.st over 7 sl. st,ch 4. 8 dc same as in row below,ch 3 in center. Ch 4 to next sl.stitches.

—6th Row—3 sl st over 5 sl. st,ch 5.-10 dc,ch 3 in center, Ch 5 to sl.sts.—7th Row— Ch 4 over each dc, going twice into center. Ch 3 over 5 chs. 1 sl. st to next 5chs. Ch 3,1 sl.st Ch 4.

PINE CONE EDGE.
First 2 rows in No.20 thread. Others in No.30 thread. It is CHAIN STITCHES only.
1st Row—1 sl.st,ch 6. 1 sl. st in material.—2nd Row— same.—3rd Row—1 sl.st in first loop. Then Ch 12.-1 sl. st in same loop. Ch 14,1 sl.st ch 16.-18.-16.–14.-12.- all in same loop.Ch 10.sk third loop.
—4th Row--Carefully straighten all long loops. 1 sl.st in first loop, ch3,1 sl.st in each loop.Ch 2 between motifs. 5th Row—Ch 4 over each 3 chs.

MOTH EDGE.
Made in No.30 thread. Is a very dainty edge for a Guest Towel.
1st Row—1 sl.st in material. Ch 7.-Then 1 sl.st in third st from hook.1 single cr. 3dc,1 dt. Then 1 sl.st in material. Repeat same little figure. Then ch 15 4 dc start in 6th st from hook. 1. s.c., 1 sl.st, ch 3.– 1 sl.st in material
2nd Row—1 sl.st in first point Ch 7,then 1 sl.st in third st. from hook. 1 s.c.,3 dc, 1 dt. 1 sl.st in second point. Ch 2, 1 dc in second dc of long loop. Ch' 2, 7 dc, ch 1 betw each in loop. -Ch 2, 1 dc in second dc of loop. Ch 2 to next point, Repeat.

—3rd Row— 1 sl.st in point Ch 5 to first space of long loop. Ch 4 to third space. Ch 4. 3 dc in center dc. Ch 4. Repeat.

THE BLOCK & POINT EDGE.
Made up in No.30... This is a beautiful application for Pillow Slips,Bed Sheets,Towels, and for Drawers or petticoats. Simply made. 1st Row—Work 1 sl.st chaining 4 in material.—2nd Row—4dc over every other 4chs, Ch 3.—3rd & 4th Rows—4dc over every 3chs.-Ch 3 over each 4dc. — 5th Row—Ch 7 over each 3 chs.—6th Row 4 sl.st, ch 4.-3 sl.st, ch 4.-4 sl.st over first loop of 7 chs.-3 sl.st, ch 4.-8 sl.st over second loop. -3 sl.st in third loop. Then ch 8 and TURN, fasten over second loop. -3 sl.st, ch 4, repeta 2 times in loop of 8chs.-3 sl.st, ch 4.-3 sl.st in third loop. Fourth loop same as first.

CASCADE EDGE.
Made in No. 30. thread. Elegant in pillow slips. Towels.
1st Row—1 sl.st in linen,ch 5. 1 dc, ch 2, 1 dc.
2nd Row–8 sl. st over 3 spaces. Ch 6, sk 3 spaces. 7 dt in the fourth space. Ch 6.
—3rd Row— 6 sl.st over 8 sl. st Ch 4, 9 sl.st over-1ch,7dt,& 1 ch.-Ch. 4.
—4th Row— 4 sl.st over 6 sl.st. Ch 5,-2 dc in one st. 11 dt over 9 sl.st- that is 5dt in center st.-2dc in one st.

Ch 5.—5th Row—2 sl.st over 4 sl st. Ch 5- 2 sl.st in 2 sts. Then 1 sl.st in each dc and dt below. 2 sl.st in next 2 sts. Ch.5.

—6th Row--Ch 6. 1 pt.st in third sl.st. Ch 7.– going back into 3rd st.ch 2. Sk 2 st. Repeat 5 times. Sk only 1 st in center. Ch 6 between motifs.

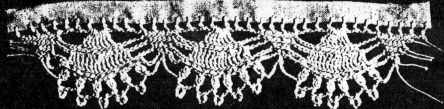

THE BLUE MOTH EDGE.
Made in 30. This is the same as the one above except first 3 rows.—1st Row—1 sl st. in linen. Ch5,1dc,ch1,1dc,ch2,1dc,ch1, 1dc,ch2.—2nd Row—1 X st over first 2 dc ch1,1 X st over next 2 dc.-ch 1.
—3rd Row—1 sl st, over first X st. Ch 7, 1 sl st in third st from hook.-1 sc,3dc,1 dt all-in 7 chs. Then 1 sl st over first single chain below. Repeat once. Ch 15, 4 dc, starting in 6th st from hook, 1 sc, 1 sl st, ch2. Fasten over third X st.—Next 2 rows same as 2nd & 3rd in Moth Edge above.

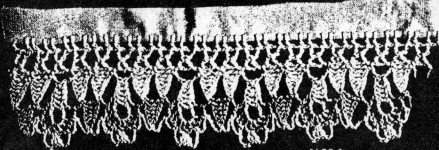

6

THE MORNING GLORY.

Made in No.30 thread. A circle of these as an insertion, leaving a half inch of material between each, in a round Table Cloth is a most beautiful creation.
1st Row—Ch 10 form ring. 20 sl.st in ring. Close.
2nd Row—Ch 10, sk 4, 1 sl.st repeat 3 times.
3rd Row—2 dc in first chain. 2 dc in third st, 2 s.c in 4th & 5th sts. Then 1 sl.st over ch. 2 S.C. 2dc.2 dt.over other. half of ch. Repeat 3 times.
—4th Row—Ch 7, 2dc over sl.st below. Ch 7,1 sl.s: over dt. Repeat 3 times.—5th Row—Ch 3,—then—1 pt.st (of 2dc),ch 3,3dt,ch3,3dt,ch3,1 pt.st—all over each 7 chs. Ch. 3, 1 sl.st over 2dc below.—6th Row—2 sl.st over first 3 chs., 3 sl.st over second 3dc., 3 sl.st over 3 dt. 3p. in center of point. Repeat in opposite direction. Same over every point.

BLACK EYED SUSAN.

Made in No.30 thread. 1st Row—Ch 8 form ring. 16 sl.st in ring.
2nd Row—Ch 6, sk 1, 1 dc, ch 3, sk 1 repeat 6 times.
3rd Row—5 sl.sts over each 3 chs.
4th Row—6 sl.st over 5 sl.sts. Ch 8 over each dc in row below. There will be 8 loops.-6 sl.st over 5 sl.sts.
5th Row—6dc,ch3,6dc in each of 8 chs.

THE FEATHER MEDALLION.

Made in No. 30 thread., 1st Row—Ch 10, form ring. 8 pt st with thread twice around hook. Ch 3 between each pt st. Close.—2nd Row—Ch 5 over each 3 chs. 1 sl.st.
—3rd Row—Ch 7 over each 5 chs. —4th Row—Ch 3, 9 dc over 7 chs, taking up back thread only. Close.
—5th Row—Ch 8, 1 dc in same st.—Ch 4, sk 4,—2dc in next st.-ch4, sk4. 1dc, ch3 & 1dc in one stitch.
—6th Row—Ch.3,3dc,ch 3, 4dc in loop. (the first 3ch count for a dc)-1 dc over first 4 chs.-Ch 4—1 dc over second 4 chs below. 4dc.3chs.4dc in loop. 1 dc over next 4chs. Repeat 6 times. —7th Row—Ch 3, 4dc over same.- 2dc, 3chs,2dc over top of 3chs. -5dc over same.-Ch 3 to next point. Repeat 7 times. —8th Row—Ch.3,-4dc with 1 ch betw each over every 7dc. 1 dc,ch 1, 1 dc over 3ch. 4dc with 1 ch betw each over next 7dc. 1 dc over 3 chs.
—9th Row—9dc and 8 picot over every point. Ch 3, 1 sl st.- ch 3 between each motif.

THE TWO-SQUARE MEDALLION

Made up in No. 30 thread. Two rows of this medallion on either side sewed to netting,makes a most beautiful door panel. Singly,one row for insertion, will work up the most elaborate curtain.
1st Row—Ch 10,form ring,ch 3.—24dc in ring.Close.
—2nd Row—Ch 10, sk 5,1 sl.st in next st. repeat 3 times.—3rd Row—Ch 3, 5dc, ch 3, 6dc over 10 chs. 6dc, ch3, 6dc over next 10 chs. repeat twice.—4th Row—Ch5, 1dt. Ch 5, 1 dt in corner.Ch 2,1 dt. Ch 5, 1 dt. Ch 2, 1 dt in corner. Ch 5, 2 dt over middle of side. repeat 3 times.
—5th Row— Ch 3, work 13 dc up to corner. Ch 3, 14 dc. repeat 3 times. —6th Row—Ch 5,—2 dt, Ch 3, 2 dt in 7th dc below. Ch 5, to corner. 1 sl.st, Ch 5, 2 dt, Ch 3, 2 dt. Ch 5, 1 sl.st in corner.Ch 5.— 2 dt, Ch 3,—2 dt in 8th st from corner.repeat three times. —7th Row—5 sl.st over 5 chs. 1 p. 2 sl.st over 2 dt.,-2 p. over next 3 chs. 2 sl.st 1 p.-5 sl. st over 5 chs. Then Ch 5, 3p. in corner.Ch 5, 5 sl. st over next 5 chs. Repeat.

PEACOCK DOILIE

This is made in No.30 thread and is shown one fourth less than actual size.
Cut linen in 3inch circle,fold back to 2¾ inches.
1st Row—Work 60 dc with 2chs betw each in linen.
—2nd Row—1 sl.st over each st. —3rd Row—Same.
—4th Row—9 sl.st-ch.6-sk.6,—2dt,ch3,2dt in next 2st.-ch.6-sk.6. Repeat 7 times over circle..
(It may become necessary to sk 7 sl st.sometimes.)
5th Row—7 sl.st over 9 sl.st.—ch.7,—3dt,ch4,3dt, in loop.Ch.7. Repeat 7 times...—6th Row—5 sl.st. over 7 sl.st.—Ch.8,—10 dt with 1 ch betw each over loop of 4 chs.- Ch. 8...—7th Row—3sl.st over 5sl st—Ch.8-10 dc with 2chs betw each over 10 dt.Ch.8.
—8th Row—1 sl.st over 3 sl.st.,—Ch.9—9 pt.st of 2dt with 3chs betw each. Ch.9.—1 sl.st.
—9th Row—Ch.9 up to first pt.st.-sl.st.—Ch.7, going back to third st fromhook,ch.2.— 1 sl.st over every 3 chs. —2 sl.st over chain between motifs.

[124]

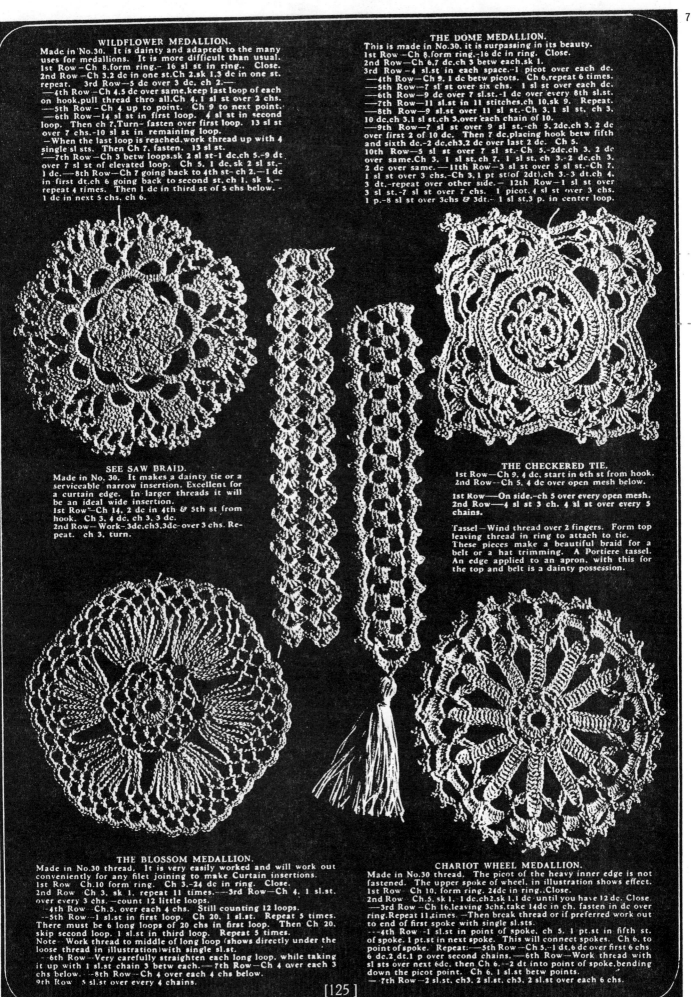

WILDFLOWER MEDALLION.

Made in No.30. It is dainty and adapted to the many uses for medallions. It is more difficult than usual.
1st Row.—Ch 8.form ring.- 16 sl st in ring.. Close.
2nd Row.—Ch 3.2 dc in one st.Ch 2.sk 1.3 dc in one st. repeat. 3rd Row.—5 dc over 3 dc, ch 2.—
—4th Row.—Ch 4.5 dc over same.keep last loop of each on hook.pull thread thro all.Ch 4, 1 sl st over 2 chs.—
—5th Row.—Ch 4 up to point. Ch 9 to next point.·
—6th Row.—14 sl st in first loop. 4 sl st in second loop. Then ch 7.Turn- fasten over first loop. 13 sl st over 7 chs. -10 sl st in remaining loop.
—When the last loop is reached.work thread up with 4 single sl sts. Then Ch 7, fasten. 13 sl st.
—7th Row.—Ch 3 betw loops.sk 2 sl st-1 dc.ch 5.-9 dt over 7 sl st of elevated loop. Ch 5, 1 dc, sk 2 sl st.-1 dc.—8th Row.—Ch 7 going back to 4th st— ch 2.—1 dc in first dt.ch 6 going back to second st, ch 1, sk 5.—repeat 4 times. Then 1 dc in third st of 5 chs below. -1 dc in next 5 chs, ch 6.

THE DOME MEDALLION.

This is made in No.30. it is surpassing in its beauty.
1st Row.—Ch 8,form ring.-16 dc in ring. Close.
2nd Row.—Ch 6,7 dc.ch 3 betw each.sk 1.
3rd Row.—4 sl.st in each space.-1 picot over each dc.
—4th Row.—Ch 9, 1 dc betw picots. Ch 6,repeat 6 times.
—5th Row.—7 sl·st over six chs. 1 sl st over each dc.
—6th Row.—9 dc over 7 sl.st.-1 dc over every 8th sl.st.
—7th Row.—11 sl.st in 11 stitches,ch 10.sk 9. Repeat.
—8th Row.—9 sl.st over 11 sl st.-Ch 3,1 sl st, ch 3, 10 dc.ch 3,1 sl st,ch 3,over each chain of 10.
—9th Row.—7 sl st over 9 sl st,-ch 5, 2dc,ch 3, 2 dc over first 2 of 10 dc. Then 7 dc.placing hook betw fifth and sixth dc.-2 dc,ch3,2 dc over last 2 dc. Ch 5.
10th Row.—5 sl st over 7 sl st.-Ch 5.-2dc,ch 3, 2 dc over same.Ch 3, 1 sl st, ch 7, 1 sl st, ch 3.-2 dc,ch 3. 2 dc over same.—11th Row.—3 sl st over 5 sl st.-Ch 7, 1 sl st over 3 chs.-Ch 3,1 pt st(of 2dt),ch 3.-3 dt.ch 4, 3 dt.-repeat over other side. — 12th Row.—1 sl st over 3 sl st. -7 sl st over 7 chs. 1 picot, 4 sl st over 3 chs. 1 p.-8 sl st over 3chs & 3dt.- 1 sl st,3 p. in center loop.

SEE SAW BRAID.

Made in No. 30. It makes a dainty tie or a serviceable narrow insertion. Excellent for a curtain edge. In larger threads it will be an ideal wide insertion.
1st Row.—Ch 14, 2 dc in 4th & 5th st from hook. Ch 3, 4 dc, ch 3, 3 dc.
2nd Row.—Work--3dc,ch3,3dc- over 3 chs. Repeat. ch 3, turn.

THE CHECKERED TIE.

1st Row.—Ch 9, 4 dc, start in 6th st from hook.
2nd Row.--Ch 5, 4 dc over open mesh below.

1st Row.——On side.-ch 5 over every open mesh.
2nd Row.——4 sl st 3 ch. 4 sl st over every 5 chains.

Tassel.—Wind thread over 2 fingers. Form top leaving thread in ring to attach to tie.
These pieces make a beautiful braid for a belt or a hat trimming. A Portiere tassel. An edge applied to an apron, with this for the top and belt is a dainty possession.

THE BLOSSOM MEDALLION.

Made in No.30 thread. It is very easily worked and will work out conveniently for any filet joining to make Curtain insertions.
1st Row.—Ch.10 form ring. Ch 3.-24 dc in ring. Close.
2nd Row.—Ch 3, sk 1. repeat 11 times.—3rd Row.—Ch 4, 1 sl.st. over every 3 chs. —count 12 little loops.
--4th Row.—Ch.5, over each 4 chs. Still counting 12 loops.
--5th Row.—1 sl.st in first loop. Ch 20, 1 sl.st. Repeat 5 times. There must be 6 long loops of 20 chs in first loop. Then Ch 20, skip second loop. 1 sl.st in third loop. Repeat 5 times.
Note.-- Work thread to middle of long loop (shows directly under the loose thread in illustration)with single sl.st.
-6th Row.—Very carefully straighten each long loop, while taking it up with 1 sl.st chain 3 betw each.— 7th Row.—Ch 4 over each 3 chs below.--8th Row.—Ch 4 over each 4 chs below.
9th Row.- 5 sl.st over every 4 chains.

CHARIOT WHEEL MEDALLION.

Made in No.30 thread. The picot of the heavy inner edge is not fastened. The upper spoke of wheel, in illustration shows effect.
1st Row.- Ch 10, form ring. 24dc in ring..Close.
2nd Row.—Ch.5, sk 1,-1 dc.ch2,sk 1,1 dc.-until you have 12 dc. Close.
—3rd Row.—Ch 16,leaving 3chs.take 14dc in ch. fasten in dc over ring.Repeat 11,times. —Then break thread or if preferred work out to end of first spoke with single sl.sts.
---4th Row.—1 sl.st in point of spoke, ch 5. 1 pt.st in fifth st. of spoke. 1 pt.st in next spoke. This will connect spokes. Ch 6. to point of spoke. Repeat:—5th Row.—Ch 5.—1 dt.6 dc over first 6 chs. 6 dc,2 dt,1 p over second chains. —6th Row.—Work thread with sl sts over next 6dc, then Ch 6.--2 dt into point of spoke,bending down the picot point. Ch 6, 1 sl.st betw points.
— 7th Row.—2 sl.st, ch3, 2 sl.st, ch3, 2 sl.st over each 6 chs.

8

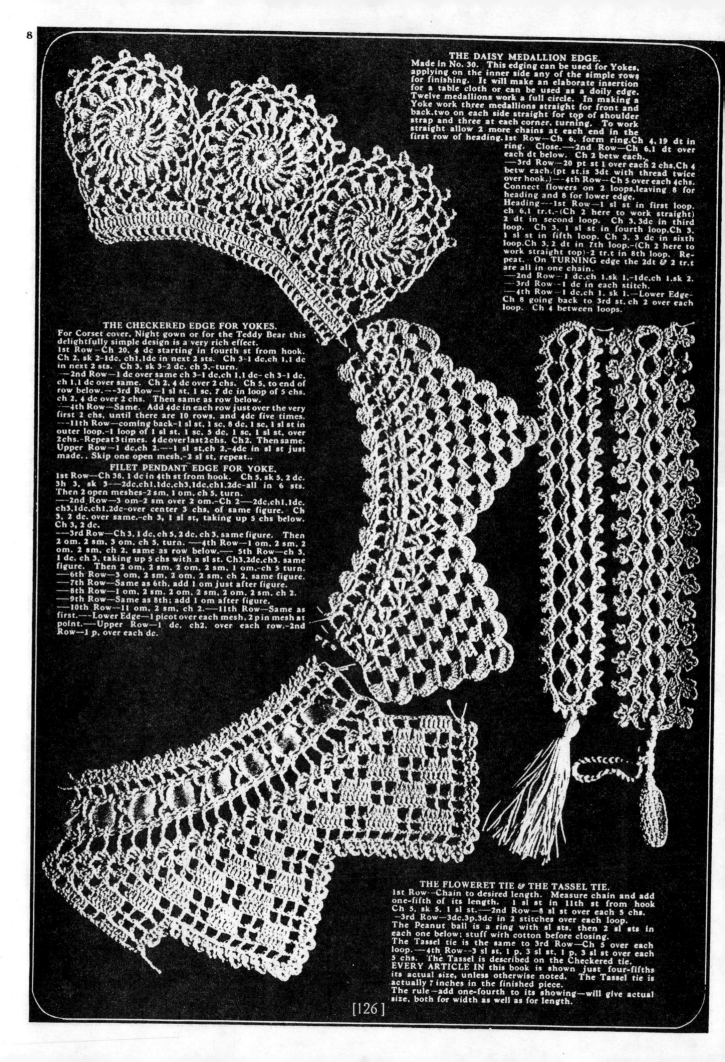

THE DAISY MEDALLION EDGE.

Made in No. 30. This edging can be used for Yokes, applying on the inner side any of the simple rows for finishing. It will make an elaborate insertion for a table cloth or can be used as a doily edge. Twelve medallions work a full circle. In making a Yoke work three medallions straight for front and back, two on each side straight for top of shoulder strap and three at each corner, turning. To work straight allow 2 more chains at each end in the first row of heading. 1st Row—Ch 6, form ring. Ch 4, 19 dt in ring. Close.—2nd Row—Ch 6, 1 dt over each dt below. Ch 2 betw each. —3rd Row—20 pt st 1 over each 2 chs. Ch 4 betw each. (pt st. is 3dt with thread twice over hook.)—4th Row—Ch 5 over each 4chs. Connect flowers on 2 loops, leaving 8 for heading and 8 for lower edge.
Heading—1st Row—1 sl st in first loop. ch 6, 1 tr.t.—(Ch 2 here to work straight) 2 dt in second loop. Ch 3, 3dc in third loop. Ch 3, 1 sl st in fourth loop. Ch 3, 1 sl st in fifth loop. Ch 3, 3 dc in sixth loop. Ch 3, 2 dt in 7th loop.—(Ch 2 here to work straight top)—2 tr.t in 8th loop. Repeat. On TURNING edge the 2dt & 2 tr.t are all in one chain.
—2nd Row—1 dc, ch 1, sk 1,—1dc, ch 1, sk 2.
—3rd Row—1 dc in each stitch.
—4th Row—1 dc, ch 1, sk 1.—Lower Edge—Ch 8 going back to 3rd st. ch 2 over each loop. Ch 4 between loops.

THE CHECKERED EDGE FOR YOKES.

For Corset cover, Night gown or for the Teddy Bear this delightfully simple design is a very rich effect.
1st Row—Ch 20, 4 dc starting in fourth st from hook. Ch 2, sk 2—1dc, ch1, 1dc in next 2 sts. Ch 3—1 dc, ch 1, 1 dc in next 2 sts. Ch 3, sk 3—2 dc. ch 3,—turn.
—2nd Row—1 dc over same ch 3—1 dc, ch 1, 1 dc— ch 3—1 dc, ch 1, 1 dc over same. Ch 2, 4 dc over 2 chs. Then to end of row below.—3rd Row—1 sl st, 1 sc, 7 dc in loop of 5 chs. ch 2, 4 dc over 2 chs. Then same as row below.
—4th Row—Same. Add 4dc in each row just over the very first 2 chs, until there are 10 rows, and 4dc five times.
—11th Row—coming back—1 sl st, 1 sc, 8 dc, 1 sc, 1 sl st in outer loop.—1 loop of 1 sl st, 1 sc, 5 dc, 1 sc, 1 sl st, over 2chs.—Repeat 3 times. 4dc over last 2chs. Ch2. Then same. Upper Row—1 dc, ch 2.—1 sl st, ch 2,—4dc in sl st just made.. Skip one open mesh,—2 sl st, repeat..

FILET PENDANT EDGE FOR YOKE.

1st Row—Ch 38, 1 dc in 4th st from hook. Ch 5, sk 5, 2 dc. 3h 3, sk 3—2dc, ch1, 1dc, ch3, 1dc, ch1, 2dc—all in 6 sts. Then 2 open meshes—2 sm, 1 om, ch 5, turn.
—2nd Row—3 om—2 sm over 2 om.—Ch 2—2dc, ch1, 1dc, ch3, 1dc, ch1, 2dc—over center 3 chs, of same figure. Ch 3, 2 dc. over same.—ch 3, 1 sl st, taking up 5 chs below. Ch 3, 2 dc.
—3rd Row—Ch 3, 1 dc, ch 5, 2 dc, ch 3, same figure. Then 2 om, 2 sm, 3 om, ch 5, turn.—4th Row—1 om, 2 sm, 2 om, 2 sm, ch 2, same as row below.—5th Row—Ch 3, 1 dc, ch 3, taking up 5 chs with a sl st. Ch3, 2dc, ch3, same figure. Then 2 om, 2 sm, 2 om, 2 sm, 1 om.—ch 5 turn.
—6th Row—3 om, 2 sm, 2 om, 2 sm, ch 2, same figure.
—7th Row—Same as 6th, add 1 om just after figure.
—8th Row—1 om, 2 sm, 2 om, 2 sm, 2 om, ch 2.
—9th Row—Same as 8th; add 1 om after figure.
—10th Row—11 om, 2 sm, ch 2.—11th Row—Same as first.—Lower Edge—1 picot over each mesh, 2 p in mesh at point.—Upper Row—1 dc, ch2, over each row.—2nd Row—1 p. over each dc.

THE FLOWERET TIE & THE TASSEL TIE.

1st Row—Chain to desired length. Measure chain and add one-fifth of its length. 1 sl st in 11th st from hook. Ch 5, sk 5, 1 sl st.—2nd Row—8 sl st over each 5 chs. —3rd Row—3dc, 3p, 3dc in 2 stitches over each loop. The Peanut ball is a ring with sl sts, then 2 sl sts in each one below; stuff with cotton before closing. The Tassel tie is the same to 3rd Row—Ch 5 over each loop.—4th Row—3 sl st, 1 p, 3 sl st, 1 p, 3 sl st over each 5 chs. The Tassel is described on the Checkered tie.
EVERY ARTICLE IN this book is shown just four-fifths its actual size, unless otherwise noted. The Tassel tie is actually 7 inches in the finished piece.
The rule—add one-fourth to its showing—will give actual size, both for width as well as for length.

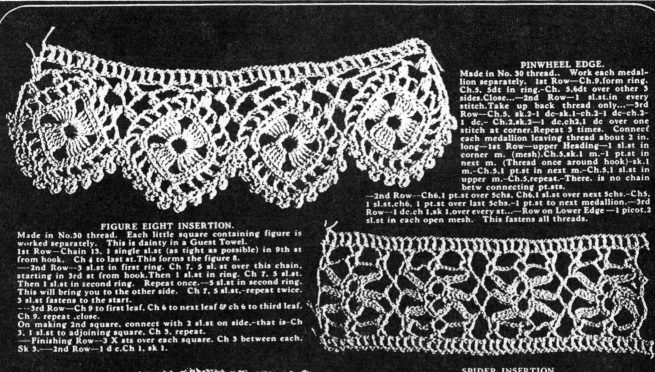

PINWHEEL EDGE.

Made in No. 30 thread.. Work each medallion separately. 1st Row—Ch.9.form ring. Ch.5, 5dt in ring.-Ch. 5,6dt over other 3 sides.Close...—2nd Row—1 sl.st.in every stitch.Take up back thread only...—3rd Row—Ch.5, sk.2-1 dc-sk.1-ch.2-1 dc-ch.2-1 dc,- Ch.2,sk.2-1 dc,ch2,1 dc over one stitch at corner.Repeat 5 times. Connect each medallion leaving thread about 2 in. long—1st Row—upper Heading—1 sl.st in corner m. (mesh).Ch.5,sk.1 m.—1 pt.st in next m. (Thread once around hook)-sk.1 m.-Ch.5,1 pt.st in next m.-Ch.5,1 sl.st in upper m.-Ch.5,repeat.-There. is no chain betw connecting pt.sts.

—2nd Row—Ch6,1 pt.st over 5chs, Ch6,1 sl.st over next 5chs.-Ch5, 1 sl.st,ch6, 1 pt.st over last 5chs.-1 pt.st to next medallion.—3rd Row—1 dc,ch 1,sk 1,over every st...—Row on Lower Edge—1 picot,2 sl.st in each open mesh. This fastens all threads.

FIGURE EIGHT INSERTION.

Made in No.30 thread. Each little square containing figure is worked separately. This is dainty in a Guest Towel.
1st Row—Chain 13. 1 single sl.st (as tight as possible) in 9th st from hook. Ch 4 to last st.This forms the figure 8.
—2nd Row—3 sl.st in first ring. Ch 7, 5 sl. st over this chain, starting in 3rd st from hook.Then 1 sl.st in ring. Ch 7, 5 sl.st. Then 1 sl.st in second ring. Repeat once.—5 sl.st in second ring. This will bring you to the other side. Ch 7, 5 sl.st,-repeat twice. 3 sl.st fastens to the start.
—3rd Row—Ch 9 to first leaf, Ch 6 to next leaf & ch 6 to third leaf. Ch 9. repeat .close.
On making 2nd square, connect with 2 sl.st on side,-that is-Ch 3, 1 sl.st to adjoining square, Ch 3, repeat.
—Finishing Row—3 X sts over each square. Ch 3 between each. Sk 3.—2nd Row—1 d c.Ch 1, sk 1.

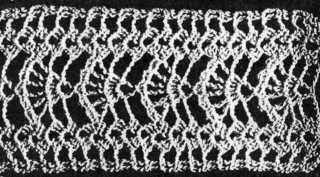

SPIDER INSERTION

Made in No. 30 thread. This is a neat light insertion for Lingerie.
1st Row--Ch 32, 1 dc in 8th st from hook. Ch 2, 1 dc in same st.-Ch 5, sk 3,-3 sl.st. Ch 5.- 1 dc,ch 2,1 dc,- ch 2,1 dc,-Ch 5, turn. —2nd Row-- 1 dc,ch 2, 1 dc over same.Ch 3,-1 sl.st over 5 chs,Ch 6. Repeat. Ch 5, turn.
—3rd Row—Same start, Ch 3, 11 dc over 6 chs. Ch 3.
—4th Row—7dc over 11 dc. sk 2dc. Ch 3.
—5th Row— Ch 5, 3 sl.st.same as first row.

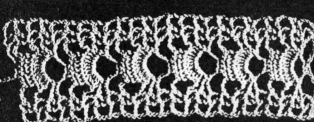

FAN INSERTION.

Made up in No. 30 thread. It is not a difficult piece and adapts itself to Curtains, door panels. Bedspreads and Lingerie.
1st Row— Ch 32.1 dc in 4th st from hook. Ch 2, sk 2,-3dc,3chs,3dc in next 6 stitches. Sk 4, ch 4,-1 dc,3chs,1 dc in next st. Repeat in opposite direction.. turn. —2nd Row—Ch 3, 1 dc, ch 2,-3dc.3ch,3dc, over same. Ch 3, 7dc over 3chs below. Repeat, turn. —3rd Row— Ch3, 1 dc, ch 2,-3dc,3ch,3dc over same. Then 6 dt with 2chs betw each,each one betw 2 dc below. Repeat, turn.—4th Row—Ch 3, 1 dc, ch 2,-3dc, 3ch,3dc over same.-1 sl.st.2 single cro. 1 sl.st,over each 2chs.

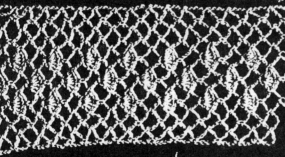

NARROW SHELL INSERTION

Made up in No.30 Thread. It is easily made. It serves for Lingerie, Table cloth, Curtain or for Bed Spread. Used in connection with medallions, there is no limit to the applications for its use.
1st Row--Ch 38, 1 sl.st in 9th st from hook, Ch 5, 1 sl.st, sk 4. Repeat 5 times.—2nd Row— Ch 6, 1 sl.st over first 5 chs below. Ch 5, 1 sl.st over next 5 ches. Repeat once. Then 1 sl.st in next sl.st below. 1 sl.st over next 5 chs. Repeat to other end.—3rd Row—Same as first Row.
4th Row--Ch 6, 1 sl.st over first 5 chs., Ch 5, 1 sl.st over next 5 chs.. 1 sh.st over next sl.st, 1 sl.st over next 5 chs.-Ch 5, 1 sl.st over next 5 chs.-1 sh. st over next sl.st.- 1 sl.st over next 5 chs.

SUNFLOWER EDGE.

Made in No. 30 thread. 1st Row--Ch 9, form ring. Ch 3, 24dc in ring. Close.—2nd Row—Ch 9, 1 sl.st in second st from hook. 2 sc, 3dc in next 5 sts. This leaves 2 chs open. Then 1 dc over 2nd dc of ring Sk 1, ch 7.- 1 sl.st in second st from hook. 2sc, 3dc. This will fill out the 7chs leaving 1 dc over ring. There are 12 petals.Connect adjoining petals as the work progresses. Heading--Ch 5, over each of the 4 upper petals. Ch5 to next flower.—2nd Row—1 dc, ch 1, sk 1.....Lower edge--4dt with 3 p. in each of the 4 petals.

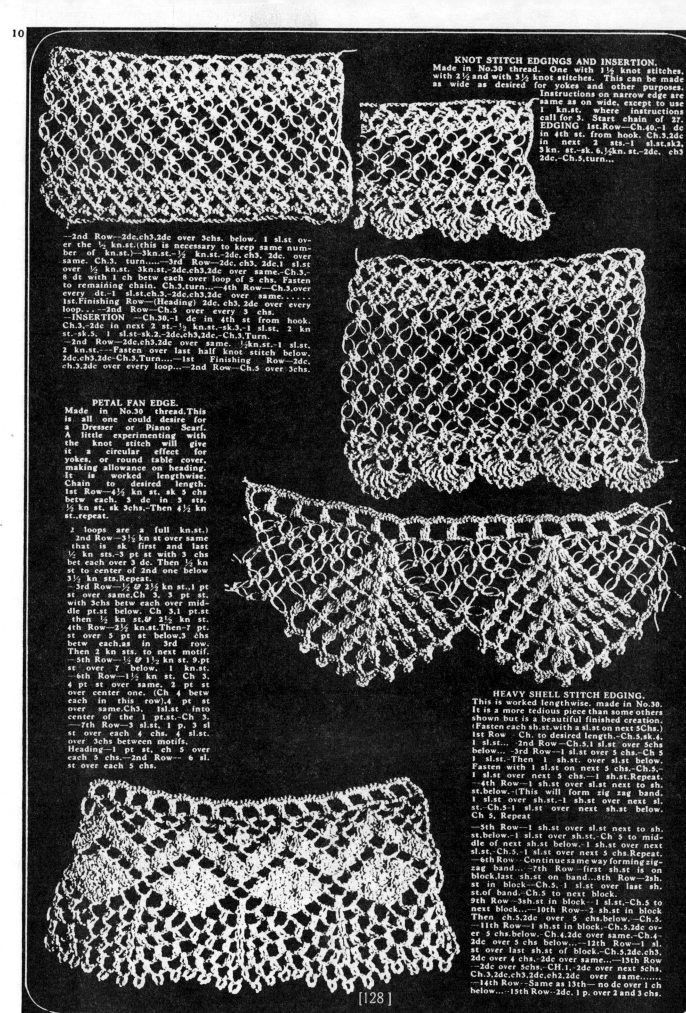

KNOT STITCH EDGINGS AND INSERTION.

Made in No.30 thread. One with 1½ knot stitches, with 2½ and with 3½ knot stitches. This can be made as wide as desired for yokes and other purposes. Instructions on narrow edge are same as on wide, except to use 1 kn.st. where instructions call for 3. Start chain of 27. EDGING 1st.Row—Ch.40.—1 dc in 4th st. from hook. Ch.3.2dc in next 2 sts.—1 sl.st.sk2, 3 kn. st.-sk. 6.½kn. st.-2dc, ch3 2dc.-Ch.5.turn...

--2nd Row--2dc.ch3.2dc over 3chs. below. 1 sl.st over the ½ kn.st.(this is necessary to keep same number of kn.st.)--3kn.st.--½ kn.st.-2dc, ch3, 2dc. over same. Ch.3. turn......--3rd Row—2dc, ch3, 2dc,1 sl.st over ½ kn.st. 3kn.st.-2dc.ch3,2dc over same.-Ch.3.- 8 dt with 1 ch betw each over loop of 5 chs. Fasten to remaining chain. Ch.3,turn...—4th Row—Ch.3.over every dt.-1 sl.st.ch.3.-2dc.ch3,2dc over same...... 1st.Finishing Row—(Heading) 2dc, ch3, 2dc over every loop...--2nd Row—Ch.5 over every 3 chs.
--INSERTION --Ch.30,-1 dc in 4th st from hook. Ch.3,-2dc in next 2 st.-!½ kn.st.-sk.3,-1 sl.st, 2 kn st.-sk.5, 1 sl.st-sk.2.-2dc,ch3,2dc.-Ch.3.Turn.
--2nd Row—2dc,ch3,2dc over same. ½kn.st.-1 sl.st, 2 kn.st.--Fasten over last half knot stitch below. 2dc.ch3.2dc-Ch.3.Turn....-1st Finishing Row—2dc. ch.3,2dc over every loop...-2nd Row—Ch.5 over 3chs.

PETAL FAN EDGE.

Made in No.30 thread.This is all one could desire for a Dresser or Piano Scarf. A little experimenting with the knot stitch will give it a circular effect for yokes, or round table cover, making allowance on heading. It is worked lengthwise. Chain to desired length. 1st Row—4½ kn st, sk 5 chs betw each. 3 dc in 3 sts. ½ kn st, sk 3chs,-Then 4½ kn st.,repeat.

2 loops are a full kn.st.) 2nd Row—3½ kn st over same that is sk first and last ½ kn sts.-3 pt st with 3 chs bet each over 3 dc. Then ½ kn st to center of 2nd one below 3½ kn sts.Repeat.
-3rd Row—½ & 2½ kn st.,1 pt st over same,Ch 3, 3 pt st, with 3chs betw each over middle pt.st below. Ch 3,1 pt.st .then ½ kn st.& 2½ kn st. 4th Row—2½ kn.st.Then—7 pt. st over 5 pt st below,3 chs betw each,as in 3rd row. Then 2 kn sts. to next motif. -5th Row—½ & 1½ kn st. 9.pt st over 7 below, 1 kn.st. -6th Row—1½ kn st. Ch 3, 4 pt st over same. 2 pt st over center one. (Ch 4 betw each in this row),4 pt st over same.Ch3, 1sl.st into center of the 1 pt.st.-Ch 3. -7th Row—3 sl.st, 1 p. 3 sl st over each 4 chs. 4 sl.st. over 3chs between motifs. Heading—1 pt st, ch 5 over each 5 chs.—2nd Row-- 6 sl. st over each 5 chs.

HEAVY SHELL STITCH EDGING.

This is worked lengthwise. made in No.30. It is a more tedious piece than some others shown but is a beautiful finished creation. (Fasten each sh.st.with a sl.st on next 5Chs.) 1st Row · Ch. to desired length.-Ch.5,sk.4. 1 sl.st... -2nd Row—Ch.5,1 sl.st over 5chs below... -3rd Row--1 sl.st over 5 chs.-Ch 5 1 sl.st.-Then 1 sh.st. over sl.st below. Fasten with 1 sl.st on next 5 chs.-Ch.5,- 1 sl.st over next 5 chs.—1 sh.st.Repeat. —4th Row—1 sh.st over sl.st next to sh. st.below.-(This will form zig zag band. 1 sl.st over sh.st.-1 sh st over next sl. st.-Ch.5-1 sl.st over next sh.st below. Ch 5, Repeat

—5th Row—1 sh.st over sl.st next to sh. st,below.-1 sl.st over sh.st.-Ch 5 to middle of next sh.st below.-1 sh.st over next sl.st,-Ch.5,-1 sl.st over next 5 chs.Repeat. —6th Row--Continue same way forming zig-zag band.--7th Row—first sh.st is on block,last sh.st on band...8th Row—2sh. st in block--Ch.5, 1 sl.st over last sh. st.of band.-Ch.5 to next block. 9th Row—3sh.st in block--1 sl.st,-Ch.5 to next block...--10th Row—2 sh.st in block Then ch.5,2dc over 5 chs.below.--Ch.5. --11th Row—1 sh.st in block.-Ch.5,2dc over 5 chs.below.-Ch.4,2dc over same.-Ch.4- 2dc over 5 chs below...--12th Row—1 sl. st over last sh.st of block.-Ch.5,2dc.ch3. 2dc over 4 chs,-2dc over same...--13th Row --2dc over 5chs.-CH.1,-2dc over next 5chs. Ch.3,2dc,ch3,2dc,ch2,2dc over same...... --14th Row—Same as 13th— no dc over 1 ch below....-15th Row—2dc, 1 p. over 2 and 3 chs.

THE PYRAMID EDGE.
Made in No. 80.—1st Row—1 sl st,ch 5,1 sl st in linen.—-2nd Row—10 sl st in each of first 2 loops,5 sl st in third loop. Then ch 5 and turn. 1 sl st over second loop,ch 5,1 sl st over first loop. Turn-10 sl st over these 5 chs and 5 sl st over part of 5 chs. Ch5 turn,1 sl st in loop just completed,10 sl st over these 5 chs.-5 sl st over each of remaining loops.

LITTLE MAIDS IN A ROW.
This is made in No.80, it will make up as a narrow edge in No.60 or 80. A very dainty Handkerchief edge. 1st Row.Ch.6, 1 slip st in linen. turn. 1 sl.st,1 s c. 3 dc, 1 dt in chain. Then ch 9, in same st in linen,turn. 1 sl.st, 1 sc. 3 dc, 1 dt over six sts of 9 chs. leaving 3 chs for loop. Ch 6 to linen leaving a space of ¾ of an inch. —2nd Row—1 sl.st, ch 4 to loop. 1 p. ch 6 going back to second st. Ch 2, 1 sl.st in loop. 1 p. ch 4, 1 sl.st ch 4.

THE HALF KNOT STITCH EDGE.
1st Row -3 sl st,1 single kn st, 3 sl st,in linen.- -2nd Row -1 sl st over 3 sl st. Ch 7 over kn st.---3rd Row -4 sl st, ch 4, 5 sl st, ch 4. 4 sl st over each loop. Made in No. 80.

One may well be proud of any of these dainty kerchiefs. The application is of course not limited to handkerchiefs alone. For Pillow slip, bed sheet, napkin and for Lingerie these edgings are ideal. All made in No.80. they stand the tub.

THE RIPPLE EDGE.
Made in No.80.-1st Row -1 sl st in linen.Ch 5, 1 dc.ch 2,1 dc.- -2nd Row -1 sl st in first dc 3dc.ch3,3dc in second dc.- -3rd Row—1 sl st in point. Ch 6 to next point.- -4th Row -1 sl st,1 sc,6 dc,1 sc,1 sl st in each loop.

BABY SHELL EDGE.
Made in No.80. Shell st is 6 dc in 1 stitch. 1st Row--1 sl st.ch 5 in linen.—2nd Row—1 sl st Ch 5,from loop to loop.- -3rd Row—1 sl st in first loop. Ch 5,1 sl st in second loop. 1 picot(5chs)—1 shell st in sl st below. 1 sl st in 3rd loop,1 p.1 sl st,ch 5 to next loop.

THE ZEPHYR, A KNOT STITCH EDGE.
Made in No.80. —1st Row -1 sl st,1 kn st in linen.—2nd Row -1 kn st over same.— -3rd Row—1 sl st,ch 6 over each kn st. -—4th Row—1 sl st over same. Ch 3, 1 sl st in center of 6 chs.-3 picots,ch 3,1 sl st over same.

CROCHETING.

EXPLANATION OF TERMS USED.

Ch.—Chain.

Sc.—Single Crochet. Having a stitch on the needle, put the needle through the work and draw the silk through both the work *and the stitch on the needle.*

Dc.—Double Crochet. Having a stitch on the needle, put the needle through the work and draw a stitch through, making two on the needle. Take up the silk again and draw it through both these stitches.

Tc. or Tr.—Treble Crochet. Having a stitch on the needle, take up the silk as if for a stitch, put the needle through the work and draw a stitch through, making three on the needle. Take up the silk and draw through two, then take up again and draw through the two remaining.

Stc. or Str.—Short Treble Crochet. Like treble, except that when the three stitches are on the needle, instead of drawing the silk through two stitches twice, it is drawn through all three at once.

Ltc. or Ltr.—Long Treble Crochet. Like treble, except that the silk is thrown twice over the needle before inserting the latter in the work. The stitches are worked off two at a time, as in treble.

S. S. means slip-stitch, which is to pass hook through a stitch of the foundation and draw thread through that and the loop on the needle without putting thread over. This is the shortest of all crochet stitches except the chain.

*—Indicates a repetition, and is used merely to save words: "*2 ch., 2 tr., 1 ch., 2 tr., repeat three times," would be equivalent to saying, "2, ch., 2 tr., 1 ch., 2 tr., 2 ch., 2 tr., 1 ch., 2 tr., 2 ch., 2 tr., 1 ch., 2 tr., 2 ch., 2 tr., 1 ch., 2 tr."

INSERTION.

This insertion, with edge to match, is lovely to trim a baby blanket. Have pale blue surah silk or ribbon under the insertion, then finish edge of blanket with the lace, or it may be used on flannel skirts.

Materials: 2 ounces BELDING'S "Pure Thread" Crochet Silk, and a steel hook.

The shapes are each crocheted from the middle and joined by a row or outside edge of picots. Each shape or leaf is begun in the middle with 8

ch., on which are worked on both sides of ch., 3 ch., *1 half tr., 2 ch., 1 tr., 2 ch., 4 long tr., 2 ch., 1 tr., 2 ch., 1 half tr., 4 ch.; repeat from * on the other side of ch.

2nd row.—3 dc. under each 2 ch. and 7 dc. under each 4 ch.

3rd row.—3 ch. for a tr., 2 tr. in the 3rd and 5th, and 3 tr. in 4th of 7 dc., and 1 tr. in each of the other dc. of previous row.

4th row.—1 dc. in each tr., with 2 dc. in the middle of the 3 tr., at each end of leaf.

5th row.—1 tr., 1 ch., 1 tr., 1 ch., 1 tr., each time missing 1 tr. between the tr. being made, 3 picots (made of 5 ch., 1 dc. in 1st ch.). then * 1 tr., 1 ch., miss 1, 1 tr. in next, 3 picots; repeat from * round the row, remembering to put

2 tr. with picots between, then in the point at each end. This completes one leaf, and all the others are worked the same.

The illustration shows how each leaf is joined to the other. A row of rosettes is crocheted between the leaf shapes and also joins them, each two being made differently. For the rosette in the center of 4 leaves make a ring of 5 ch.

1st row.—6 ch., *1 tr., 3 ch.; repeat from * 6 times, 1 dc. in 3rd of 6 ch.

2nd row.—In the 2nd of 3 ch., 1 dc., 1 half tr., 1 tr., 1 half tr., 1 dc.; in the center or at 1 tr., join to the end picots of the leaves.

For the rosettes between each group of 4 leaves make 10 ch. and join in a ring.

1st row.—21 tr. under the ch.

2nd row.—A row of tr. and picots like around the leaves, and joining as seen in cut.

For the small shapes looking like triangles, make 13 ch., 1 dc. in each of the 6 stitches, 3 dc. in next, 1 dc. in each of next 6 stitches; turn.

2nd row.—5 dc., miss 5 dc. in middle, 5 dc. Now place both middle edges of this triangle together and close with 5 sc., and break off thread.

3rd row.—1 tr., a picot, 1 ch., 1 tr., 1 ch., 1 tr., 1 ch., 1 tr., 3 picots, miss 1 dc., 1 ch., 1 tr., 1 ch., 1 tr., 1 ch., 1 tr. at the points of triangles, 3 picots, 3 tr. with 1 ch. between each, 1 picot, 1 tr.; fasten securely and break off.

On each side are made 3 rows, thus:

1st row.—11 tr. in 1 picot, 8 ch., 1 tr. in middle of another group of picots, 8 ch., 1 dc. in each stitch across the triangle, 8 ch., and so on across the row.

2nd row.—1 tr., miss 1 st., 1 tr. in next.

3rd row.—1 tr., 3 ch., miss 3 st., 1 tr. in next.

Lace to Match Above.—Each leaf is commenced in the center with 8 ch.

1st row.—1 half tr. (half tr., you draw the silk through all 3 stitches at once) in the 8th st. of ch.; 2 ch., 1 tr. in 7th; 2 ch., 1 long tr. in the 6th; 2 ch., 1 long tr. in the 5th; 2 ch., 1 long tr. in the 4th; 2 ch., 1 long tr. in the 3rd; 2 ch., 1 tr. in the 2nd; 2 ch., 1 half tr. in the 1st; 4 ch.; repeat this down the other side of ch.; 1 st. in 1st half tr.

2nd row.—3 dc. under each 2 ch.; 7 dc. under each 4 ch.; 1 sc. in 1st dc.

3rd row.—3 ch., 1 tr. in each dc., with 2 tr. in the 3rd and 5th, and 3 tr. in the 4th of each 7 dc.; 1 dc. in the top of the 3 ch; break off thread neatly.

4th row.—(*a*) 1 tr. in the middle of the 3 tr. at point of leaf; 3 picots (a picot is made of 5 ch., 1 dc. in 1st of the 5 ch.), 1 tr. in same stitch the last tr. is in; *1 ch., miss 1, 1 tr. in next; 1 ch., miss 1, 1 tr. in next; 3 picots; miss 1; 1 tr. in next; repeat from * 4 times; 1 ch.,

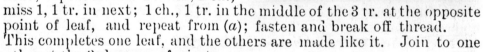

miss 1, 1 tr. in next; 1 ch., 1 tr. in the middle of the 3 tr. at the opposite point of leaf, and repeat from (*a*); fasten and break off thread.

This completes one leaf, and the others are made like it. Join to one another at the 3rd group of picots.

The triangular shapes are begun with 15 ch.; 1 dc. in each st. of ch.; turn; 1 dc. in each of 5 dc. (taking up the back loop), miss 5 dc.; 1 dc. in each of the next 5 dc.; fold these 10 stitches together and join with 1 sc. in each of 5 dc. Break off thread, and have the joining turned on the wrong side of lace. Now join the shape of the leaves in this way:

1 tr. in 1st st., 2 ch. and join with a dc. to the 2nd picot of the group directly after the group at the point of leaf; 2 ch., 1 dc. in 1st ch. after tr.; 1 ch., 1 tr. in next; 1 ch., 1 tr. in next; 3 picots, joining the 2nd picot to the corresponding one of the next group around leaf; 1 tr. in next; 1 ch., 1 tr. in next; 1 ch., 1 tr. in extreme point of shape; 3 picots, joining the 2nd one under the 2 picots that are joined together at sides of leaf, 1 tr. in the same st. the last tr. is in; 1 ch., 1 tr. in next;

1 ch., 1 tr. in next; 3 picots, joining the 2nd picot to the corresponding one of next leaf; 1 tr., 1 ch., 1 tr., 1 picot, joining to the 2nd picot of the group before the extreme point of leaf, 1 tr. at end of the triangular shape.

The top edge is made thus:

1st row.—1 tr. in the 2nd picot of the group at the point of leaf; 8 ch., *1 dc. under each st. across the triangular shape, 8 ch., 1 tr. in the 2nd of next group of picots; 8 ch., and repeat from * across the length.

2nd row.—1 tr. 1 ch., miss 1, 1 tr. in next; repeat.

3rd row.—This row is of cross tr., made thus : 1 half tr. under 1st 1 ch.; work off 2 loops; 1 tr. under next 1 ch.; now work off all the loops on hook; 2 ch., 1 tr. in the center where the tr. and long tr. are crossed; 1 chain; repeat.

4th row.—1 tr. under 2 ch., 1 ch., 1 tr. under 1 ch.; repeat.

GREEK PATTERN.

Use BELDING's "Pure Thread" Crochet Silk, and a steel hook.

Make a chain of 36 stitches.

1st row.—Tr. in 8th st., 3 tr. in next 3 stitches, ch 2, tr. in 3rd st. ch. 2, tr. ch. 3rd st., ch. 2, tr. in 3rd st., ch. 2, tr. in 3rd st., ch. 2, tr. in 3rd st., 3 tr. in next 3 stitches, ch. 2, tr. in 3rd st., ch. 2, tr. in 3rd st.; turn.

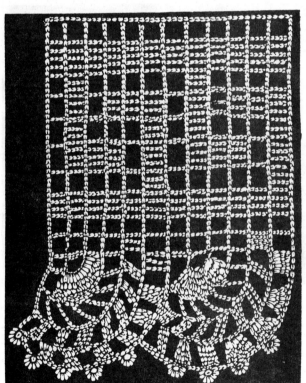

2nd row.—Ch. 6, tr. in last tr. of 1st row, ch. 2, tr. in next tr. of last row, ch. 2, 4 tr. in 4th tr. of last row, ch. 2, tr. in next tr., 15 tr. in next 15 stitches, ch. 2, tr. in 3rd st. of ch.; turn.

3rd row.—Ch. 5, 4 tr. in 4 tr. of last row, ch. 2, tr. in 3rd st., ch. 2, tr. in 3rd st., ch. 2, tr. in 3rd st., 3 tr. in next 3 stitches, ch. 2, 4 tr. in 4 tr. of last row, ch. 2, tr. in next tr., ch. 2, tr. in next tr., 12 tr. in ch. of 6; turn.

4th row.—Ch. 2, tr. between first 2 tr., ch. 2, tr. between 3rd and 4th tr., ch. 2, tr. between 5th and 6th tr., ch. 2, tr. between 7th and 8th tr., ch. 2, tr. between 9th and 10th tr., ch. 2, tr. between 11th and 12th tr., ch. 2, tr. on last tr. of group, ch. 2, tr. in next tr., ch. 2, 4 tr. in next 4 tr., ch. 2, 4 tr. in next 4 tr., ch. 2, tr. in next tr., 3 tr. in next 3 stitches, ch. 2, 4 tr. in next 4 tr., ch. 2, tr. in 3rd stitch of ch.; turn.

5th row.—Ch. 5, 4 tr. in 4 tr., ch. 2, 4 tr. in next 4 tr., ch. 2, tr. in 1st tr., ch. 2, tr. in 4th tr., ch. 2, 4 tr. in next 4 tr., ch. 2, tr. in next tr., 2 tr. under 2 ch., ch. 2, 2 tr. under 2 ch.; repeat to end of row; turn.

6th row.—Ch. 4, single crochet in top of last tr., 3 tr. under 2 ch., * ch. 4, single crochet in top of last tr., 3 tr. under 2 ch., * repeat what comes between the stars 3 times, 3 tr. under 2 ch., 3 tr. under next 2 ch., ch. 2, tr. in 3rd st., ch. 2, tr. in next tr., 15 tr. in next 15 stitches, ch. 2, 4 tr. in next 4 tr., ch. 2, tr. in 3rd st. of ch. This finishes one scallop. Join the 3rd and 5th rows with single crochet in spaces between the groups of 3rd tr. cr.

POINT LACE EDGE.

This beautiful design is composed of stars worked separately and joined together by bars of chain stitch with purls at intervals. Four stars are required for each scallop, and these are joined together in the center by the purls at the top of the leaflet and again round the outside, leaving only one leaflet of each star free.

For the Star.—9 ch., miss last and work back 1 sc., 4 dc., 1 sc., leave the last 2 chain, pass the silk behind the work and begin again on the other side of the chain already worked on, 1 sc., 2 dc., 1 tr., purl of 4, 2 tr., purl, 1 tr., in same as last, 1 tr. in top, purl, 1 tr. in same, 1 tr. in next, purl, 1 tr., 2 dc., 1 sc., 2 dc. on 2 chain left from foundation. Repeat this 3 times to form 1 star; fasten off.

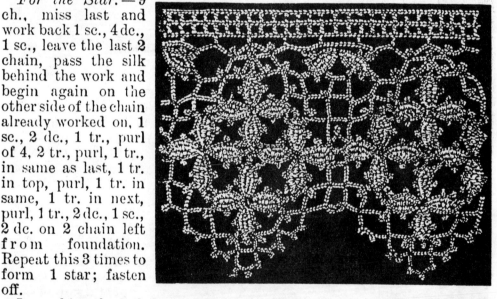

In working the 2nd star, join it to the 1st by 2 top purls of 2 following leaflets; join the 3rd to the 2nd in the same way, and join the 4th to the 3rd and to the 1st. This completes 1 pattern. Continue the groups of stars, joining them together by the top purl of 1 leaflet left free, until a sufficient length has been worked, then begin the connecting bars.

1st row.—1 sc. in 4th purl of outside leaflet of right hand star, 11 ch., 1 sc. in 2nd purl of next leaflet of next star, purl, 11 ch., 1 sc. in 2nd purl of top leaflet, purl, 13 ch., sc. in 4th purl of same leaflet, purl, 11 ch., sc. in 2nd purl of next leaflet, purl, 11 ch., sc. in 4th purl of leaflet of next star, purl, 11 ch., sc. in 2nd purl of next leaflet, 3 ch., begin round next scallop.

2nd row.—1 sc. in center stitch of 1st 11 ch., 5 ch., purl, 5 ch., sc. in next 11, 4 ch., purl, 2 ch., purl, 4 ch., sc. in next 11, 3 ch., purl, 2 ch., purl, 3 ch., sc. in 4th of 13th. 4 ch., purl, 2 ch., purl, 2 ch.. purl, 4 ch., sc. in 10th of 13 ch., 3 ch.. purl, 2 ch., purl, 3 ch., sc. in 11, 4 ch., purl, 2 ch., purl, 4 ch., sc. in 11, 5 ch., purl, 5 ch., sc. in 11. 3 ch., repeat from the beginning of row, joining the first purl to the last. This completes the outside edge.

SPIDER WEB LACE.

1st row.—12 ch., join in a ring and work 11 double into one side only, 2 ch., repeat.
2nd row.—7 double on 11 double. missing 2 at the beginning and 2 at the end, 7 ch., 3 long tr. on 3 center double of next ring, 7 ch., repeat.

3rd row.—5 double on 7 double, 7 ch., then 2 groups of 3 tr., divided by 3 ch., above long tr., 7 ch., repeat.
4th row.—3 double on 5 double, 7 ch., 3 tr. on 3 tr., 2 ch., 3 tr. on ch., 2 ch., 3 tr. on tr., 7 ch., repeat.
5th row.—1 double, 7 ch., 3 tr. on tr., 2 ch., 3 tr., 3 ch., 3 tr., 2 ch., 3 tr. on last group, 7 ch., repeat.
6th row.—3 tr. on 1st 3 tr., 3 ch.. repeat till there are 5 groups of tr., and begin again. Work 11 double into the rings on the other side, and 2 slip-stitches on 2 ch. between the rings, then repeat from the 2nd row.

For the edge work a row of loops of 5 ch., with 1 double in each loop of 3 ch., and a 2nd row of dc. worked close together. The heading also consists of 2 rows; work slip-stitches along the center group of 3 tr., 5 ch., 1 long tr. into side of scallop, 2 ch., 1 long tr. into next scallop, 5 ch., repeat. Above this work a row of 1 tr., 1 ch.

HEADING.

Make a sufficient number of half stars and begin the bars again between the scallops.
1st row.—1 sc. in 4th purl of outside leaflet of star, 11 ch., sc. in 2nd purl of next leaflet, purl, 11 ch., sc. in 4th purl of next leaflet, purl, 11 ch., sc. in 2nd purl of top leaflet, purl, 11 ch., sc. in 4th purl of same leaflet, purl, 11 ch., sc. in 2nd purl of next leaflet, purl, 11 ch., sc. in 4th purl of next leaflet, purl, 11 ch., sc. in 2nd purl of last leaflet, 3 ch., purl, 3 ch., repeat.
2nd row.—Sc. in 1st 11 ch., 5 ch., purl, 5 ch., * sc. in next 11, 5 ch., join to top purl of half star, 5 ch., sc. in next 11, purl, 11 ch., sc. in 11

above top of star, purl, 11 ch., sc. in next 11, purl, 5 ch., join to top purl of right-hand leaflet of half-star, 5 ch., sc. in next 11, 5 ch., purl, 5 ch., sc. in last 11, 5 ch., sc. in 1st 11 of next scallop, 5 ch., purl, 4 ch., sc. in 1st purl of left-hand leaflet of half star, 4 ch., sc. in corresponding purl of right-hand leaflet, 4 ch., sc. in purl of last 11, 5 ch., join to the back of the purl last worked to close the square, 5 ch., repeat from *.

3rd row.—1 dc. between leaflets of half star, 9 ch., purl reversed, 9 ch., sc. in 11 ch. near top of star, purl, 11 ch., sc. in 11 ch. on other side of top leaflet, purl, 9 ch., purl, 9 ch., repeat.

4th row.—1 tr. in center of 1st 9 ch., 8 ch., 1 tr. in 5th of 2nd 9 ch., 8 ch., 1 tr. in 6th of 11 ch., 8 ch., 1 tr. in 5th of 9 ch., 8 ch., 1 tr. in next 9 ch., 8 ch., repeat.

5th row.—1 tr., 2 ch., miss 2, repeat.

6th row.—1 tr. on tr., 2 ch., repeat.

OPEN-WORK EDGE.

The lace is worked the short way on a foundation of 34 ch.

1st row.—7 ch., miss 3 of foundation, 3 tr., 7 ch., 1 tr., missing 6, 3 ch., 1 tr. in same, 5 ch., miss 4, 1 tr., 3 ch., 1 tr. in same, 5 ch., miss 4, 1 tr., 3 ch., 1 tr. in same, 7 ch., miss 6, 3 tr., 3 ch., miss 3, 1 tr., 7 ch., turn.

2nd row.—3 tr. on 3 tr., 6 ch., 4 tr. in loop of 3 ch., 5 ch., 4 tr. in next loop, 5 ch., 4 tr. in last loop, 6 ch., 3 tr. on 3 tr., 3 ch., miss 3, 1 tr., 7 ch., turn.

3rd row.—3 tr., 5 ch., 5 tr., with 1 ch. after each, on 4 tr., increasing in the center of group, 5 ch., 5 tr. and ch. on 4, 5 ch., 5 tr. and ch. on 4, 5 ch., 3 tr. on 3, 3 ch., miss 3, 1 tr., 7 ch., turn.

4th row.—3 tr. on 3 tr., 3 ch., 1 double in 2nd of 5 ch., 3 ch., 1 double in 4th, 3 ch., 1 double on 1st of 5 tr., 3 ch., 1 double in 3rd, 3 ch., 1 double in 5th, make 15 of these loops, then 3 ch., 3 tr. on tr., 3 ch., miss 3, 1 treble, 7 ch., turn.

5th row.—Same as the 1st.

6th row.—Same as the 2nd.

7th row.— Same as the 3rd.

8th row.—Like 4th, but after the single tr. at end, instead of working the 7 ch. to turn, make 12 ch. and join back to last tr. of 7th row, 1 ch., join to end of 6th row, turn and work 28 tr. in the loop of 12 ch.; continue the foundation for 2 rows, then

For the Border Work.—*5 ch., 1 dc. in 4th of tr., repeat from * 6 times round scallop, turn, 2 slip stitches along foundation, then loops of 5 ch. round the scallop; work 2 rows of the foundation, and round the scallop 7 loops of 7 ch.; slip stitches along foundation to end of 1st row, turn; 5 tr. with 1 ch. after each tr. in the loops of 7 ch., with 2 ch. between the groups; after the last 2 ch. join to foundation, 3 ch., turn and work round the scallop again 1 tr., 1 ch., repeat on 5 tr., 2 ch., 1 dc. 2 in ch. between groups of 5 tr.; after the last group join to foundation; turn and work round each group 3 loops of 5 ch.. Continue the foundation for 10 rows, then begin another scallop.

SHELL LACE EDGE.

The lace is worked throughout the short way on a foundation of 28 ch.

1st row.—6 ch. to turn, 3 tr., 3 ch., miss 3, 3 tr., 3 ch., 3 tr., 3 ch., 3 tr., 6 ch., 1 single in last 2 ch., turn.

2nd row.—12 tr. in loop of 6 ch., then 3 ch., 3 tr. in loop of 3 ch. 4 times, 6 ch., turn.

3rd row.—3 tr., 3 ch., as before, 4 times; then 1 tr., 1 ch. 10 times round scallop, missing the 1st 2 tr., 5 ch., turn.

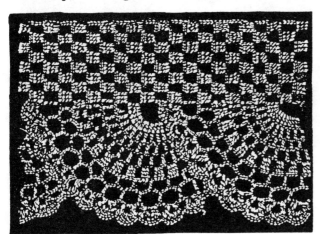

4th row.—1 tr., 2 ch. in each 1 ch., 1 tr. in 3 ch., 2 ch., 1 tr. in same, then 3 ch., 3 tr. to end of row, 6 ch., turn.

5th row.—Same as 3rd row to scallop, then 1 tr., 3 ch. 11 times round scallop, 4 ch., turn.

6th row.—3 tr. in each loop of 3 ch. round scallop divided by 2 ch., 11 groups in all, then 3 tr., 3 ch. to end of row, 6 ch., turn.

7th row.—Same as 3rd row to scallop, 2 ch. after last 3 tr., then 1 tr. in loop of 2 ch., 4 ch. 11 times round scallop, 6 ch., turn.

8th row.—Same as last row, but with 5 ch. instead of 4, 3 tr., 3 ch. to end of row, 6 ch., turn.

9th row.—4 groups of 3 tr., 3 ch., to scallop; round the scallop work 2 tr., 3 ch., 2 tr. in each loop of 5 ch., 2 ch., turn.

10th row.—1 double, 5 tr., 1 double in each loop of 3 ch. round scallop, 11 times in all, 4 ch., finish the row as before, 6 ch., turn and repeat from the 1st loop, joining the loop of 6 ch. at the end of the row to the first group of tr. round scallop. Continue joining the rows in this way to the preceding scallop, taking care not to join them beyond the 5th group of tr.

IMITATION NET EDGE.

The lace is worked the short way on a foundation of 20 ch.

1st row.—9 ch., miss 3 of foundation, 1 tr. in 4th, 5 ch., miss 3, 1 tr., repeat to end and work 2 tr. in last 2 stitches, 4 ch., turn.

2nd row.—1 tr. on 2nd tr., 2 ch., 1 tr. in center st. of 5 ch., 5 ch., 1 tr., repeat 3 times, 2 ch., 1 tr. in 3rd beyond last tr., 9 ch., turn.

3rd row.—Same as the 1st.

4th row.—1 tr. on 2nd tr., 2 ch., 1 tr., 5 ch., 1 tr., 2 ch., 4 tr. in 2nd of 5 ch., 5 ch., 1 tr., 5 ch., 1 tr., 2 ch., 1 tr., 9 ch., turn.

5th row.—1 tr., 5 ch., 4 tr. in 4th of next 5 ch., 1 ch., 4 tr. in last of 2 ch., 2 ch., 1 tr., 5 ch., 2 tr., 4 ch., turn.

6th row.—1 tr., 2 ch., 1 tr., 2 ch., 4 tr. on 2nd of 2 ch., 1 ch., 4 tr. on 1 ch., 1 ch., 4 tr. on 2nd of 5 ch.. 5 ch., 1 tr., 2 ch., 1 tr., 9 ch., turn.

7th row.—1 tr., 5 ch., 4 tr. in 1 ch., 1 ch., 4 tr. in 1 ch., 2 ch., 1 tr. on last of 4 tr., 5 ch., 2 tr., 4 ch., turn.

8th row.—1 tr., 2 ch., 1 tr., 5 ch., 1 tr. on 1st of 4 tr., 2 ch., 4 tr. on 1 ch., 5 ch., 1 tr., 5 ch., 1 tr., 2 ch., 1 tr.; now begin the scallop; * 11 ch., 1 single in loop at end of 6th row, 5 ch., single into 6th of 11 ch., repeat from *, making 3 loops of chain connected by bars of 5 ch., then 5 ch., join to foundation at end of 4th row, 3 single on foundation, 5 ch., turn, 1 tr. in last bar of 5 ch., 5 ch., repeat round scallop, making 9 loops in all, then work 2 rows of the plain open foundation ;

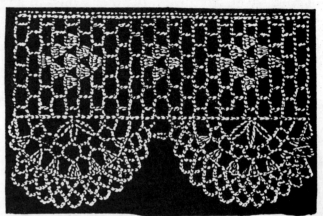

at the end of the 2nd row work round the scallop 5 ch., 3 tr. in loop of 5 ch., 3 ch., repeat all round, ending with 5 ch., join to foundation, turn and work back 15 loops of 5 ch., 1 double, into first and last of each group of 3 tr. Continue the foundation ; in the center of the 2nd row begin another of the groups of 4 tr.; at the end work loops of 7 chain; 1 single in center of 5 ch. all round the scallop, join to foundation, turn and work back similar loops of 9 ch. each ; there should be 17 of these in all. Continue the foundation for 2 more rows with 2 groups of 4 tr. in the 1st, and 1 group in the 2nd, then begin again at the 1st row.

After the 1st scallop those that follow are joined together at the 2nd loop of 9 ch., on the outside edge, thus : 9 ch., join to loop of previous scallop, 4 ch., 1 sc. in 5th of 9 ch., 4 ch., 1 sc. in next scallop.

VANDYKE EDGE.

Chain 19 stitches.

1st row.—5 ch., miss 2, 1 tr., 2 ch., miss 2, 3 tr. in next, 2 ch., 2 tr., 2 ch., 2 tr., 2 ch., 3 tr., turn.

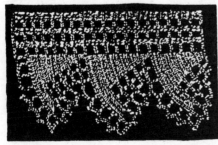

2nd row.—3 ch., 2 tr. on tr., 2 ch., 2 tr., 2 ch., 2 tr. 2 ch., 6 tr. above 3 of last row, 2 ch., 1 tr., 2 ch., 1 tr., turn.

3rd row.—5 ch., 1 tr.. 2 ch., 8 tr. on 6 of last row, 2 ch., 2 tr., 2 ch., 2 tr., 2 ch., 3 tr., turn.

4th row.—3 ch., 2 tr., 2 ch., 2 tr., 2 ch., 2 tr., 2 ch., 10 tr. on 8 tr., 2 ch., 1 tr., 2 ch., 1 tr., turn.

5th row.—3 ch., 20 tr. ending on 1st of 10 tr. in last row, 2 ch., 2 tr., 2 ch., 2 tr., 2 ch., 3 tr., turn.

6th row.—3 ch., 2 tr., 2 ch., 2 tr., 2 ch., 2 tr., 2 ch., 3 tr. on 1st of 21,
  2 ch., miss 2, 1 tr., 3 ch., 1 tr., 3 ch., 1 tr., 2 ch., p. of 3, 2 ch., 1 tr.,
  2 ch., p., 2 ch., 1 tr., 2 ch., p., 2 ch., 1 tr. in point., 2 ch., p., 2 ch.,
  1 tr. in same, 2 ch., p., 2 ch., 1 tr. in chain of 3rd row, 2 ch., p., 2 ch.,
  1 tr. in 2nd row, 2 ch., p., 1 tr. in 1st row, 2 ch., fasten off to last 2 ch.
  before the purls of last scallop. Commence again at the 1st row on 2nd
  single tr. of last row.

Another way of working this edging is to repeat the pattern of the fans
until a sufficient length has been worked, and then to add the edge as a
separate row worked round the scallops.

ROSE EDGE.

The roses are worked separately and joined together afterwards.
  Chain 16 and join round for center of rose.
1st row.—1 tr., 3 ch., miss 1 ch., repeat, making 8 tr.
2nd row.—5 double in each loop of 3 ch.
3rd row.—3 double on 3 center of 5 double, 4 ch., repeat.
4th row.—1 double, 7 tr., 1 double, in each loop of 4 ch.
  This completes a rose.   Now begin working the heading.
1st row.—1 double long tr., in a scallop of rose, * 2 ch., 1 long tr. in

next scallop, 3 ch., 1 long tr. in same, 2 ch., 1 double long tr. in next scallop, 4 ch. Now begin the loop between two roses, 5 ch., 1 long tr. in same scallop as double long tr., 4 ch., 1 long tr. in next scallop, 1 long tr. in scallop of another rose, 4 ch., 1 long tr. in next
scallop, 4 ch., close the ring by working a slipstitch in 1st of 5 ch., 4
  ch., 1 double long tr., in same scallop, repeat from *.
2nd row.—1 tr., 1 ch., miss 1, repeat.
  Turn the work and begin the edge on the other side.
1st row.—1 long tr., in side scallop of rose, joining that worked from the
  loop in heading, * 2 ch., 1 long tr. in next scallop, 5 ch., 1 long tr.
  in same, repeat from * twice more and then from the beginning
  of row.
2nd row.—1 tr., 2 ch., miss 1, round each scallop, omitting the 2 ch. between trebles at the corners.
3rd row.—1 single in scallop, 3 ch., p. of 4 ch., 3 ch., repeat 6 times
  round each scallop.

CLOVER LEAF EDGE.

This edge is rich in finish when made with BELDING's " Pure Thread "
Crochet Silk.   It is composed of shells and leaves.
  Work 4 shells, as follows: 7 ch., turn, in 4th stitch work [3 dc., 1 ch.,
3 dc.] (shell) 3 ch., 1 dc. in end stitch; turn, 7 ch. [3 dc., 1 ch., 3 dc.], all

in center of shell below; turn, take up 2nd stitch, draw silk through stitch and loop, same 3rd and 4th stitches. Now with 3 ch. commence

shell, 2 dc., 1 ch., 3 dc., 3 ch., 1 dc. in 4th st. of loop; turn, 7 ch., shell.

For clover leaf, now make 15 ch., turn, leaving 6 stitches for stem, 1 sc. in 7th st. of ch., making a loop; turn, make 3 loops in this one, as follows: 3 ch., 1 dc., 3 ch., 1 dc., 7 ch., uniting the last at base, where loop was made, with 1 sc. Turn, put needle under and in 1st loop (3 ch., 1 dc.), work 1 sc., 1 dc., 3 tr.; now put needle through upper stitch of 2nd shell, draw silk through, and finish scallop in same loop, viz.: 3 tr., 1 dc., 1 sc.

Second loop.—1 sc., 1 dc., 6 tr., 1 dc., 1 sc. Third loop the same. 6 sc. on the 6 ch. of stem, and 3 sc. on shell.

Then with 3 ch. commence shell to repeat pattern.

Between the 6 tr. of 2nd lobe of leaf fasten to 3rd lobe of preceding leaf, same as 1st lobe is united to shell.

STAR EDGING.

Make a row of ch. the required length.

1st row.—8 tr. into foundation, 10 ch., turn and join back to the 4th tr.— this forms a sort of V; work back on the last 5 of the 10 ch., 1 single, 1 double, 3 tr.—this forms the 1st point of the star; 6 ch., work back as before, missing the ch. last worked, and make 3 more points in the same way, work back on the 1st 5 of 10 ch., 3 tr., 1 double, 1 single—

this completes the star; 8 tr. into foundation, make another star, joining to point of the first one.

2nd row.—1 single into 1st point of star, 3 ch., single into next point of same star, 4 ch., single into next star, repeat.

3rd row.—All tr.

4th row.—14 tr., make a star similar to those in the 1st row, but 1 ch. and 1 tr. stitch longer, 4 tr. into foundation, turn the work, 4 ch., join to point of star, 6 ch., join to next point, 6 ch., join to next point, 6 ch., join to next point, 4 ch., join with 3 slip-stitches along the foundation, turn, work back tr. into all the loops of ch., 4 tr. on 4 of 3rd row. turn, and work round the scallop a series of 14 loops of 3 ch. separated by 1 tr., 3 slip-stitches along foundation, tr. as before, turn, and work for the outside edging of the scallop, 2 tr. into the same stitch, 3 ch.,

2 tr. into the same as before, 2 tr. into next small scallop, repeat all round, then continue the tr. above the tr. of 3rd row, 17 stitches, and begin another star and scallop.

WHEEL LACE.

Begin this lace by winding silk 35 times round a lead pencil (that has not been sharpened), slip off, and fill this ring with 50 dc., and fasten in 1st st.

6 ch., skip 1 st., 1 dc. in next st., * 2 ch., skip 1 st., 1 tr. in next st.; repeat from * all round the ring. There will be 26 tr. when done. Now begin at the beginning again, and make another ring as far as the 1st

tr., then fasten to 1st ring by the following directions: * Put the hook in any tr. of the 1st ring, and draw silk through, 2 ch., skip 1 st. of 2nd ring, 1 tr. in next st.; repeat from * twice (only putting the hook in the next tr. instead of *any* tr.) Now proceed and finish the ring the same as 1st ring.

In fastening the 3rd ring to the 2nd, only leave 10 tr. at the top, and 10 tr. at the bottom of ring (all the rest of the rings are fastened like the above), fasten the silk between the 9th and 10th tr. of top of lace, * 8 ch., skip 2 tr., fasten with a sc.; repeat from * until you come to where the rings were joined. 8 ch., skip 1 tr., fasten with sc. * 8 ch., skip 2 tr., fasten with sc.; repeat from the last * until you come round to the bottom of the lace where the rings were joined. 3 ch., skip 1 tr. in next ring, fasten with sc., * 8 ch., skip 2 tr., fasten with sc., repeat from * until you come round from where you started; 2 ch., fasten in the center of 1st loop, 4 ch., 2 tr. in same loop, * 3 tr. in next loop; repeat from * 8 times; 9 ch., fasten with sc. in center of the same loop that the last 3 tr. were in; 5 ch., fasten with sc. in same st. * 9 ch., fasten with sc. in center st. of next loop, 5 ch., fasten with sc. in same st., repeat from * until you come round to the loop before where the rings were fastened, 9 ch. fasten in the center of next loop. 5 ch., fasten in same loop, repeat from * until you come round to the top. Fasten with sc. in 1st tr., 3 ch., skip 1 st., 1 tr. in next st, * 2 ch., skip 1 st., 1 tr. in next st. Repeat from * all across top. Fill the middle of rings with needle and silk.

TRIMMING FOR DRESSES.

Silk passementerie is very expensive to buy, while clever crocheters can make their own, and also make it to sell, if wished. The patterns given herewith are very simple, but effective when finished.

Four designs are given—Panel for skirt, Border for overskirt, Collar and Cuff. The panels are made of rings, and the rest is made of rings and half circles.

To make the rings: Make a chain of 18 ch. and join in a ring, and in this ring make 36 dc.; 1 sc. in the first dc.; turn.

2nd row.—1 dc. in each dc. of previous row, taking care to insert the hook in the back loop of each stitch: 1 sc. in the first dc.; turn.

3rd row.—* 3 dc.; 4 ch., 1 dc. in first of the ch.; repeat from * across the row, when there should be 12 picots of 4 ch. each. Cut off thread and fasten neatly.

To make the half circle: 1 dc. in the center of the 3 st. between 2 picots, 14 ch., 1 dc. in the third picot, 14 ch., 1 dc. in the center of 3 dc., after the second picot from the one the last dc. was in; turn.

2nd row.—20 dc. under each 14 ch.; turn.

3rd row.—1 dc. in each st., omitting 2 st., the last of 20 st. on first 14 ch., and the first of the 20 dc. on the last 14 ch.; turn.

4th row.—3 dc., a picot; repeat until there are 10 picots, remembering to omit the 2 st. in the center.

The pendants for the panel on skirt are worked over round, wooden button molds, or beads, thus: 5 ch., close in a ring, and in the ring 19 tr.

2nd & 3rd rows.—28 dc.; that is 2 dc. in each tr.

4th row.—28 tr. The mold is then slipped in and the work finished with 3 rows of dc., gradually

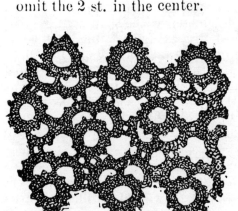

PANEL FOR SKIRT.

BORDER FOR OVERSKIRT.

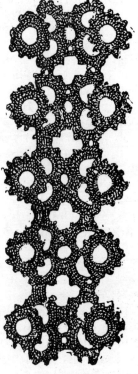

STAND-UP COLLAR.

CUFFS.

decreased until the mold can easily be covered, a few stitches with a needle securely fastening it in place. The cord on which the pendant hangs is made of 20 ch., in which are worked 1 dc. in each stitch. The illustrations sh   how the work is joined together.

PIN-WHEEL.

The wheel containing 12 spokes and called the Pin-Wheel is very pretty and used to decorate chair-scarfs, easel-drapes, etc. It may be made as follows :

Ch. 8, join round.

1st round.—Ch. 5, 1 tr. under ch. 8, * ch. 1. 1 tr. under ch. 8, repeat from * 9 times, ch. 1, join in 3d ch. of ch. 5.

2nd round.—Ch. 8, turn and work 12 tr. over the ch. 8, 1 tr. in 2nd hole of 1st round.

3rd row.—Turn, ch. 8, 1 tr. in top of 6th tr., ch. 2, 1 tr. in top of 8th tr., ch. 2. 1 tr. in 10th, ch. 2, 1 tr. in last tr.

4th round.—Turn, ch. 5, 1 tr. in tr., ch. 2., 1 tr. in next tr., ch. 2, 1 tr. in next tr., 11 tr., under ch. 8, 1 tr. in next hole, in 1st round.

Repeat 3rd and 4th rounds 10 times. You will now have 12 spokes. Put 1 sc. under ch. 8 at commencement of 1st spoke, and continue working up the spoke in sc. Turn work over, 1 tr. in 6th tr. of 12th spoke, ch. 2, 1 tr. in 8th tr., ch. 2, 1 tr. in 10th, ch. 2, 1 tr in 12th, turn, ch. 5, 1 tr. in tr., ch. 2, 1 tr. in tr., ch. 2, fasten in end of spoke.

BRASS RING CROCHET.

Common brass curtain rings are used for this work. They are filled with shades of BELDING's " Pure Thread " Crochet Silk, and are used for mats, small hand-bags, tidies, etc.

For a Mat.—Thirty-seven curtain rings and four shades of one color of silk are necessary. Commence by covering one ring for the center of mat with the lightest shade of silk; work fifty double crochets over the ring ; cover six rings in the same way with the next shade, then twelve with the third shade, and eighteen with the last. Place the lightest shade in the center, arrange the six rings of the next shade round it and sew them to the center ring where they touch it, and to each of the others at their junctions. Arrange the twelve rings round the six and sew as before, and eighteen round the twelve. The side of the mat where the rings are sewn together will be the wrong side; keep it still upon that side, and finish the rings with working an eight-pointed star in filoselle in the center of each. Make a fringe round the mat by cutting filoselle in lengths of 4 inches, and looping these lengths into the outer edges of the outside circle of rings. The rings can be ornamented with a cross of white beads in their centers, and a fringe of white beads an inch long round the outside.

To Form a Bag.—One hundred and one rings are required, covered with double crochet in colors, according to taste. Sew the rings together in the shape of a cup. First or center, one ring ; second row, six rings ; third row, twelve rings ; fourth row, sixteen rings ; fifth row, twenty rings ; sixth row, twenty-two rings ; seventh row, twenty-four rings. Above the last ring work a row of crochet, 3 tr. into the top of a ring, 5 ch., and 3 tr. into the next ring. Repeat 5 ch. and 3 tr. to the end of row.

2nd row.—1 tr. and 2 ch. into every 3rd stitch on foundation. Repeat 2nd row 11 times.

14th row.—2 tr. and 3 ch., missing 3 foundation stitches for the 3 ch. Line the bag with soft surah silk; run a ribbon in and out of the last crochet row to draw it up, and finish the lower part with a silk tassel.

JAPANESE WHORL.

1st round.—Twelve singles into the ring, join by a slip-stitch.

2nd round.— * One single into first single of previous row, 2 singles into second, repeat from * five times more, join by a slip-stitch.

Each of the six divisions is worked separately, all being attached to the central ring and connected with each other as the work progresses. The work on the first division now proceeds as follows : 12 chain, turn, and do 1 slip-stitch into first chain (the first chain after turning is the one last formed), 20 singles around the 12 chain, join by a slip-stitch to second single of the central ring, turn, and work back, doing one single into outer vein of each of the 20 singles just formed ; turn ; work towards ring, * 1 single into outer vein of each of 4 singles, 4 chain ; repeat from * three times more ; 1 single into each of next 4 singles, join to third stitch of ring. This completes first division ; commence the second by working 1 slip-stitch into fourth stitch of ring, 12 chain,  join to second picot (the picots are the small circles caused by the 4 chain) of first division by a slip-stitch into the little ring ; turn, and work hereafter as in first division. The third, fourth and fifth divisions are worked like the second ; the sixth and last division must be joined to the first. This is done while forming the picot, when, after doing the second of the 4 chain, the point of first division is secured to the picot by a slip-stitch, which counts for third of the 4 chain in this picot, the fourth being then added, and work continued to a finish at the joining by a slip-stitch in last stitch of the circle.

For a tidy, procure one yard of China silk. Hem-stitch sides, and a wide hem on one end of tidy. On the other end place 12 pin-wheels. Six across bottom, 2, and 1 on top, 2 and 1 on top. Tie in a heavy fringe. Use the Japanese whorl same way.